Rurouni Kenshin

—RESTORATION—

Story and Art by
Nobuhiro Watsuki

1

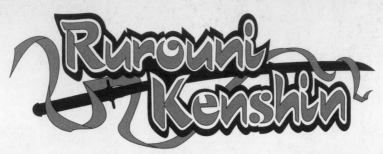

Rurouni Kenshin

RESTORATION

Calligraphy by Keita Amemiya

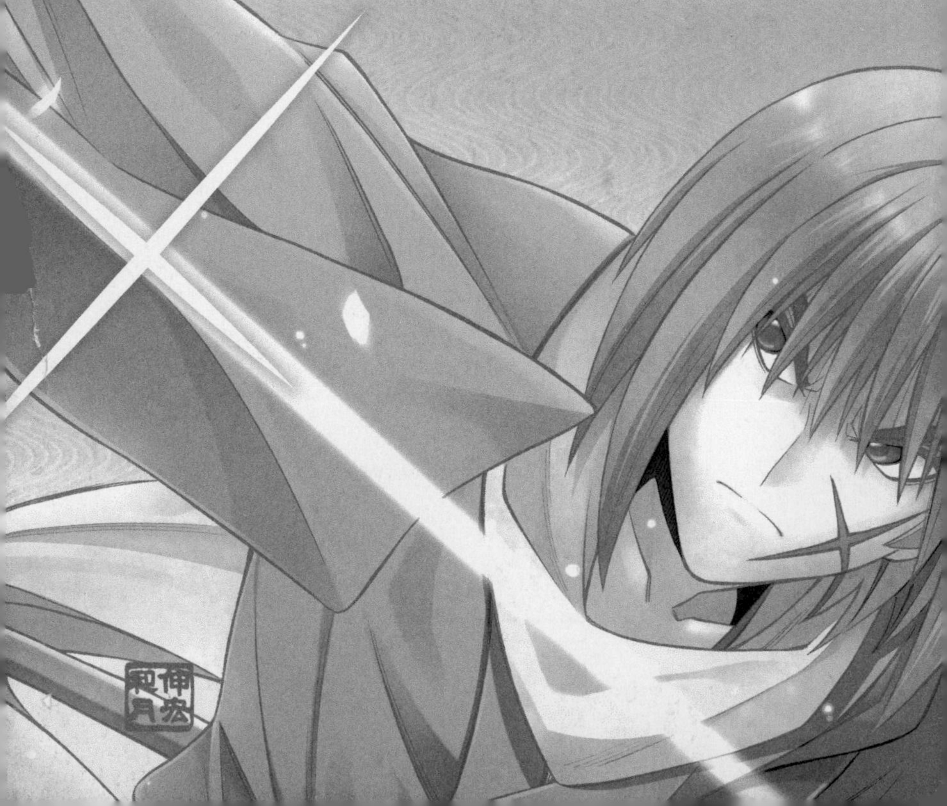

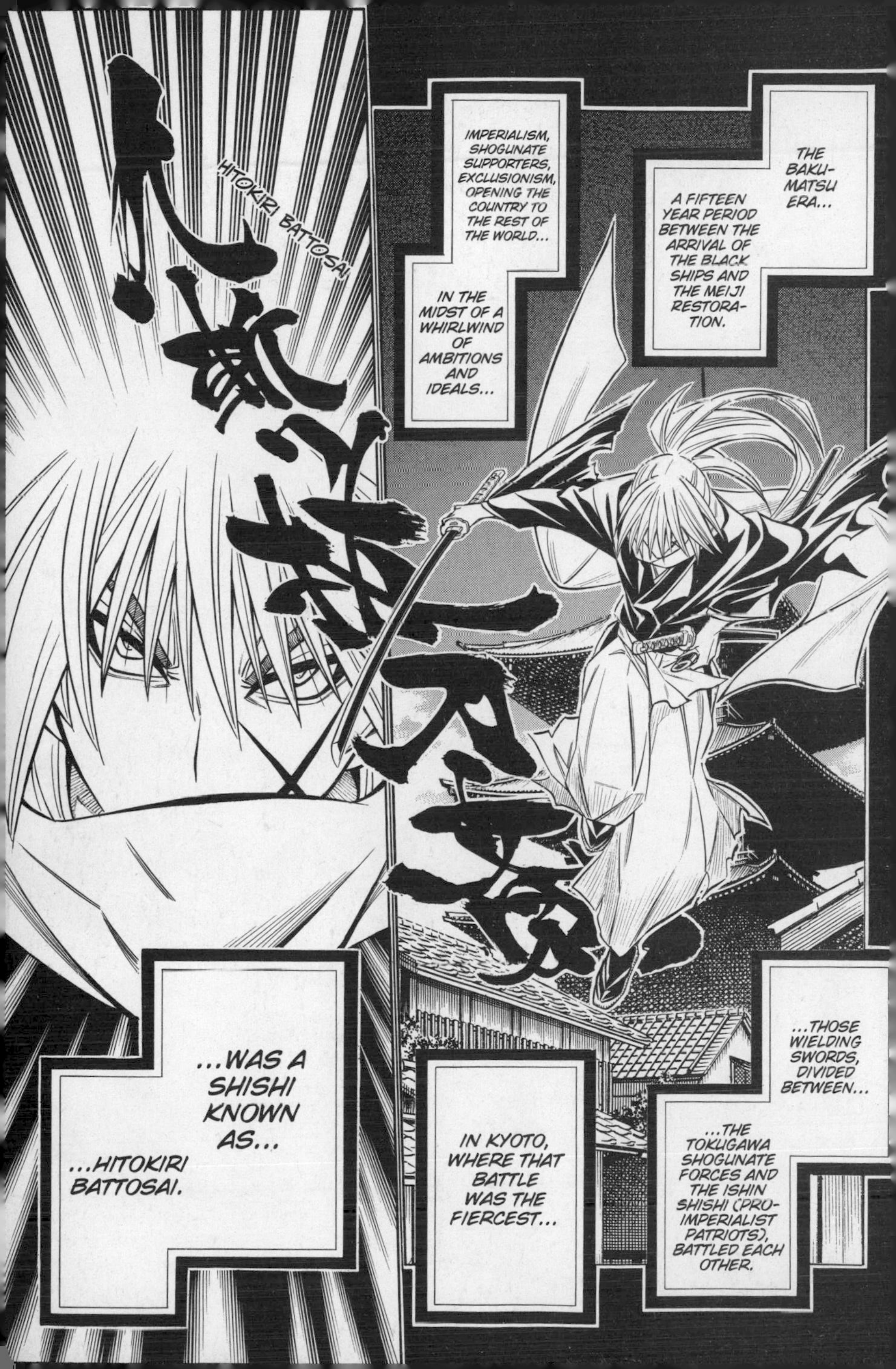
THE BAKU-MATSU ERA...
A FIFTEEN YEAR PERIOD BETWEEN THE ARRIVAL OF THE BLACK SHIPS AND THE MEIJI RESTORA-TION.
IMPERIALISM, SHOGUNATE SUPPORTERS, EXCLUSIONISM, OPENING THE COUNTRY TO THE REST OF THE WORLD...
IN THE MIDST OF A WHIRLWIND OF AMBITIONS AND IDEALS...
...THOSE WIELDING SWORDS, DIVIDED BETWEEN...
...THE TOKUGAWA SHOGUNATE FORCES AND THE ISHIN SHISHI (PRO-IMPERIALIST PATRIOTS), BATTLED EACH OTHER.
IN KYOTO, WHERE THAT BATTLE WAS THE FIERCEST...
...WAS A SHISHI KNOWN AS...
...HITOKIRI BATTOSAI.
HITOKIRI BATTOSAI

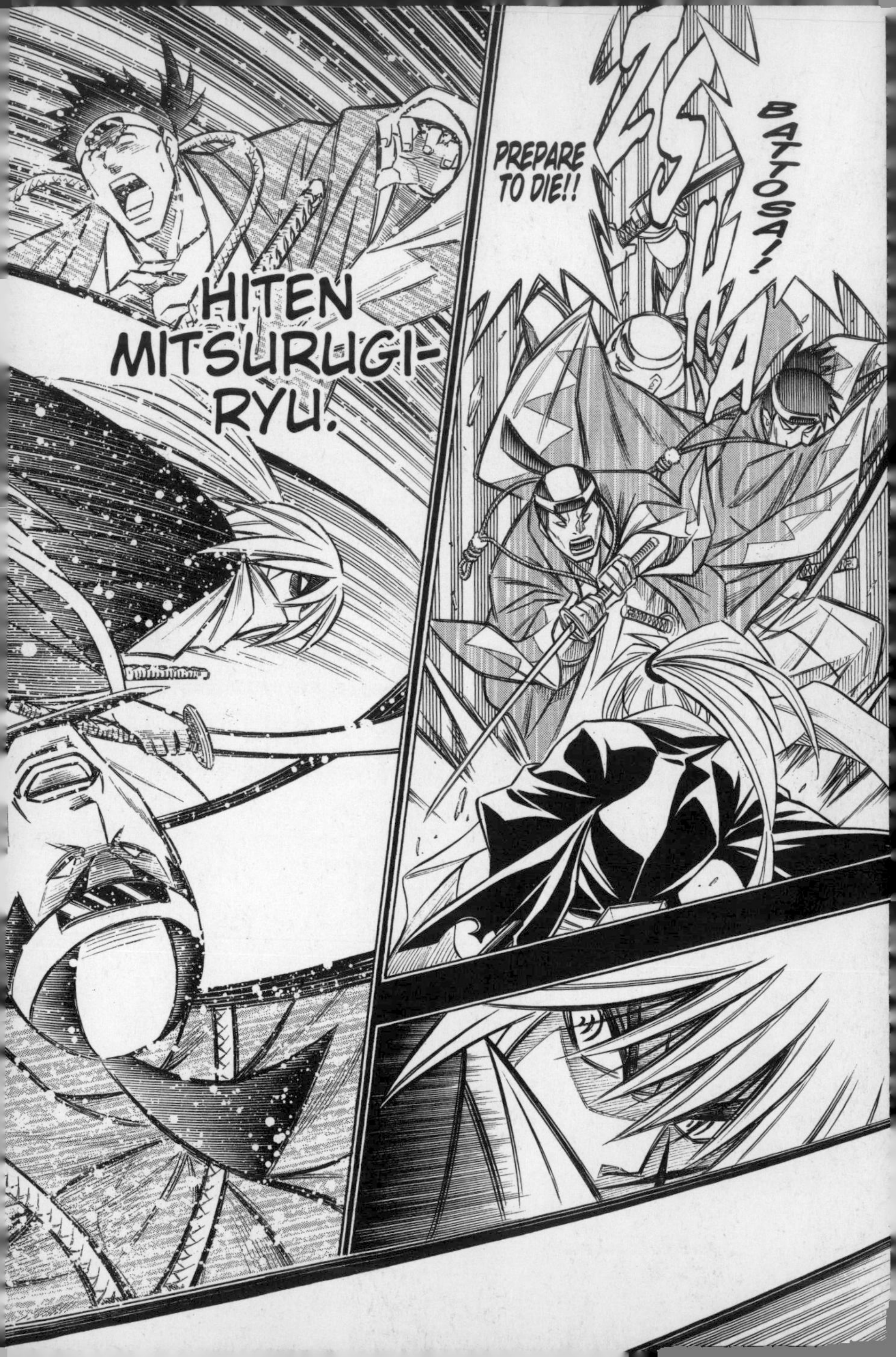
ZSHA
BATTOSA!!
PREPARE TO DIE!!
HITEN MITSURUGI-RYU.

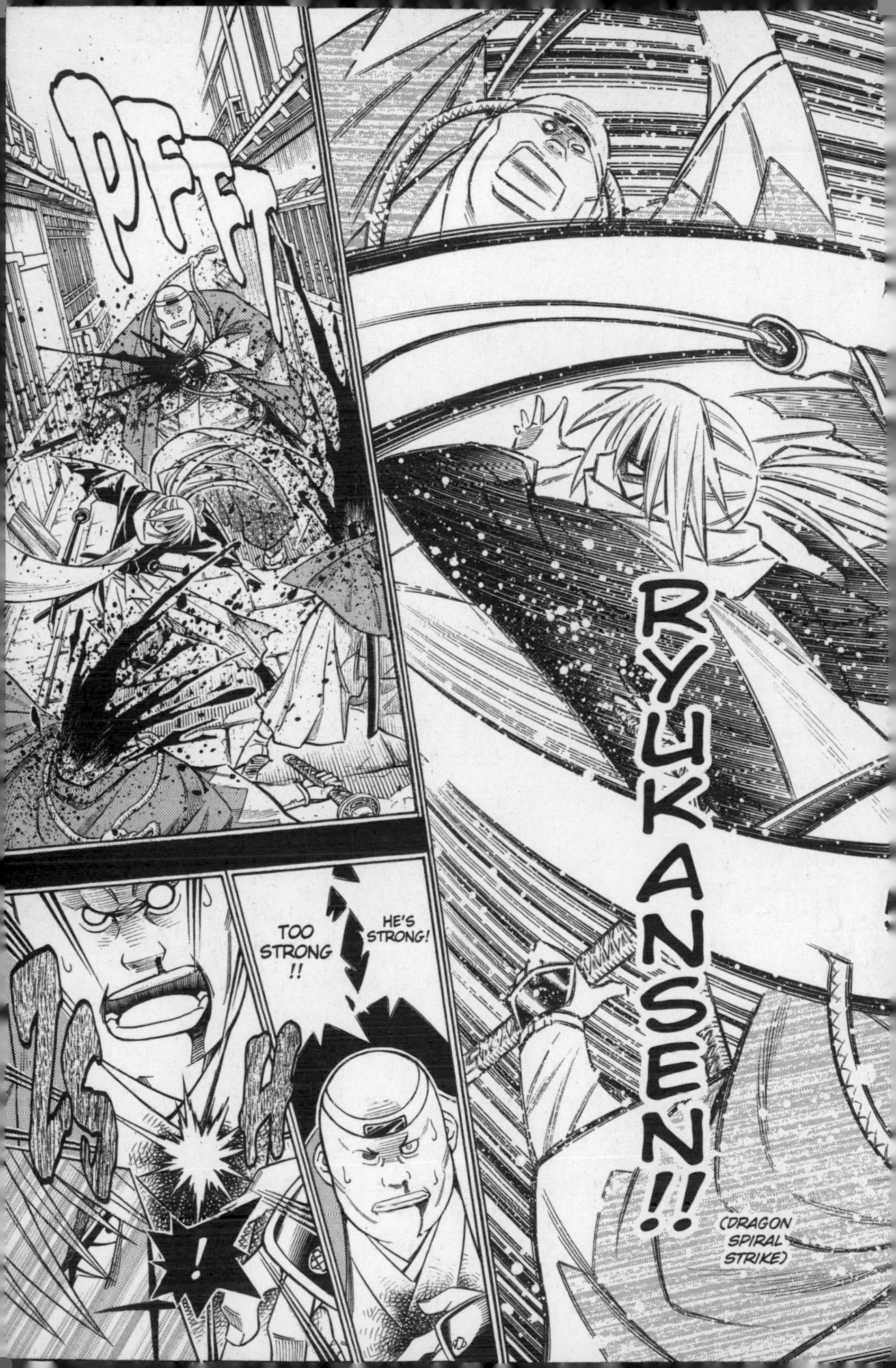
RYUKANSEN!!
(DRAGON SPIRAL STRIKE)
PFFT
HE'S STRONG!
TOO STRONG !!
!

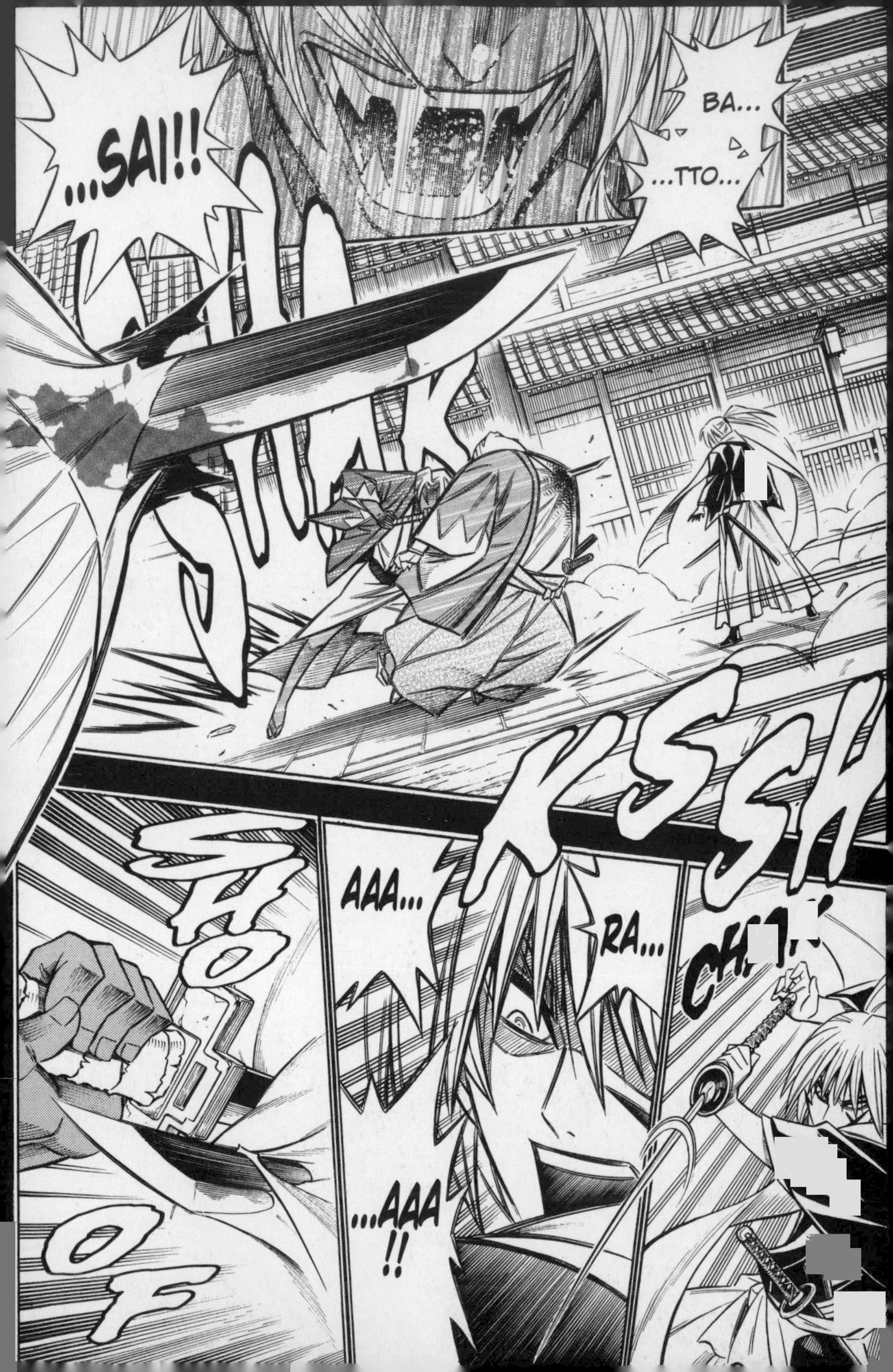
BA...
...TTO...
...SAI!!
KSSH
RA...
AAA...
...AAA!!

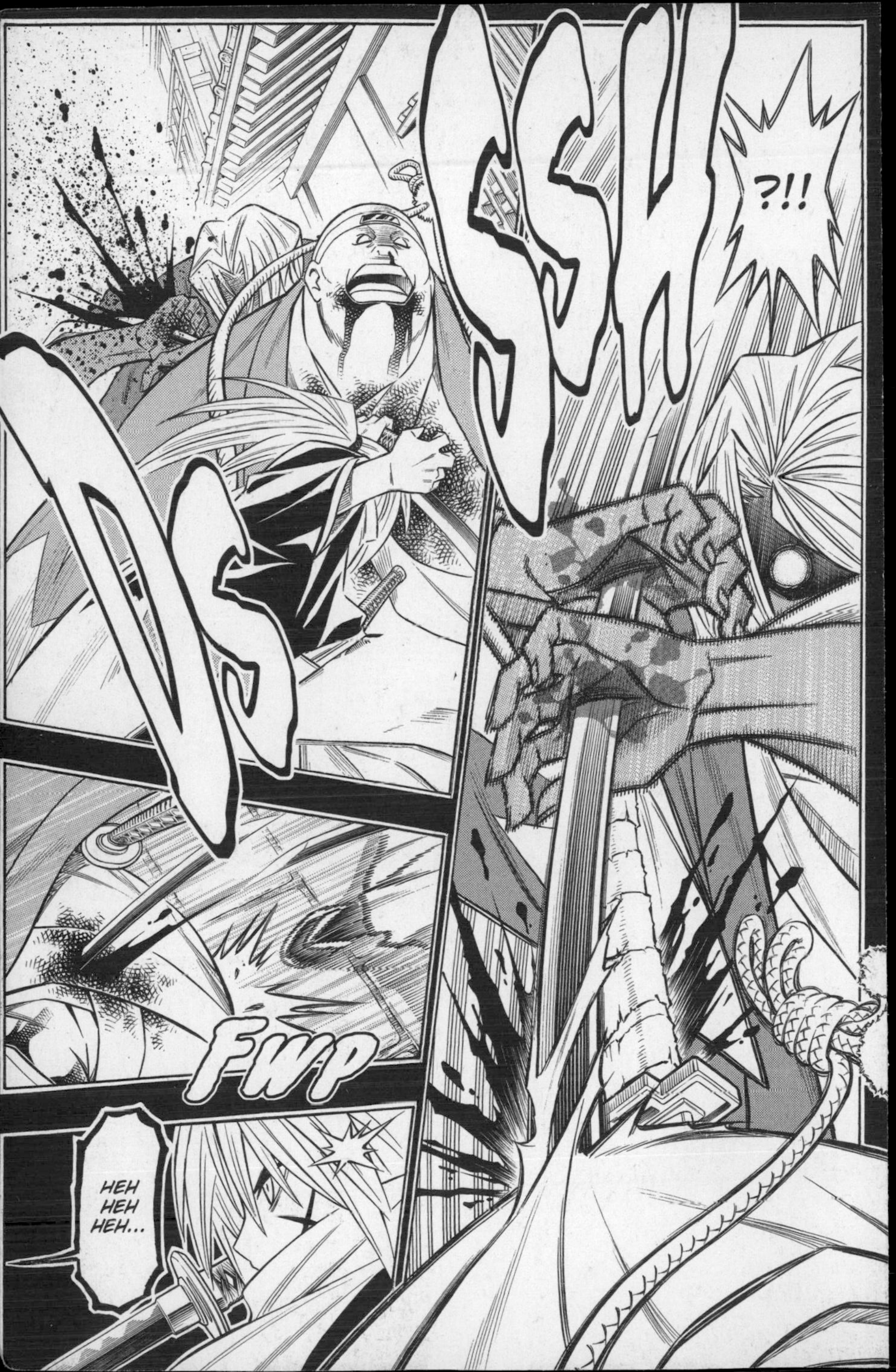
?!!
FWP
HEH HEH HEH...

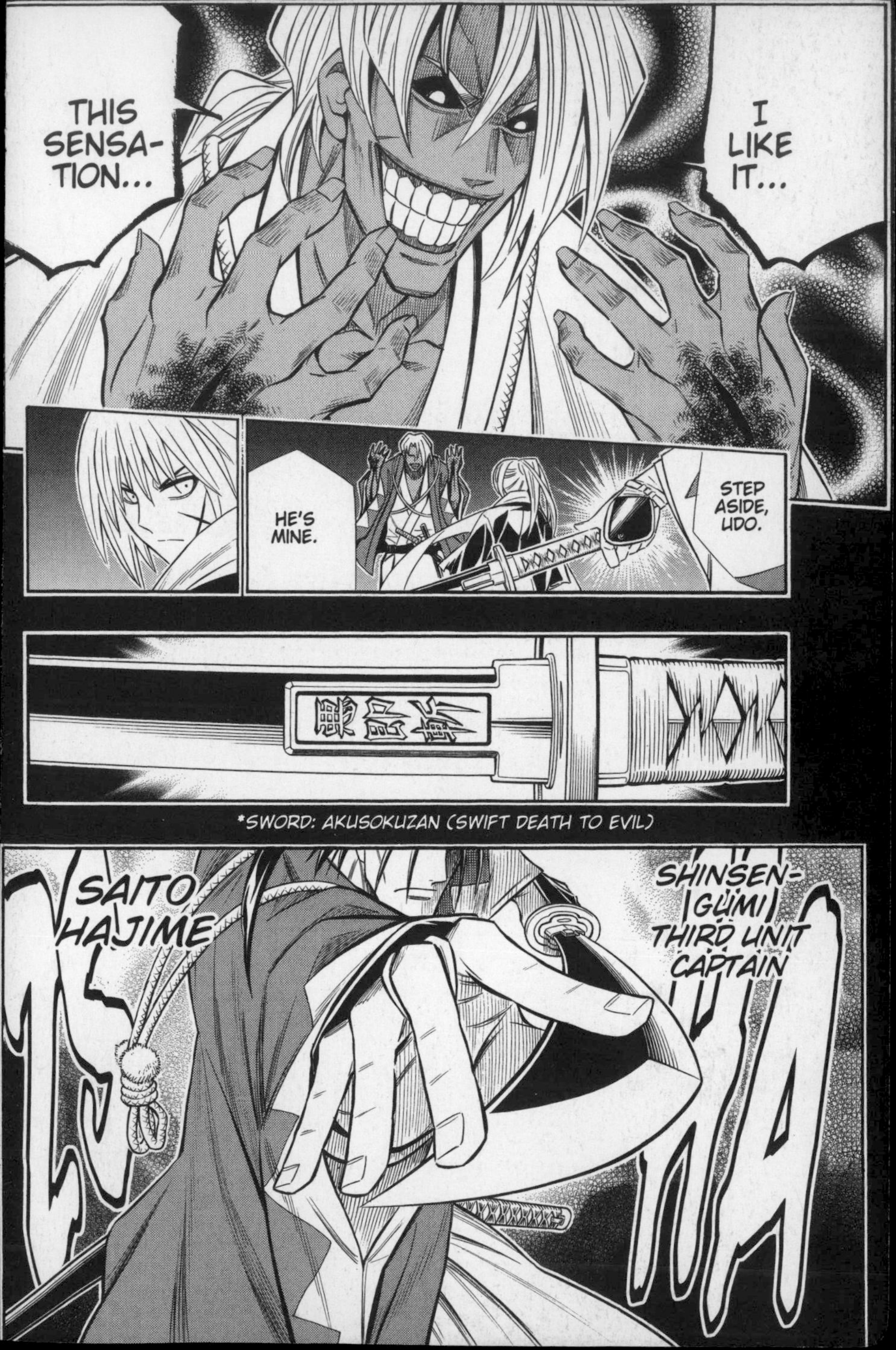
I LIKE IT...
THIS SENSATION...
STEP ASIDE, UDO.
HE'S MINE.
SHINSEN-GUMI THIRD UNIT CAPTAIN
SAITO HAJIME
*SWORD: AKUSOKUZAN (SWIFT DEATH TO EVIL)

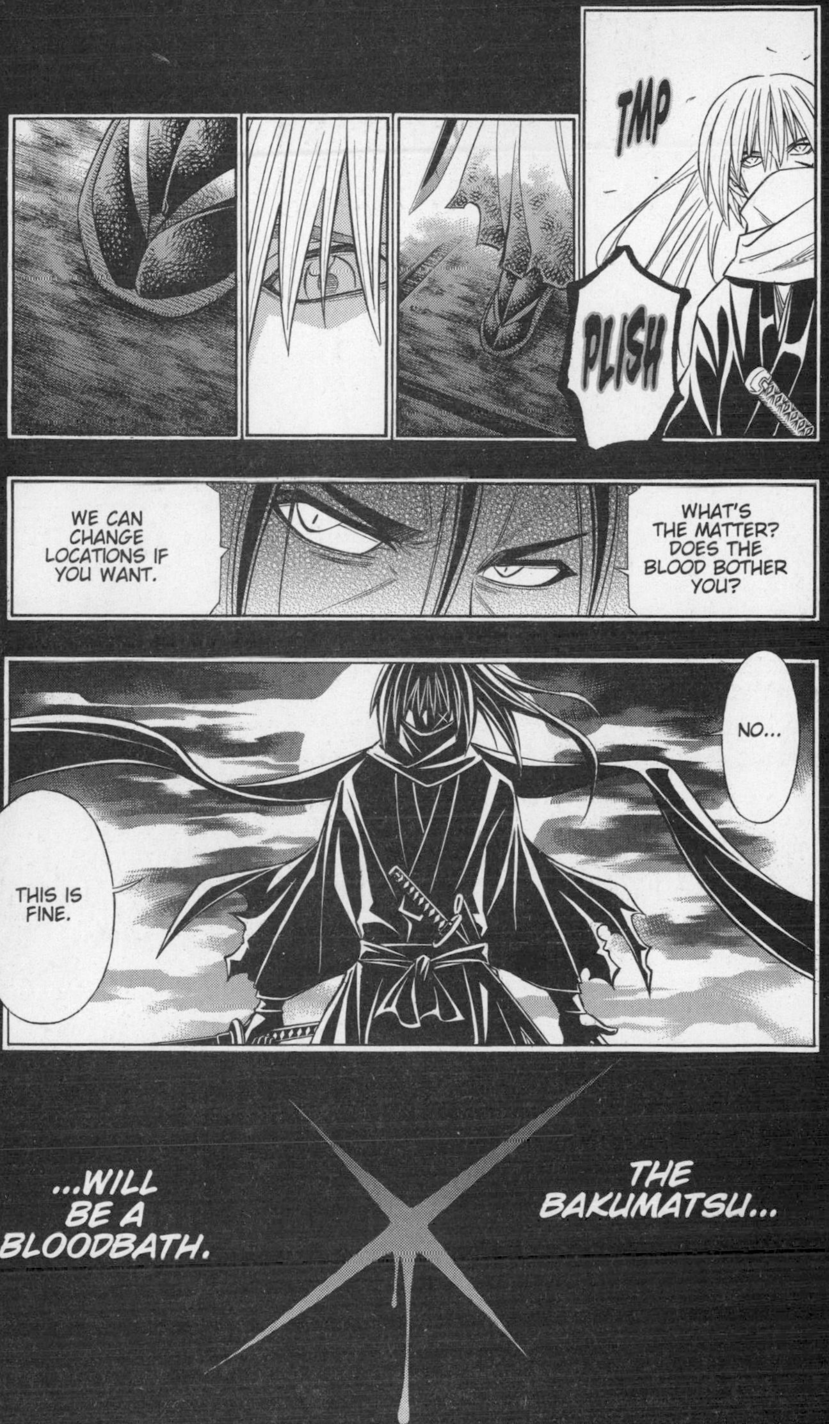
TMP
PLISH
WHAT'S THE MATTER? DOES THE BLOOD BOTHER YOU?
WE CAN CHANGE LOCATIONS IF YOU WANT.
NO...
THIS IS FINE.
THE BAKUMATSU...
...WILL BE A BLOODBATH.

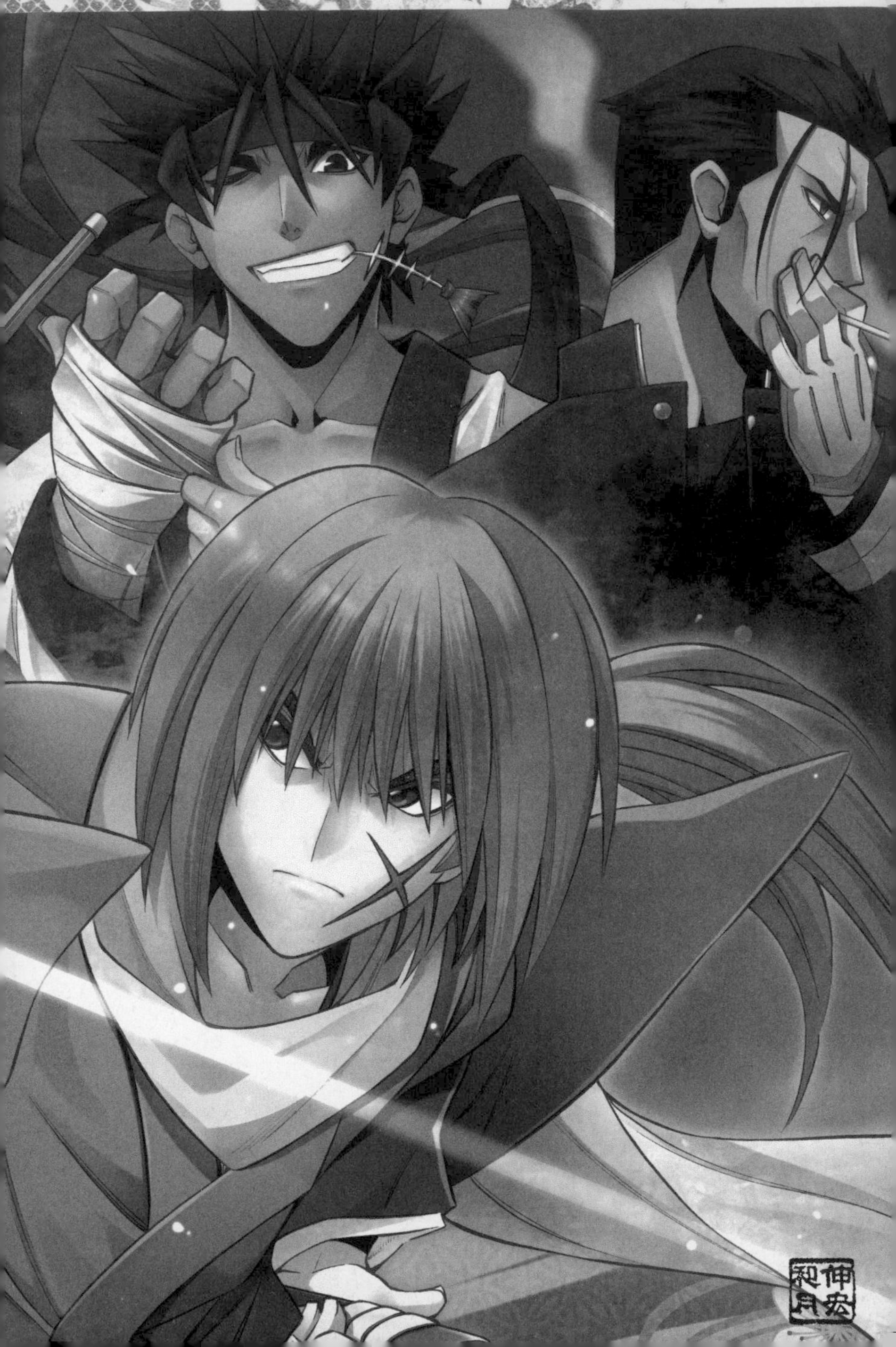
伸宏
和月

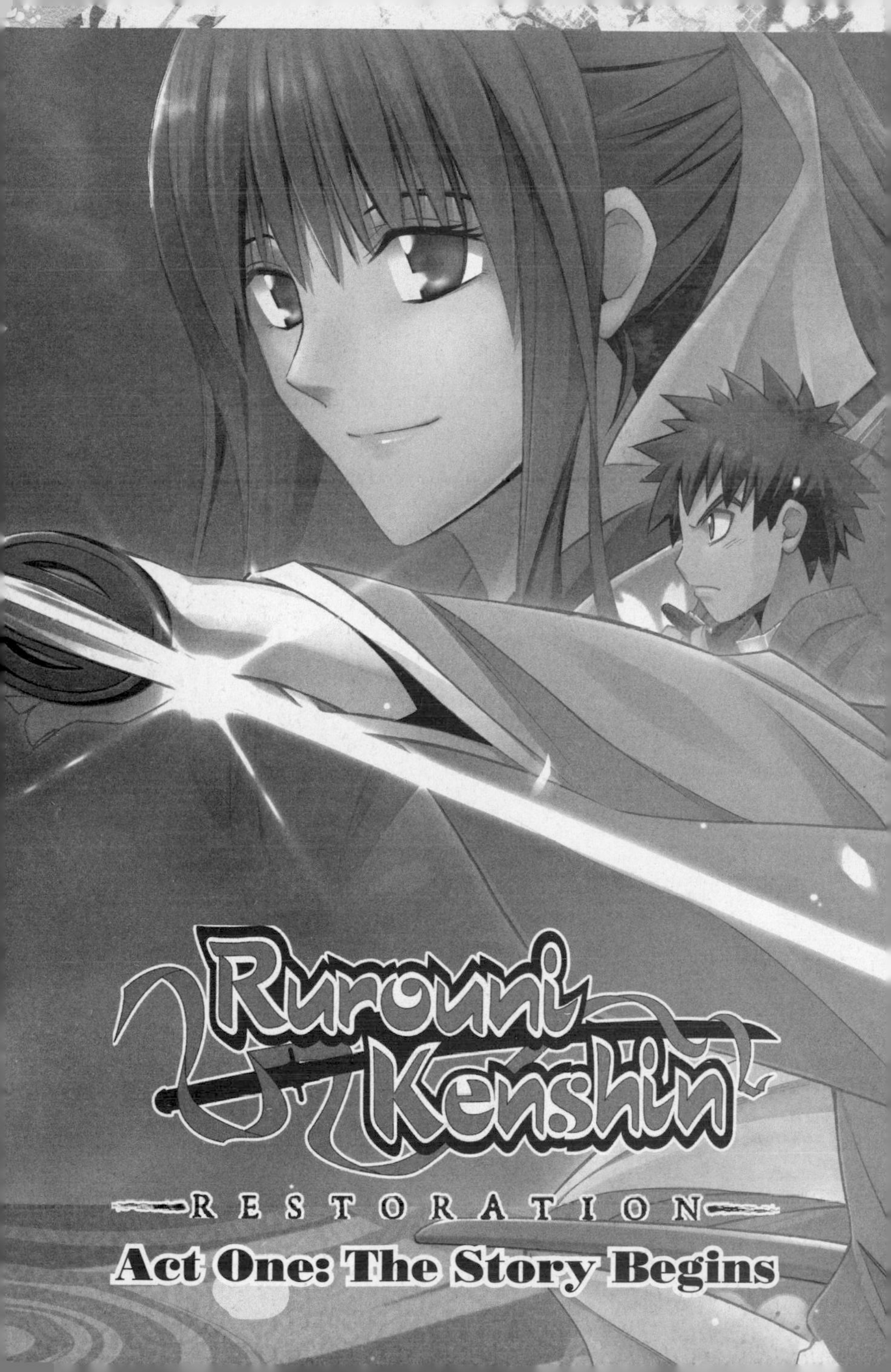
Rurouni Kenshin
RESTORATION
Act One: The Story Begins

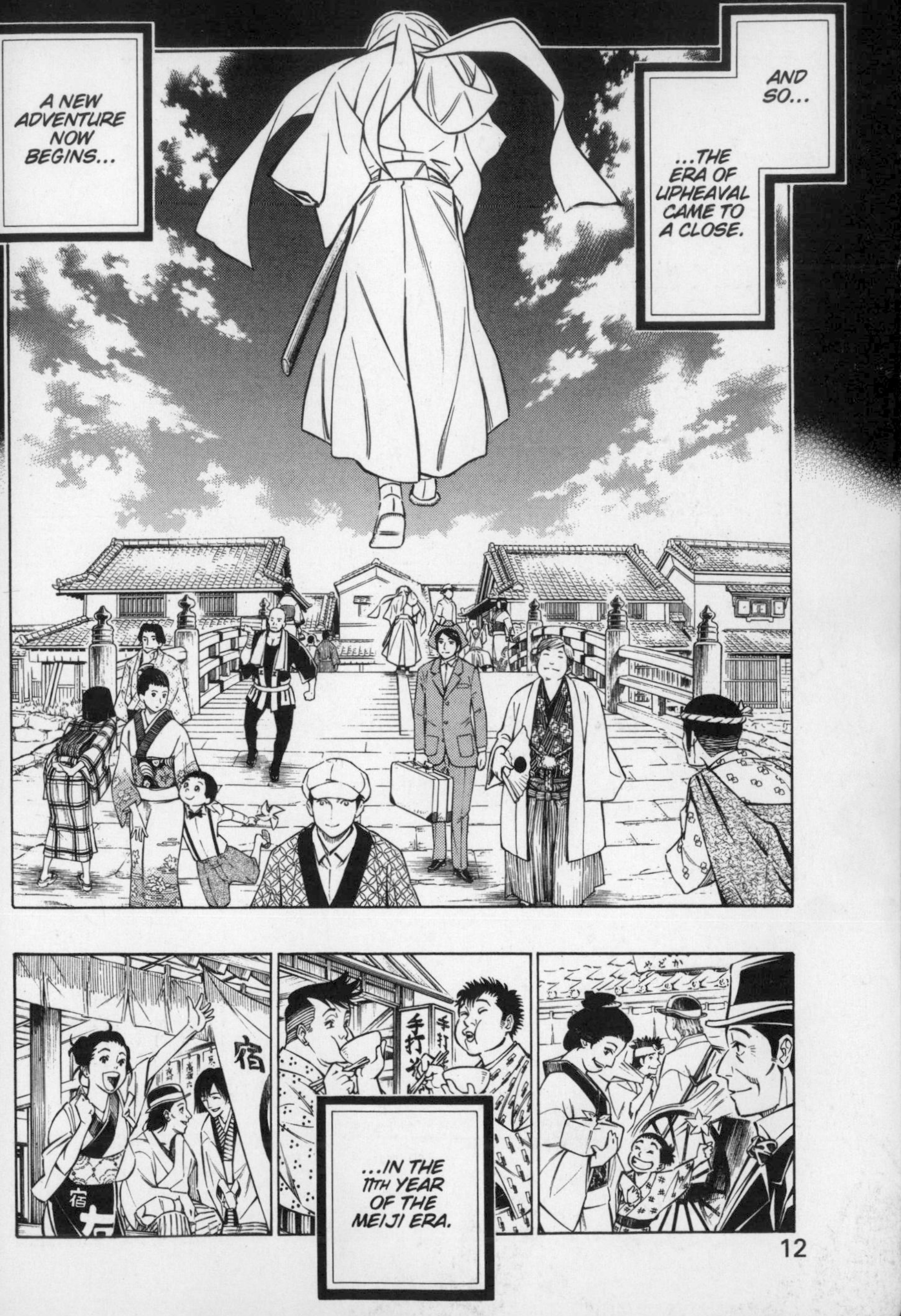
AND SO...
...THE ERA OF UPHEAVAL CAME TO A CLOSE.
A NEW ADVENTURE NOW BEGINS...
...IN THE 11TH YEAR OF THE MEIJI ERA.

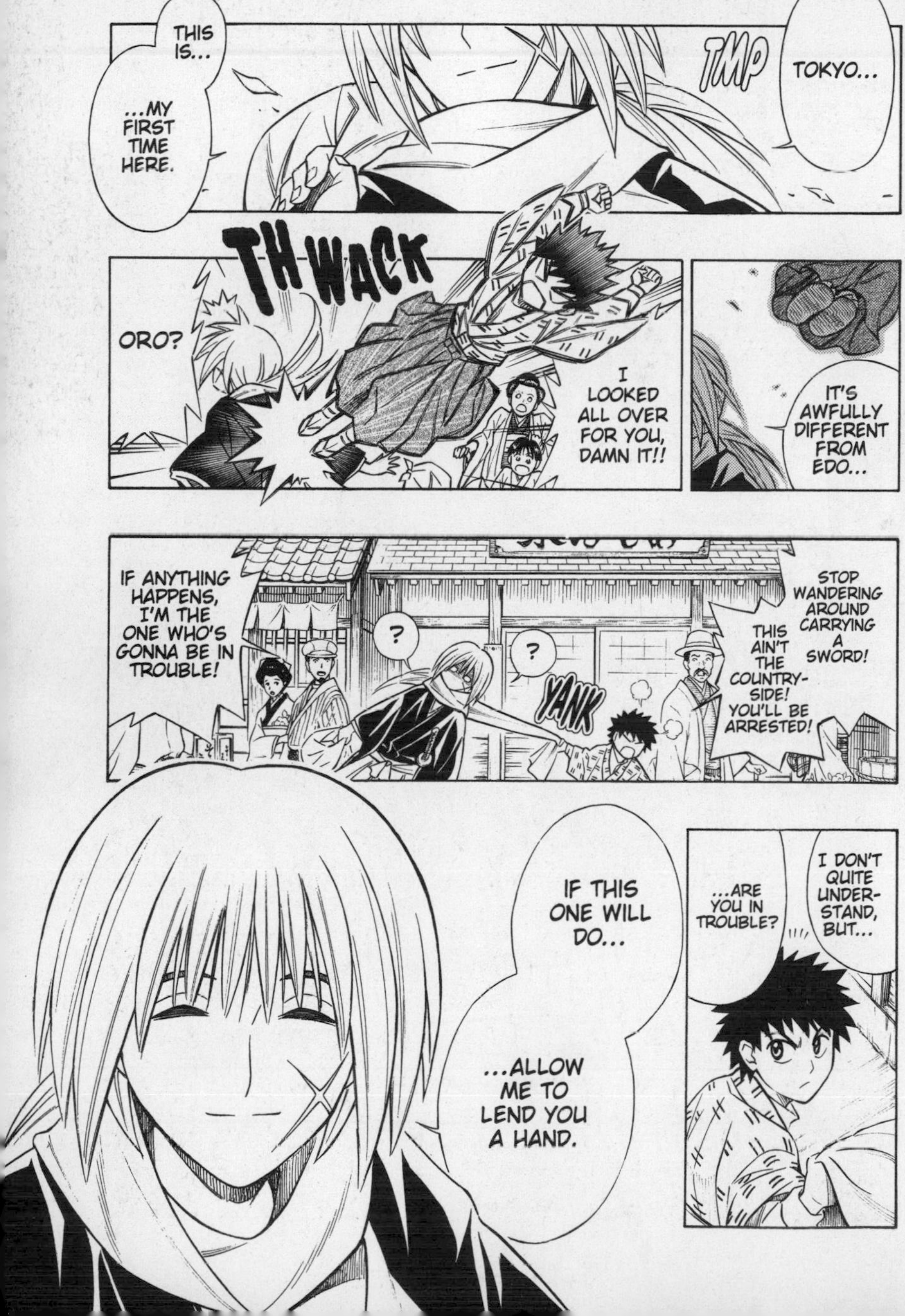
TMP
TOKYO...
THIS IS...
...MY FIRST TIME HERE.
IT'S AWFULLY DIFFERENT FROM EDO...
THWACK
I LOOKED ALL OVER FOR YOU, DAMN IT!!
ORO?
STOP WANDERING AROUND CARRYING A SWORD!
THIS AIN'T THE COUNTRYSIDE! YOU'LL BE ARRESTED!
YANK
?
?
IF ANYTHING HAPPENS, I'M THE ONE WHO'S GONNA BE IN TROUBLE!
I DON'T QUITE UNDERSTAND, BUT...
...ARE YOU IN TROUBLE?
IF THIS ONE WILL DO...
...ALLOW ME TO LEND YOU A HAND.

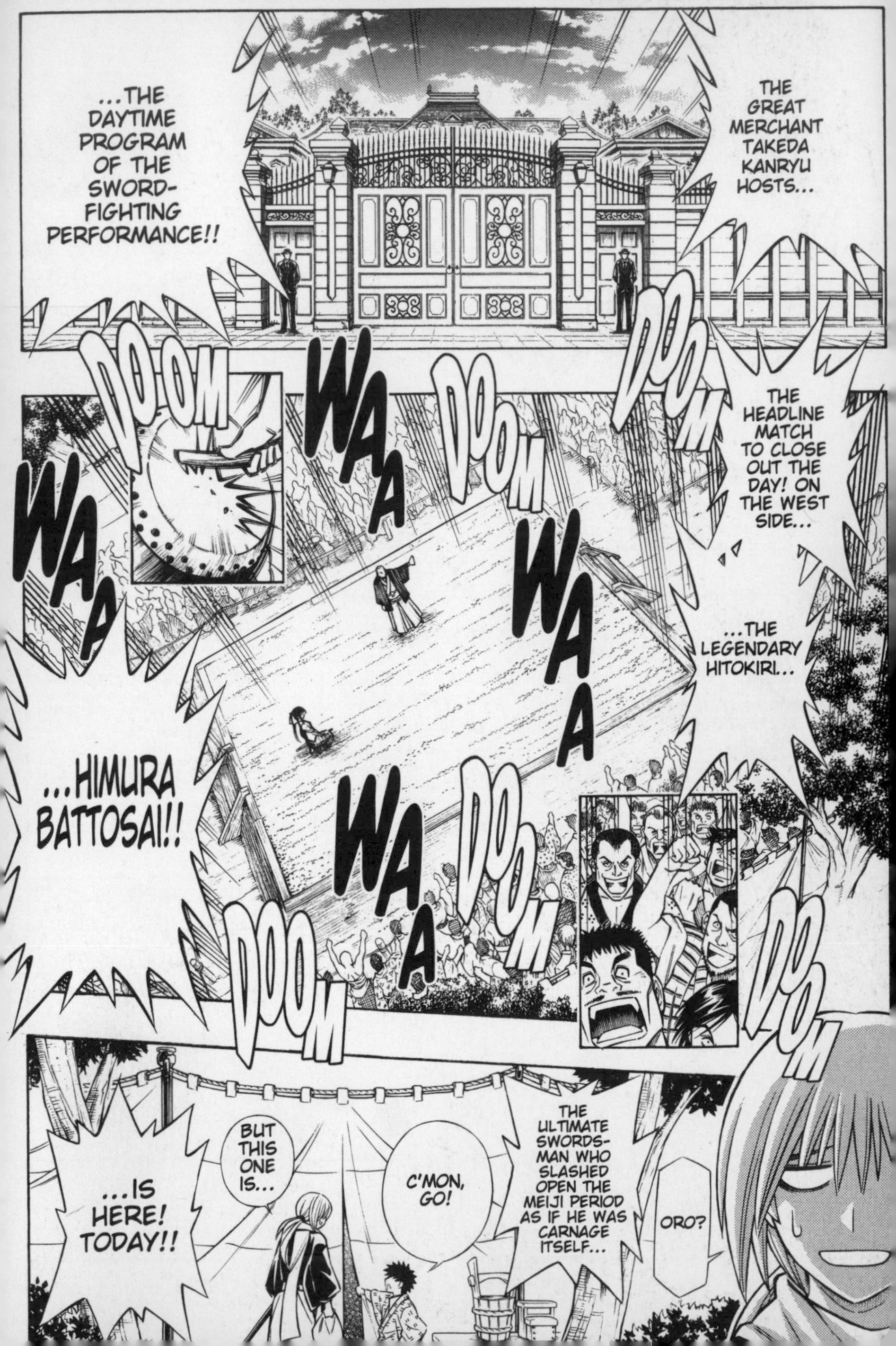
THE GREAT MERCHANT TAKEDA KANRYU HOSTS...
...THE DAYTIME PROGRAM OF THE SWORD-FIGHTING PERFORMANCE!!
DOOM
THE HEADLINE MATCH TO CLOSE OUT THE DAY! ON THE WEST SIDE...
WAA
DOOM
WAA
DOOM
WAA
...THE LEGENDARY HITOKIRI...
...HIMURA BATTOSAI!!
DOOM
WAA
DOOM
DOOM
ORO?
THE ULTIMATE SWORDS-MAN WHO SLASHED OPEN THE MEIJI PERIOD AS IF HE WAS CARNAGE ITSELF...
C'MON, GO!
BUT THIS ONE IS...
...IS HERE! TODAY!!

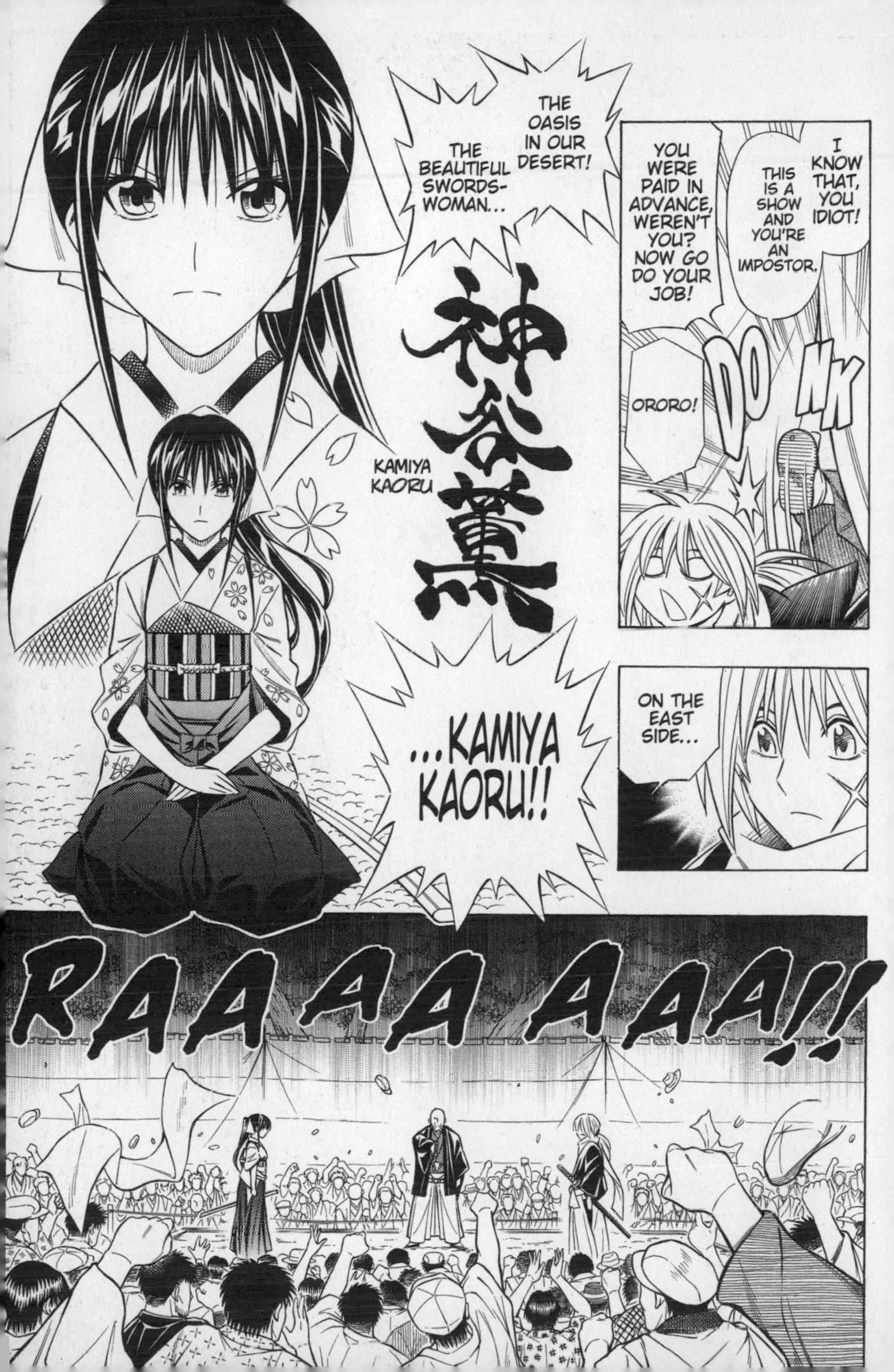
I KNOW THAT, YOU IDIOT!
THIS IS A SHOW AND YOU'RE AN IMPOSTOR.
YOU WERE PAID IN ADVANCE, WEREN'T YOU? NOW GO DO YOUR JOB!
DONK
ORORO!
ON THE EAST SIDE...
THE OASIS IN OUR DESERT!
THE BEAUTIFUL SWORDSWOMAN...
神谷薫
KAMIYA KAORU
...KAMIYA KAORU!!
RAAAAAAA!!

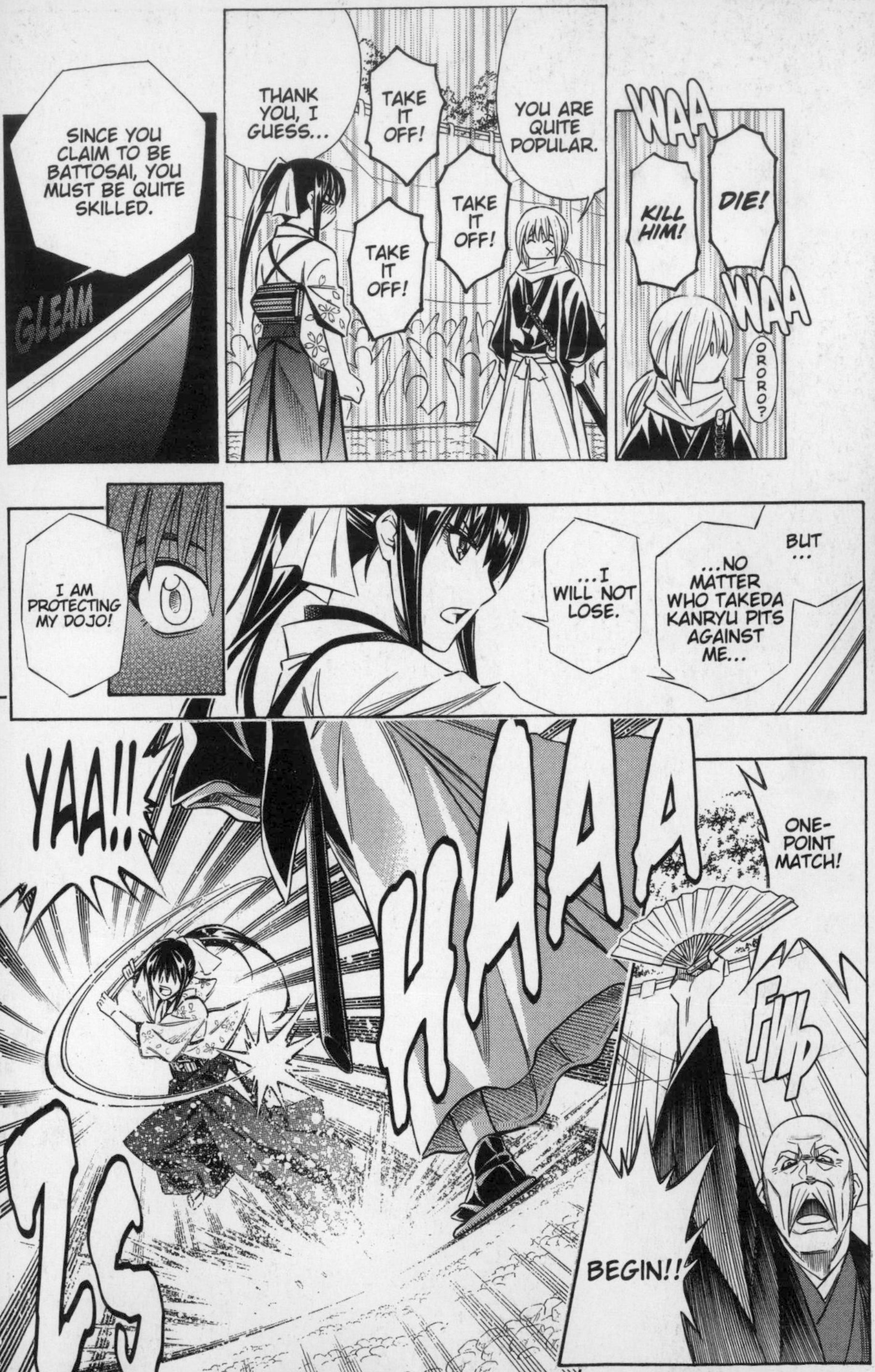

WAA
DIE!
KILL HIM!
WAA
ORORO?
YOU ARE QUITE POPULAR.
TAKE IT OFF!
TAKE IT OFF!
THANK YOU, I GUESS...
TAKE IT OFF!
SINCE YOU CLAIM TO BE BATTOSAI, YOU MUST BE QUITE SKILLED.
GLEAM
BUT...
...NO MATTER WHO TAKEDA KANRYU PITS AGAINST ME...
...I WILL NOT LOSE.
I AM PROTECTING MY DOJO!
ONE-POINT MATCH!
FWIP
BEGIN!!
WAAA
YAA!!
TS

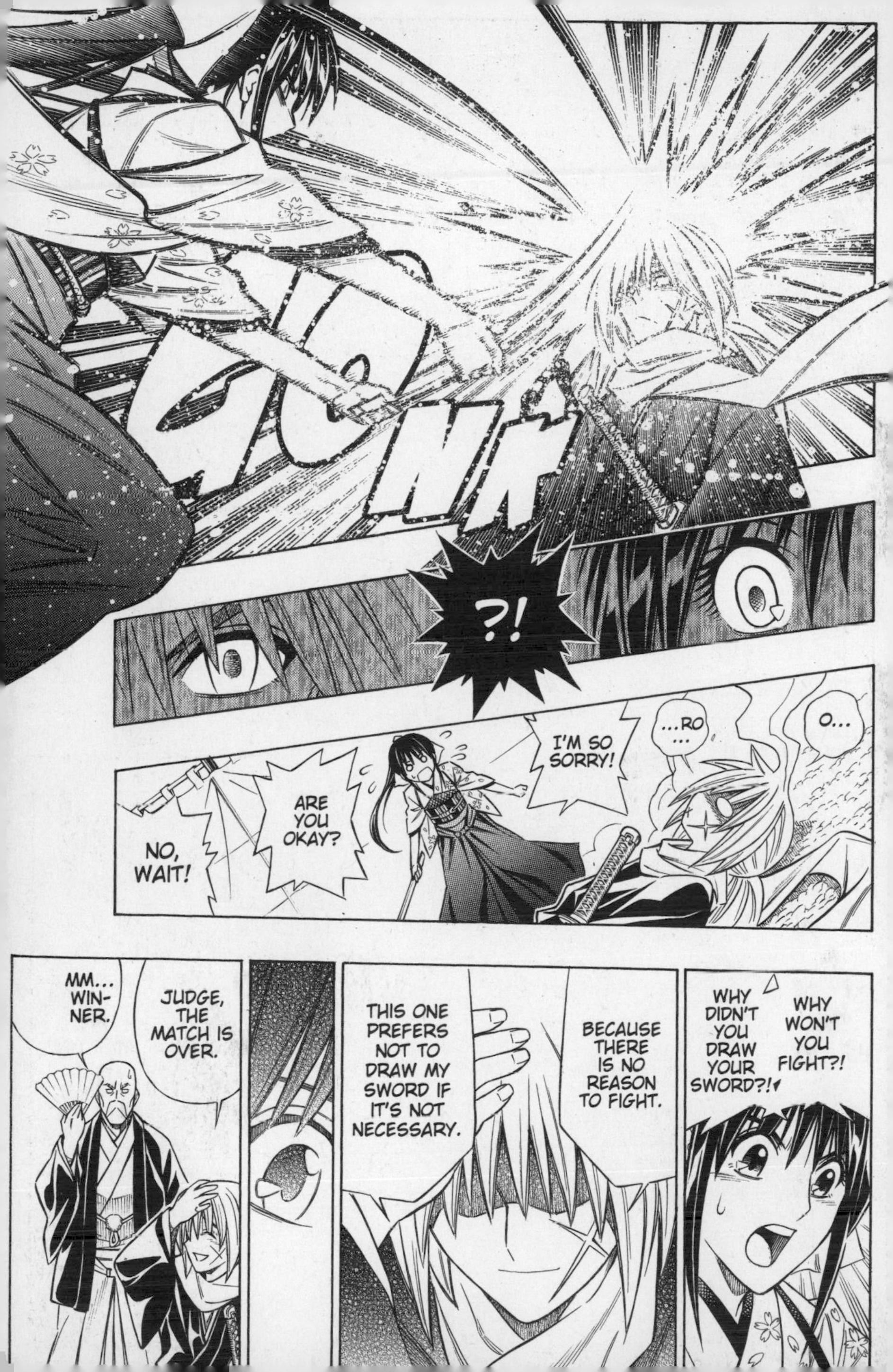
CLONK
?!
O...
...RO...
I'M SO SORRY!
ARE YOU OKAY?
NO, WAIT!
WHY WON'T YOU FIGHT?!
WHY DIDN'T YOU DRAW YOUR SWORD?!
BECAUSE THERE IS NO REASON TO FIGHT.
THIS ONE PREFERS NOT TO DRAW MY SWORD IF IT'S NOT NECESSARY.
JUDGE, THE MATCH IS OVER.
MM... WIN-NER.

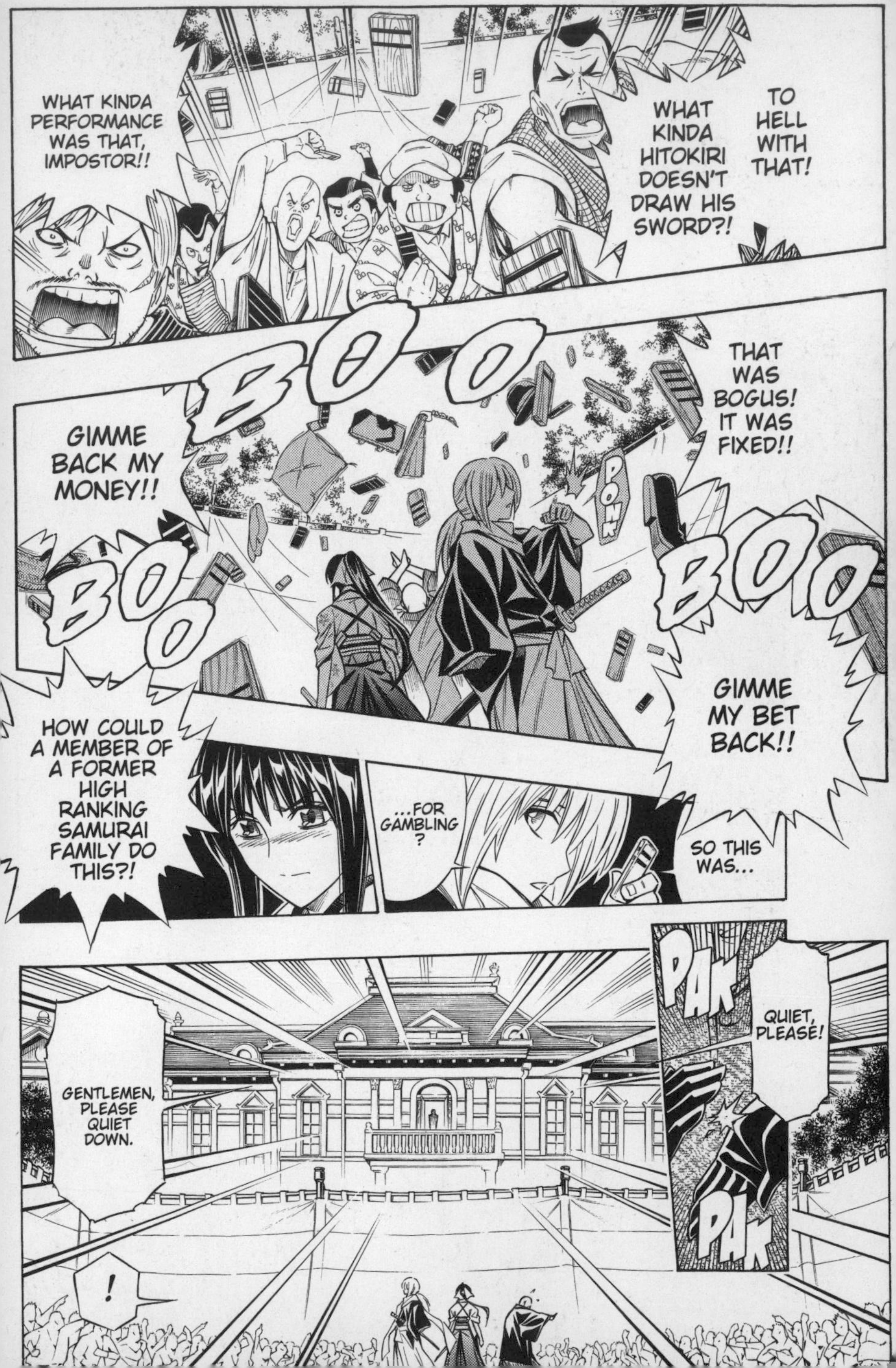
TO HELL WITH THAT!
WHAT KINDA HITOKIRI DOESN'T DRAW HIS SWORD?!
WHAT KINDA PERFORMANCE WAS THAT, IMPOSTOR!!
THAT WAS BOGUS! IT WAS FIXED!!
BOO
GIMME BACK MY MONEY!!
PONK
BOO
BOO
GIMME MY BET BACK!!
SO THIS WAS...
...FOR GAMBLING?
HOW COULD A MEMBER OF A FORMER HIGH RANKING SAMURAI FAMILY DO THIS?!
PAK
QUIET, PLEASE!
PAK
GENTLEMEN, PLEASE QUIET DOWN.
!

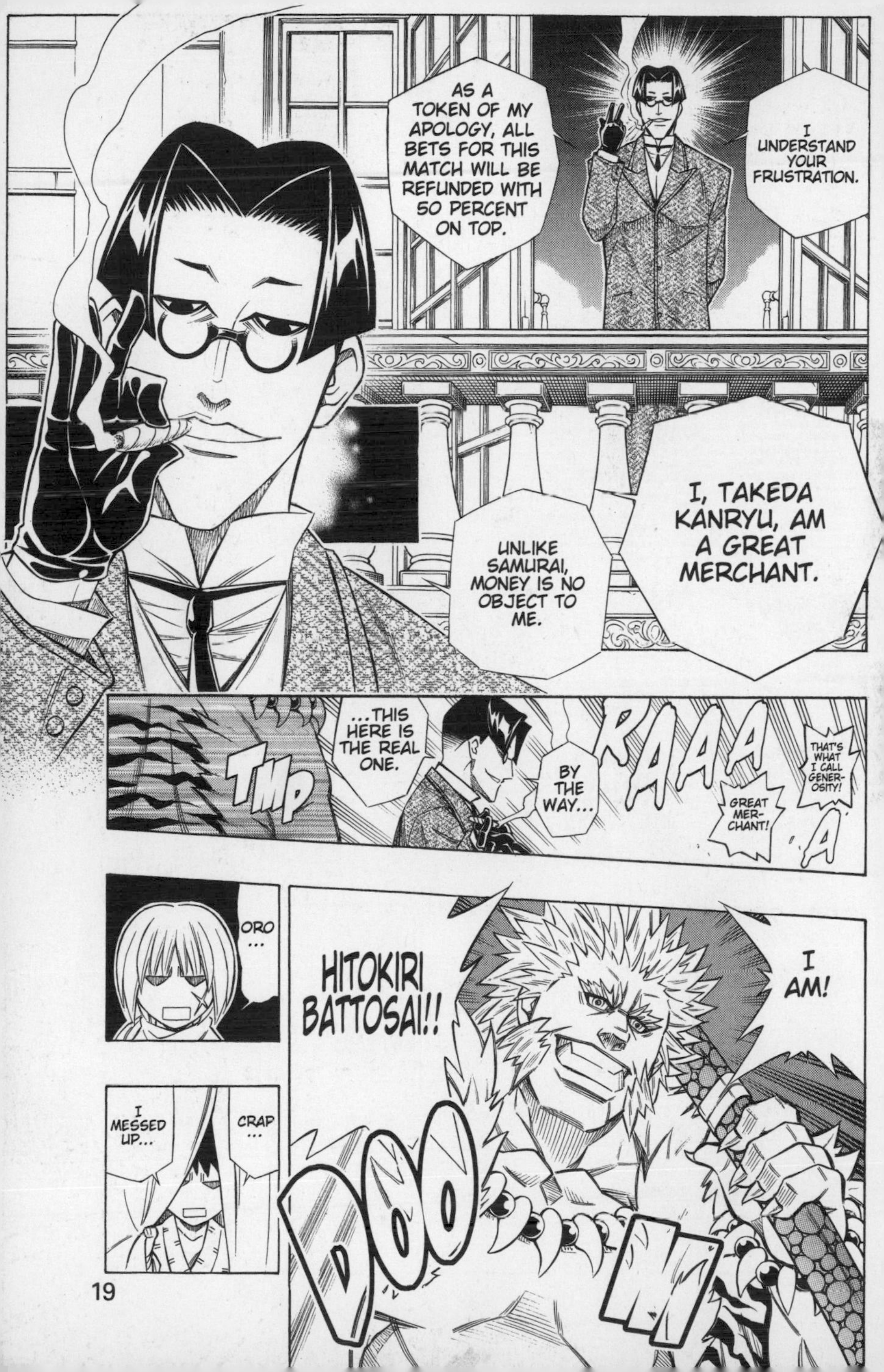
I UNDERSTAND YOUR FRUSTRATION.
AS A TOKEN OF MY APOLOGY, ALL BETS FOR THIS MATCH WILL BE REFUNDED WITH 50 PERCENT ON TOP.
I, TAKEDA KANRYU, AM A GREAT MERCHANT.
UNLIKE SAMURAI, MONEY IS NO OBJECT TO ME.
THAT'S WHAT I CALL GENER-OSITY!
GREAT MER-CHANT!
RAAAA
A
BY THE WAY...
...THIS HERE IS THE REAL ONE.
TMP
I AM!
HITOKIRI BATTOSAI!!
DOOM
ORO...
CRAP...
I MESSED UP...

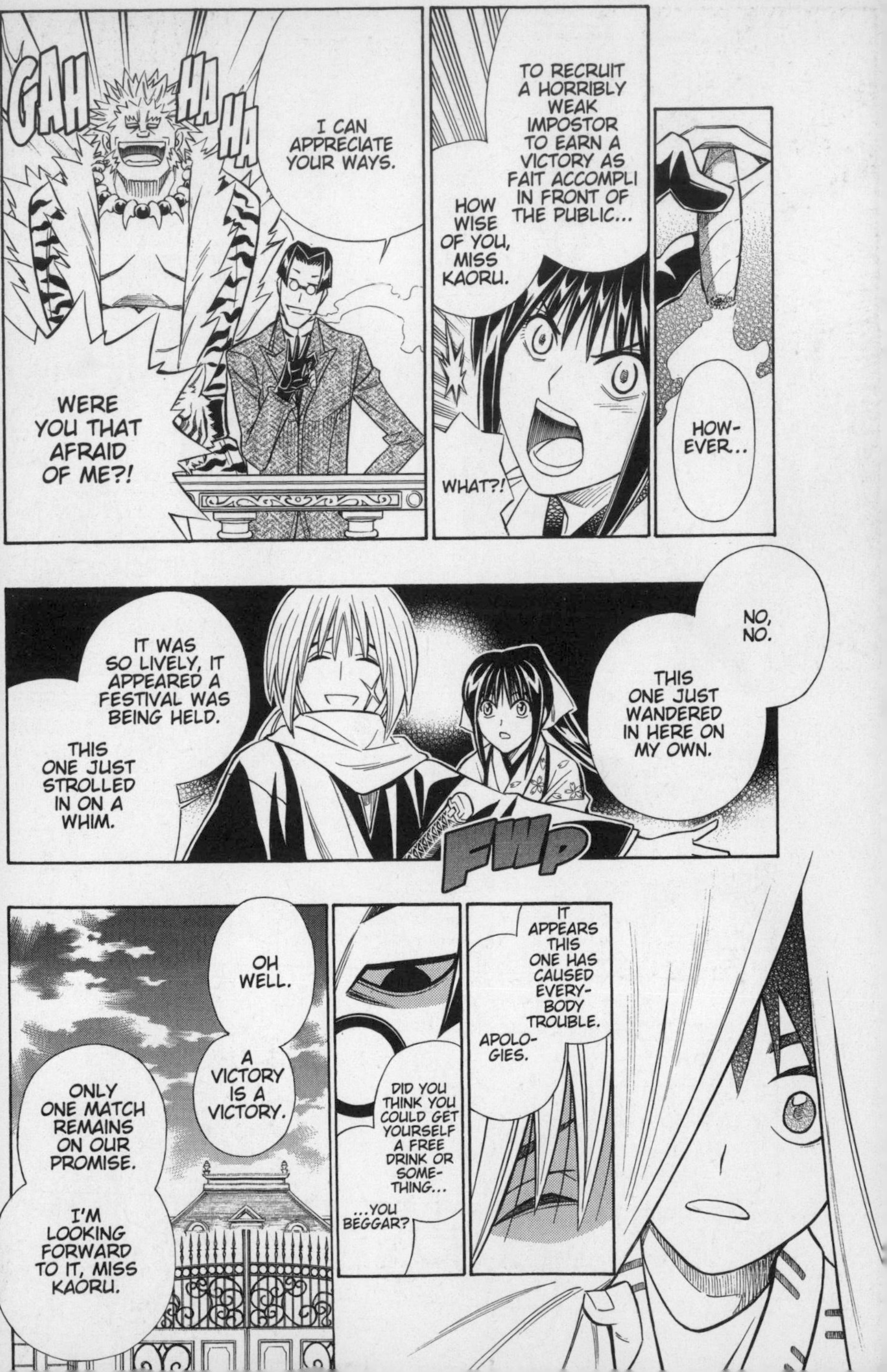
HOW-EVER...
TO RECRUIT A HORRIBLY WEAK IMPOSTOR TO EARN A VICTORY AS FAIT ACCOMPLI IN FRONT OF THE PUBLIC...
HOW WISE OF YOU, MISS KAORU.
WHAT?!
I CAN APPRECIATE YOUR WAYS.
GAH HA HA HA
WERE YOU THAT AFRAID OF ME?!
NO, NO.
THIS ONE JUST WANDERED IN HERE ON MY OWN.
FWP
IT WAS SO LIVELY, IT APPEARED A FESTIVAL WAS BEING HELD.
THIS ONE JUST STROLLED IN ON A WHIM.
IT APPEARS THIS ONE HAS CAUSED EVERY-BODY TROUBLE.
APOLO-GIES.
DID YOU THINK YOU COULD GET YOURSELF A FREE DRINK OR SOME-THING...
...YOU BEGGAR?
OH WELL.
A VICTORY IS A VICTORY.
ONLY ONE MATCH REMAINS ON OUR PROMISE.
I'M LOOKING FORWARD TO IT, MISS KAORU.

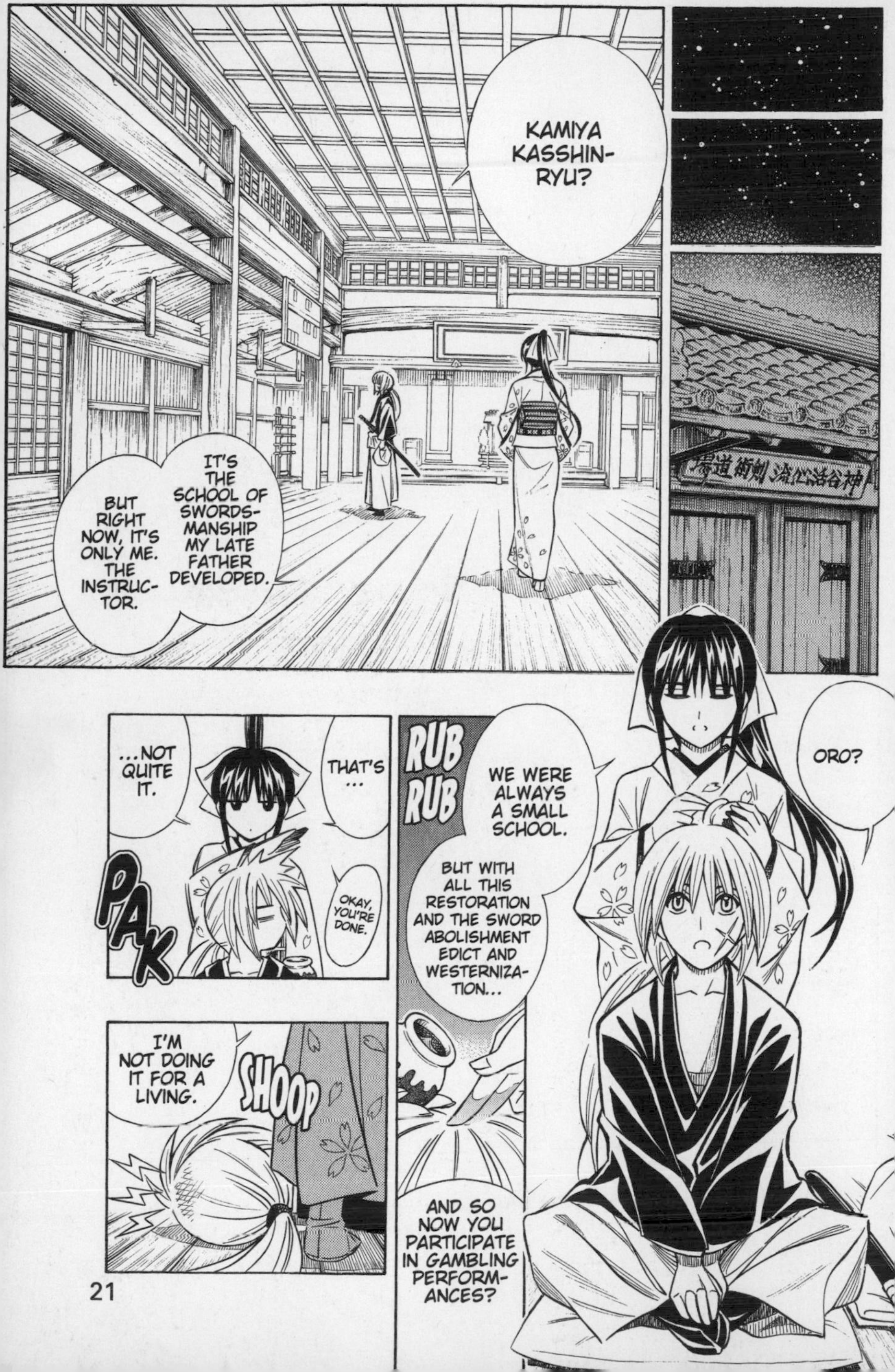
神谷活心流剣術道場
KAMIYA KASSHIN-RYU?
IT'S THE SCHOOL OF SWORDSMANSHIP MY LATE FATHER DEVELOPED.
BUT RIGHT NOW, IT'S ONLY ME. THE INSTRUCTOR.
ORO?
RUB RUB
WE WERE ALWAYS A SMALL SCHOOL.
BUT WITH ALL THIS RESTORATION AND THE SWORD ABOLISHMENT EDICT AND WESTERNIZATION...
AND SO NOW YOU PARTICIPATE IN GAMBLING PERFORMANCES?
THAT'S ...
...NOT QUITE IT.
OKAY, YOU'RE DONE.
PAK
SHOOP
I'M NOT DOING IT FOR A LIVING.

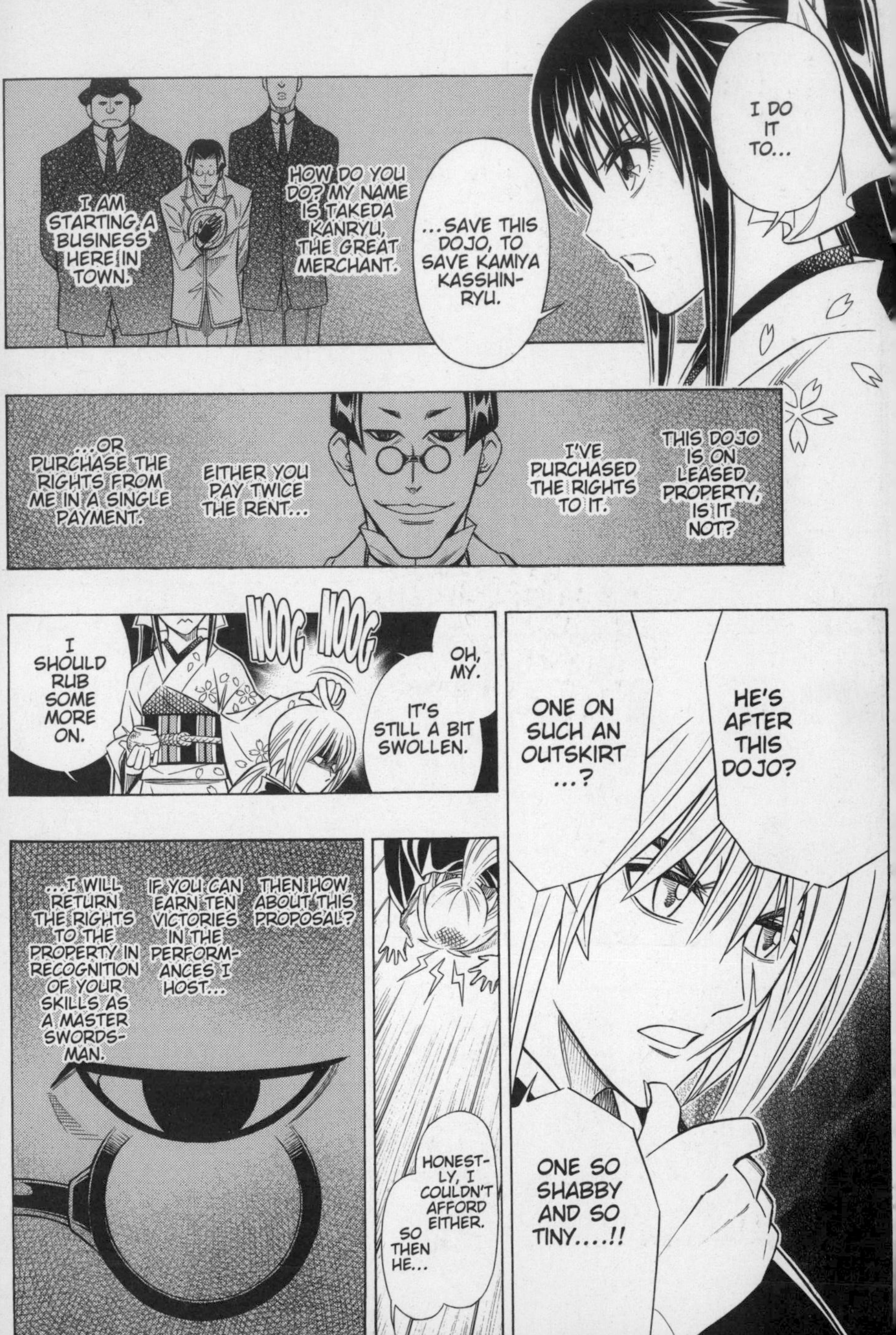
I DO IT TO...
...SAVE THIS DOJO, TO SAVE KAMIYA KASSHIN-RYU.
HOW DO YOU DO? MY NAME IS TAKEDA KANRYU, THE GREAT MERCHANT.
I AM STARTING A BUSINESS HERE IN TOWN.
THIS DOJO IS ON LEASED PROPERTY, IS IT NOT?
I'VE PURCHASED THE RIGHTS TO IT.
EITHER YOU PAY TWICE THE RENT...
...OR PURCHASE THE RIGHTS FROM ME IN A SINGLE PAYMENT.
HE'S AFTER THIS DOJO?
ONE ON SUCH AN OUTSKIRT ...?
ONE SO SHABBY AND SO TINY....!!
OH, MY.
IT'S STILL A BIT SWOLLEN.
NOOG NOOG
I SHOULD RUB SOME MORE ON.
HONESTLY, I COULDN'T AFFORD EITHER.
SO THEN HE...
THEN HOW ABOUT THIS PROPOSAL?
IF YOU CAN EARN TEN VICTORIES IN THE PERFORMANCES I HOST...
...I WILL RETURN THE RIGHTS TO THE PROPERTY IN RECOGNITION OF YOUR SKILLS AS A MASTER SWORDSMAN.

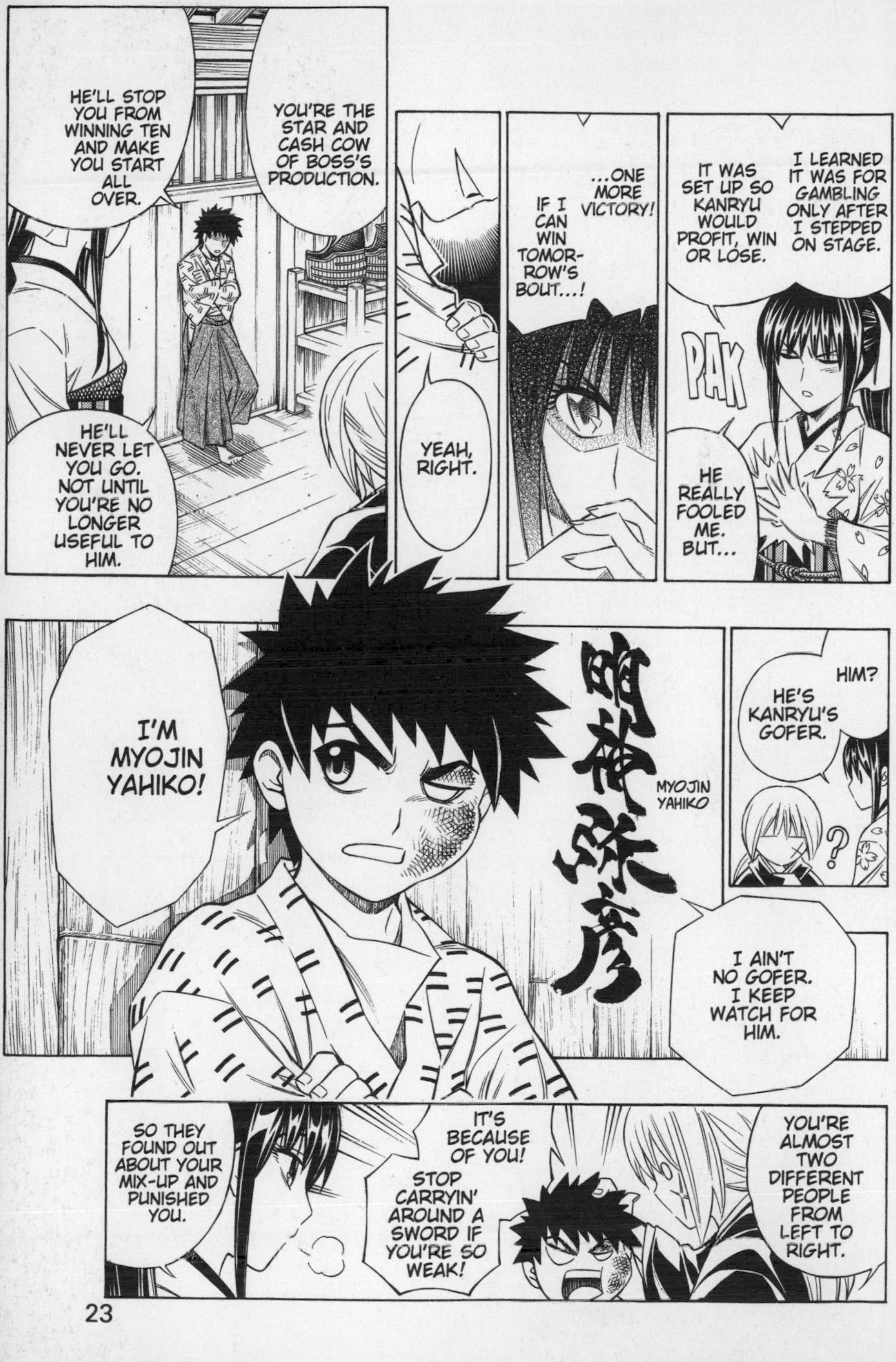
I LEARNED IT WAS FOR GAMBLING ONLY AFTER I STEPPED ON STAGE.
IT WAS SET UP SO KANRYU WOULD PROFIT, WIN OR LOSE.
PAK
HE REALLY FOOLED ME. BUT...
...ONE MORE VICTORY!
IF I CAN WIN TOMOR-ROW'S BOUT...!
YEAH, RIGHT.
YOU'RE THE STAR AND CASH COW OF BOSS'S PRODUCTION.
HE'LL STOP YOU FROM WINNING TEN AND MAKE YOU START ALL OVER.
HE'LL NEVER LET YOU GO. NOT UNTIL YOU'RE NO LONGER USEFUL TO HIM.
HIM?
HE'S KANRYU'S GOFER.
?
I AIN'T NO GOFER. I KEEP WATCH FOR HIM.
明神弥彦
MYOJIN YAHIKO
I'M MYOJIN YAHIKO!
YOU'RE ALMOST TWO DIFFERENT PEOPLE FROM LEFT TO RIGHT.
IT'S BECAUSE OF YOU!
STOP CARRYIN' AROUND A SWORD IF YOU'RE SO WEAK!
SO THEY FOUND OUT ABOUT YOUR MIX-UP AND PUNISHED YOU.

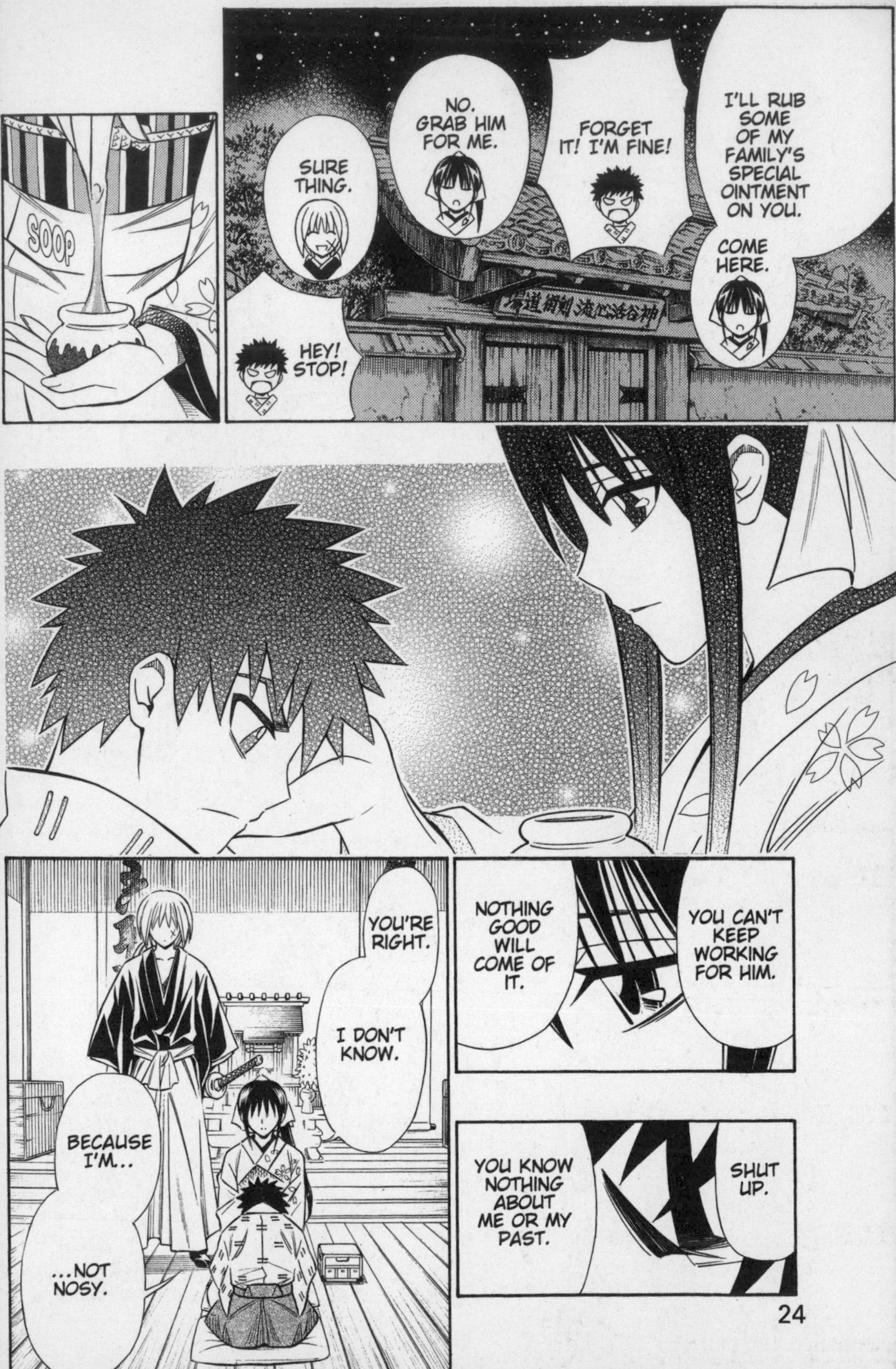

I'LL RUB SOME OF MY FAMILY'S SPECIAL OINTMENT ON YOU.
COME HERE.
FORGET IT! I'M FINE!
NO. GRAB HIM FOR ME.
SURE THING.
HEY! STOP!
SOOP
YOU CAN'T KEEP WORKING FOR HIM.
NOTHING GOOD WILL COME OF IT.
SHUT UP.
YOU KNOW NOTHING ABOUT ME OR MY PAST.
YOU'RE RIGHT.
I DON'T KNOW.
BECAUSE I'M...
...NOT NOSY.

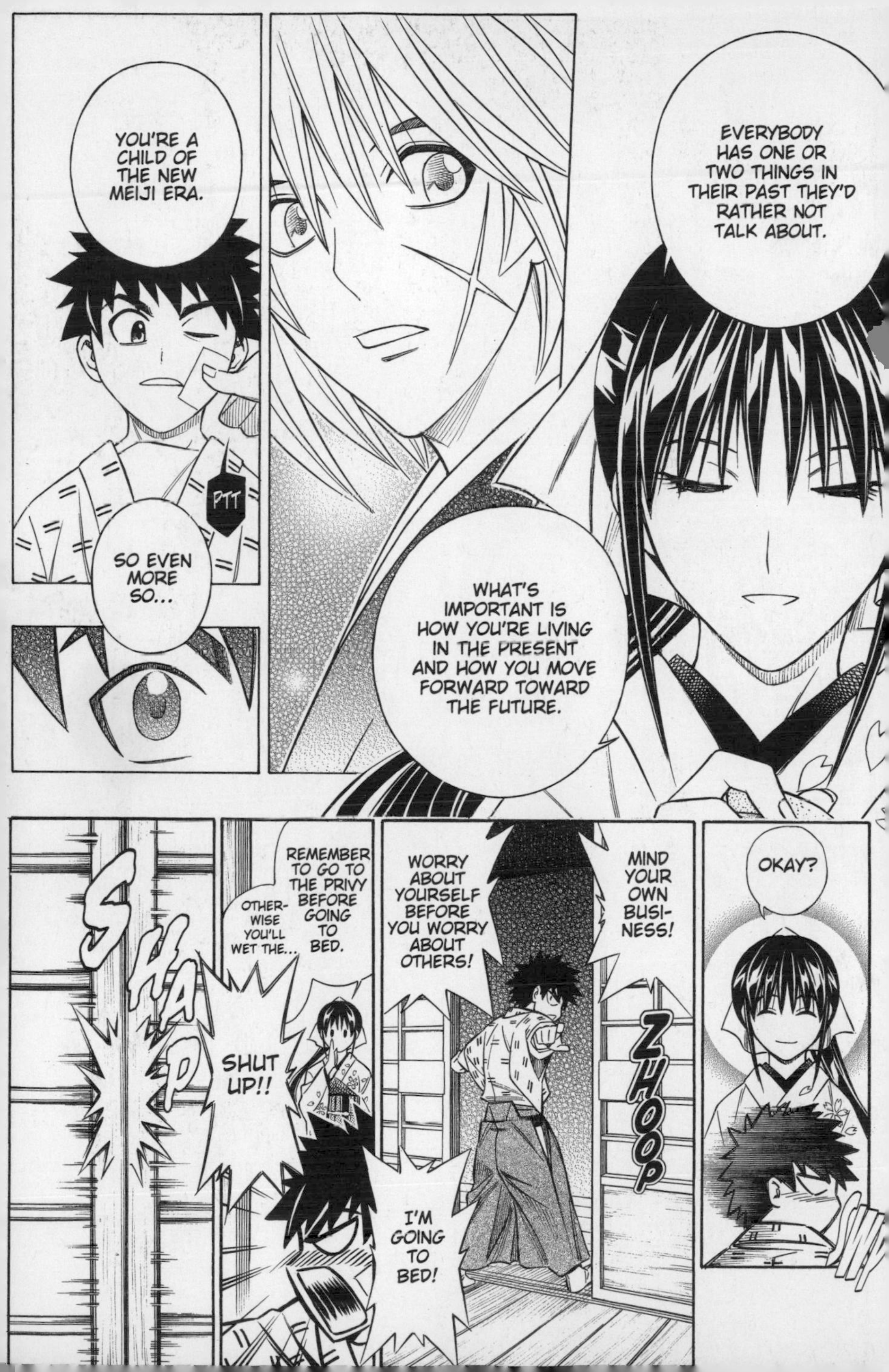
EVERYBODY HAS ONE OR TWO THINGS IN THEIR PAST THEY'D RATHER NOT TALK ABOUT.
WHAT'S IMPORTANT IS HOW YOU'RE LIVING IN THE PRESENT AND HOW YOU MOVE FORWARD TOWARD THE FUTURE.
YOU'RE A CHILD OF THE NEW MEIJI ERA.
PTT
SO EVEN MORE SO...
OKAY?
MIND YOUR OWN BUSI-NESS!
ZHOOP
WORRY ABOUT YOURSELF BEFORE YOU WORRY ABOUT OTHERS!
I'M GOING TO BED!
REMEMBER TO GO TO THE PRIVY BEFORE GOING TO BED.
OTHER-WISE YOU'LL WET THE...
SHUT UP!!
SHAP

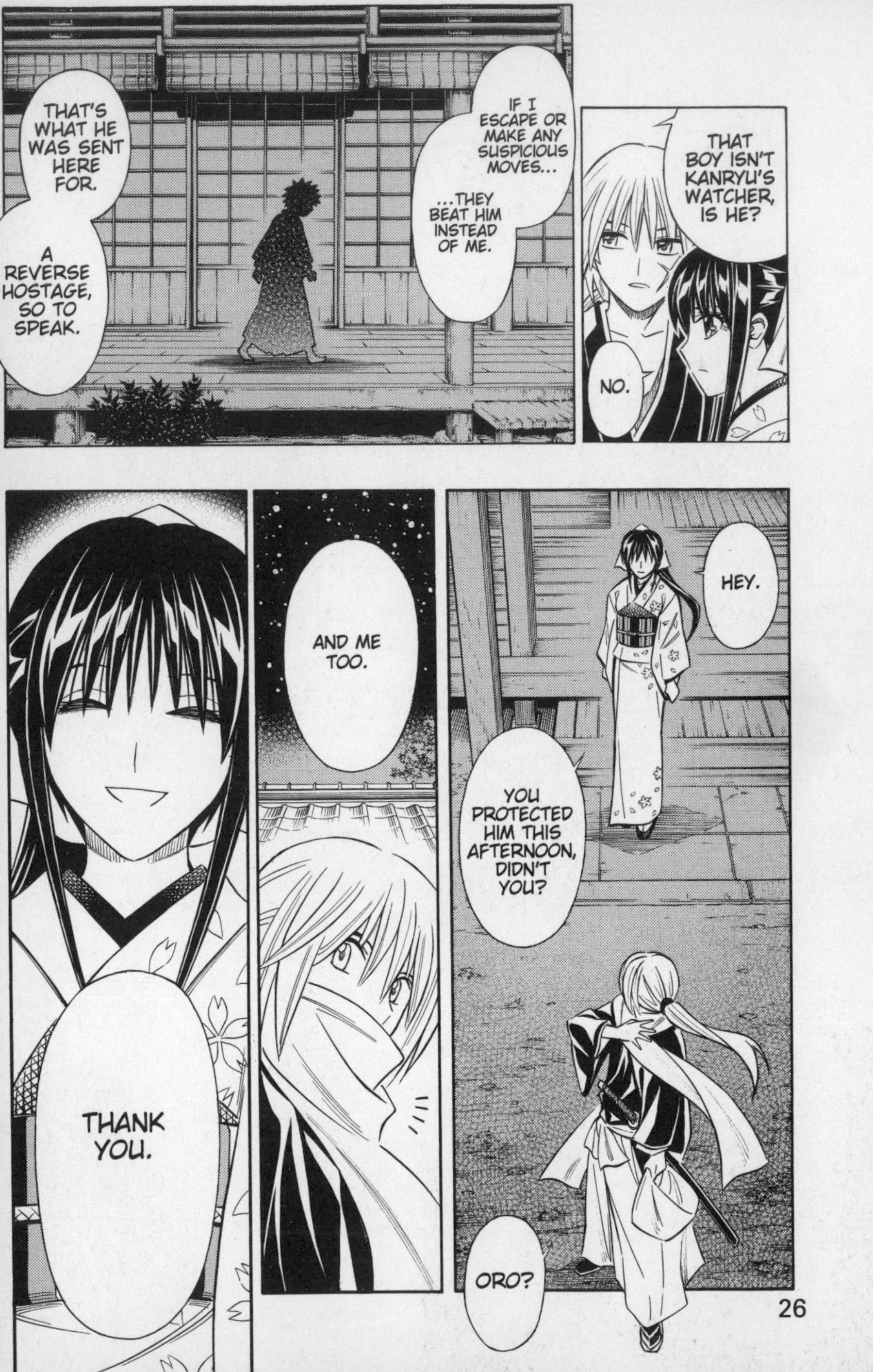
THAT BOY ISN'T KANRYU'S WATCHER, IS HE?
NO.
IF I ESCAPE OR MAKE ANY SUSPICIOUS MOVES...
...THEY BEAT HIM INSTEAD OF ME.
THAT'S WHAT HE WAS SENT HERE FOR.
A REVERSE HOSTAGE, SO TO SPEAK.
HEY.
YOU PROTECTED HIM THIS AFTERNOON, DIDN'T YOU?
ORO?
AND ME TOO.
THANK YOU.

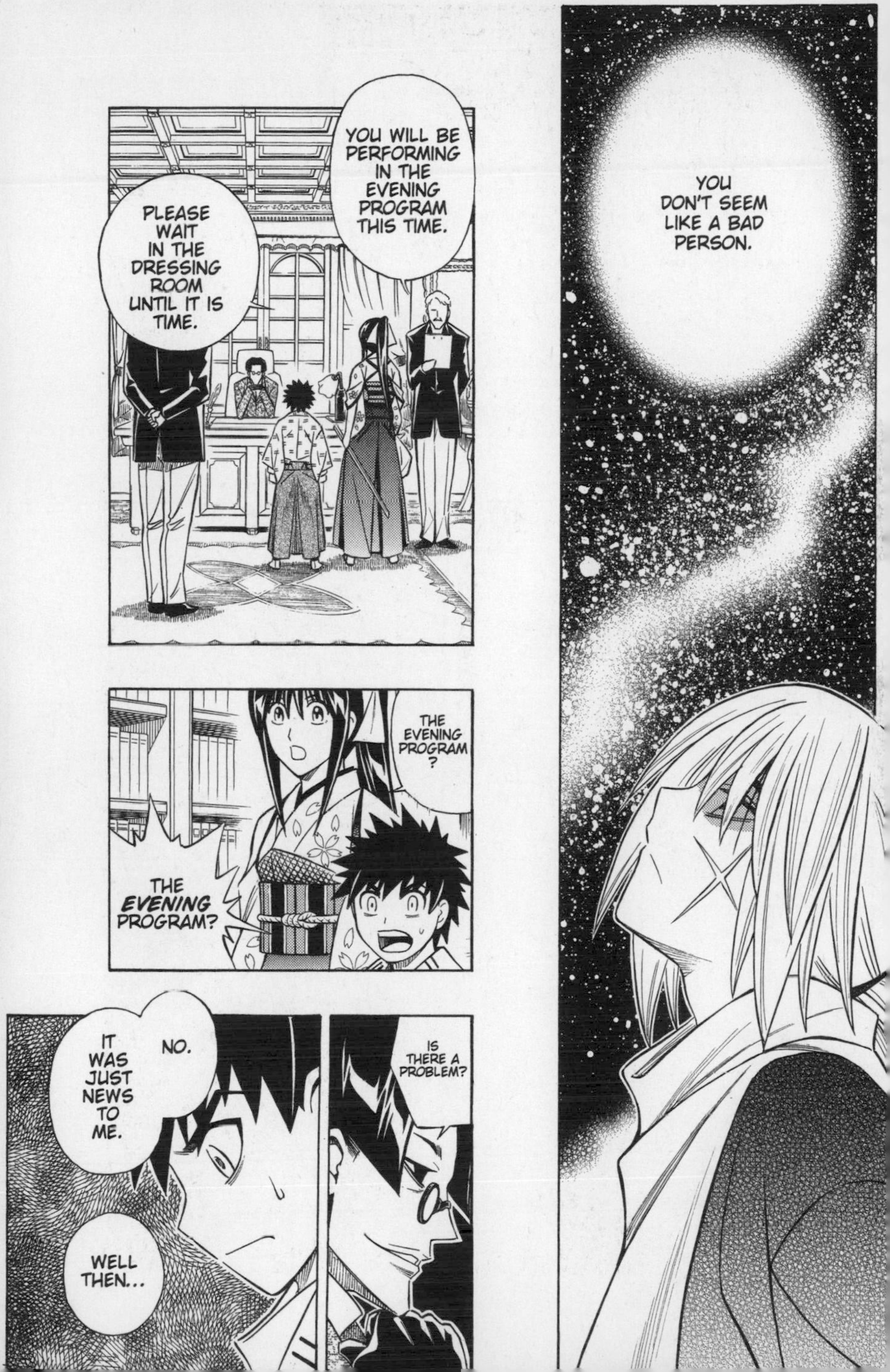
YOU DON'T SEEM LIKE A BAD PERSON.
YOU WILL BE PERFORMING IN THE EVENING PROGRAM THIS TIME.
PLEASE WAIT IN THE DRESSING ROOM UNTIL IT IS TIME.
THE EVENING PROGRAM?
THE *EVENING* PROGRAM?
IS THERE A PROBLEM?
NO.
IT WAS JUST NEWS TO ME.
WELL THEN...

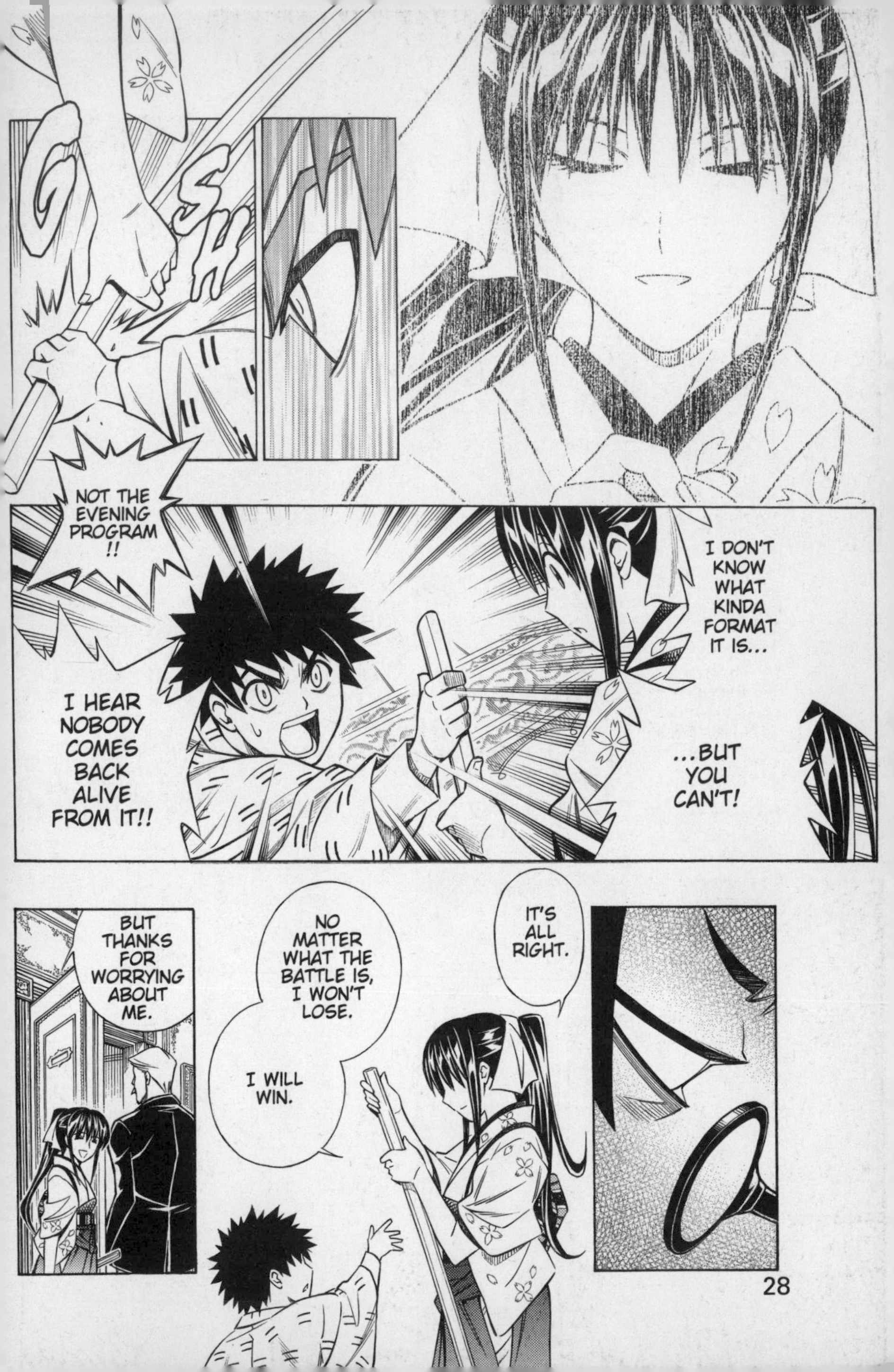
G
S
H
NOT THE EVENING PROGRAM!!
I DON'T KNOW WHAT KINDA FORMAT IT IS...
...BUT YOU CAN'T!
I HEAR NOBODY COMES BACK ALIVE FROM IT!!
IT'S ALL RIGHT.
NO MATTER WHAT THE BATTLE IS, I WON'T LOSE.
I WILL WIN.
BUT THANKS FOR WORRYING ABOUT ME.

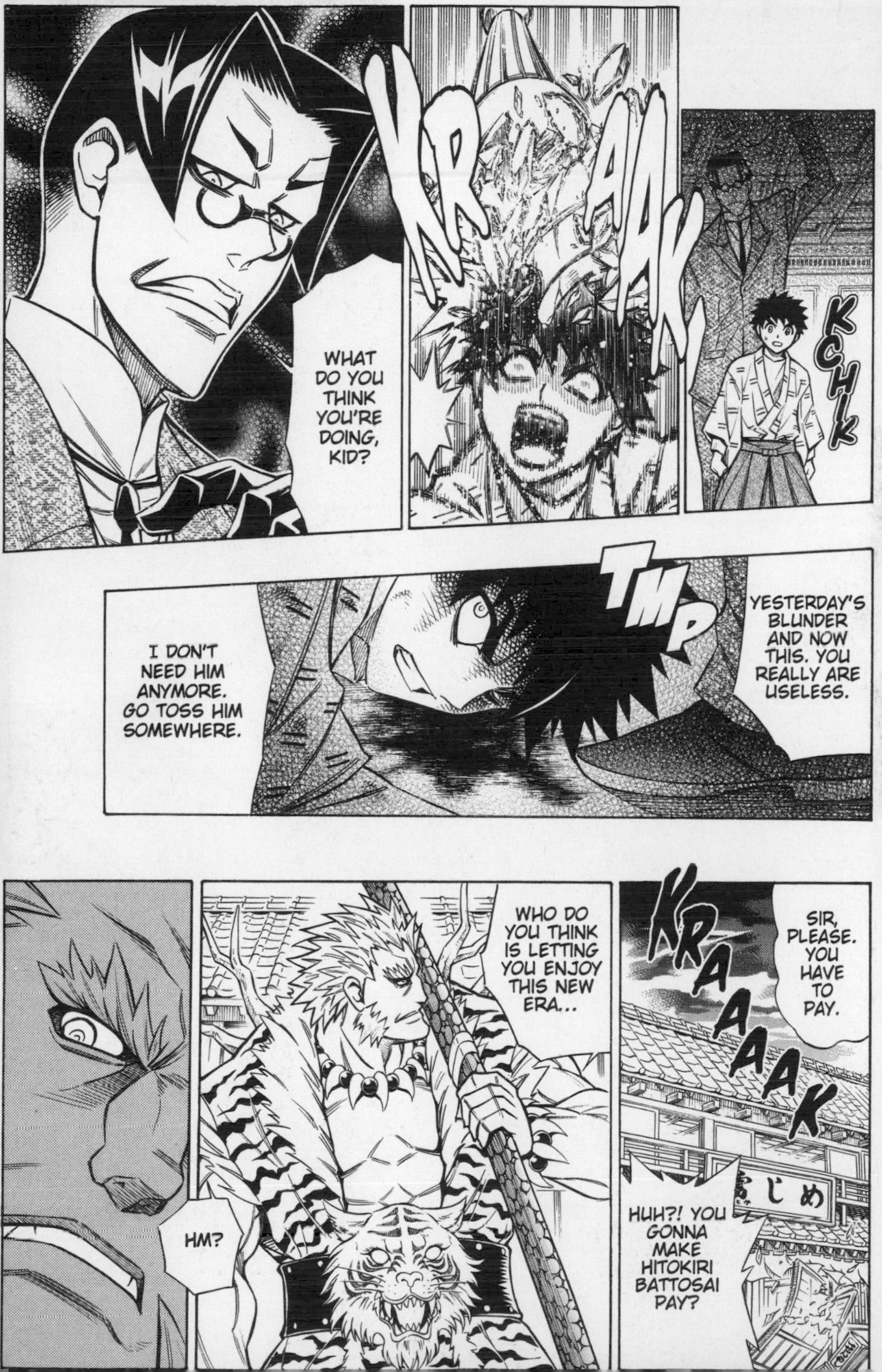

KCHK
KRAAK
WHAT DO YOU THINK YOU'RE DOING, KID?
YESTERDAY'S BLUNDER AND NOW THIS. YOU REALLY ARE USELESS.
TMP
I DON'T NEED HIM ANYMORE. GO TOSS HIM SOMEWHERE.
SIR, PLEASE. YOU HAVE TO PAY.
KRAAAAK
HUH?! YOU GONNA MAKE HITOKIRI BATTOSAI PAY?
WHO DO YOU THINK IS LETTING YOU ENJOY THIS NEW ERA...
HM?

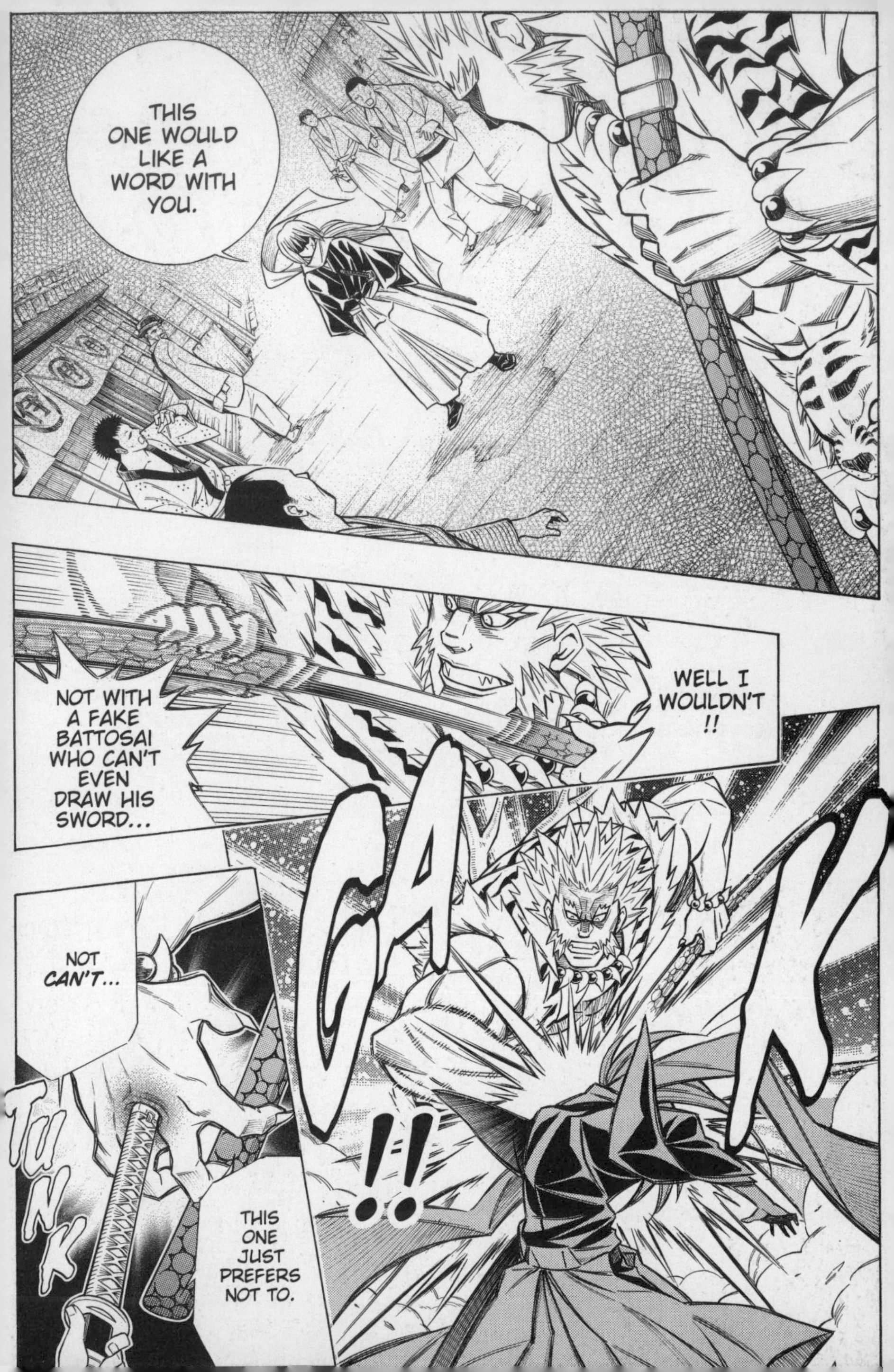
THIS ONE WOULD LIKE A WORD WITH YOU.
WELL I WOULDN'T !!
NOT WITH A FAKE BATTOSAI WHO CAN'T EVEN DRAW HIS SWORD...
GAN !!
NOT *CAN'T*...
THIS ONE JUST PREFERS NOT TO.
TUNK

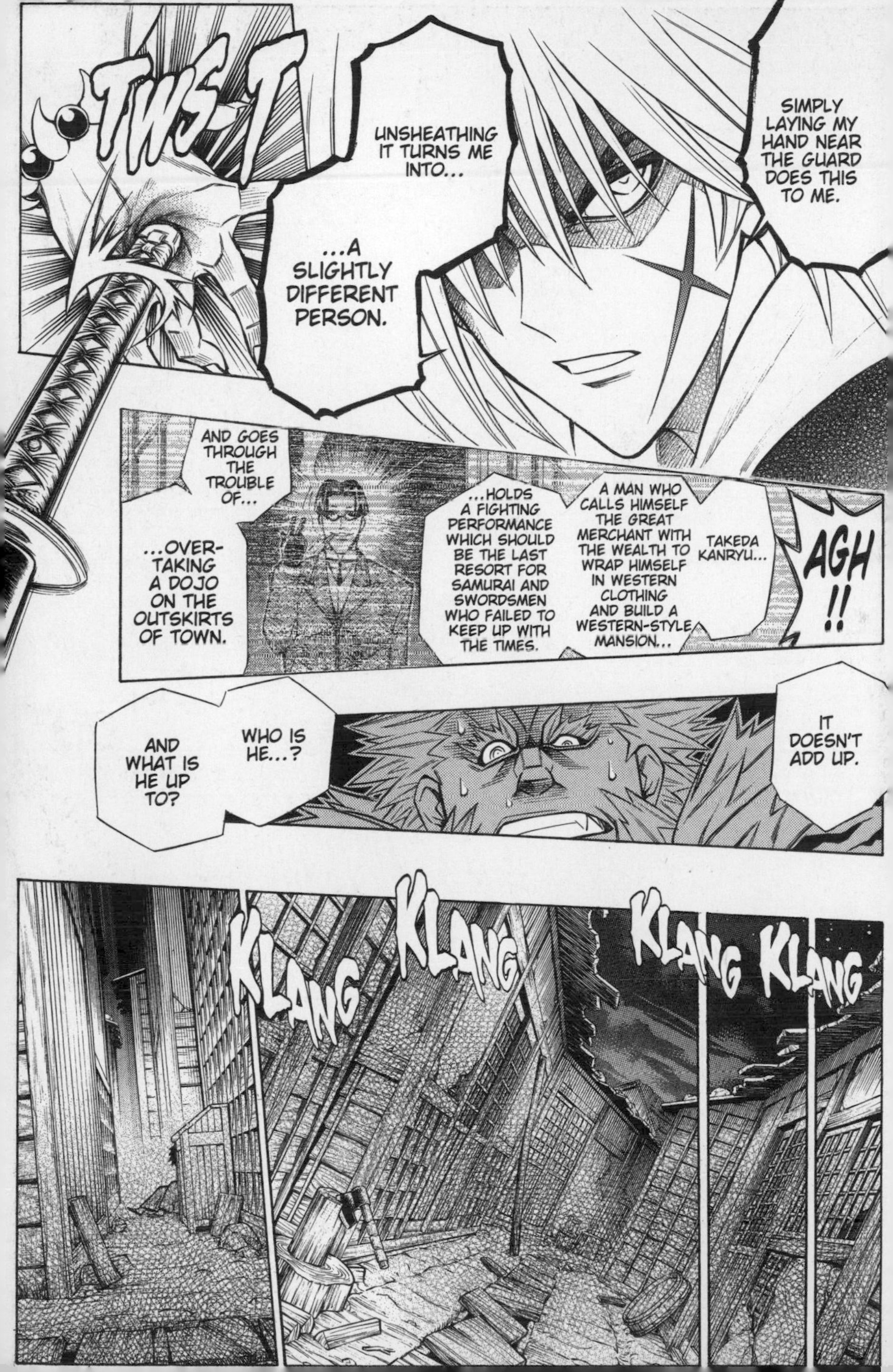
SIMPLY LAYING MY HAND NEAR THE GUARD DOES THIS TO ME.
UNSHEATHING IT TURNS ME INTO...
...A SLIGHTLY DIFFERENT PERSON.
TWIST
AGH!!
TAKEDA KANRYU...
A MAN WHO CALLS HIMSELF THE GREAT MERCHANT WITH THE WEALTH TO WRAP HIMSELF IN WESTERN CLOTHING AND BUILD A WESTERN-STYLE MANSION...
...HOLDS A FIGHTING PERFORMANCE WHICH SHOULD BE THE LAST RESORT FOR SAMURAI AND SWORDSMEN WHO FAILED TO KEEP UP WITH THE TIMES.
AND GOES THROUGH THE TROUBLE OF...
...OVER-TAKING A DOJO ON THE OUTSKIRTS OF TOWN.
IT DOESN'T ADD UP.
WHO IS HE...?
AND WHAT IS HE UP TO?
KLANG KLANG
KLANG
KLANG
KLANG

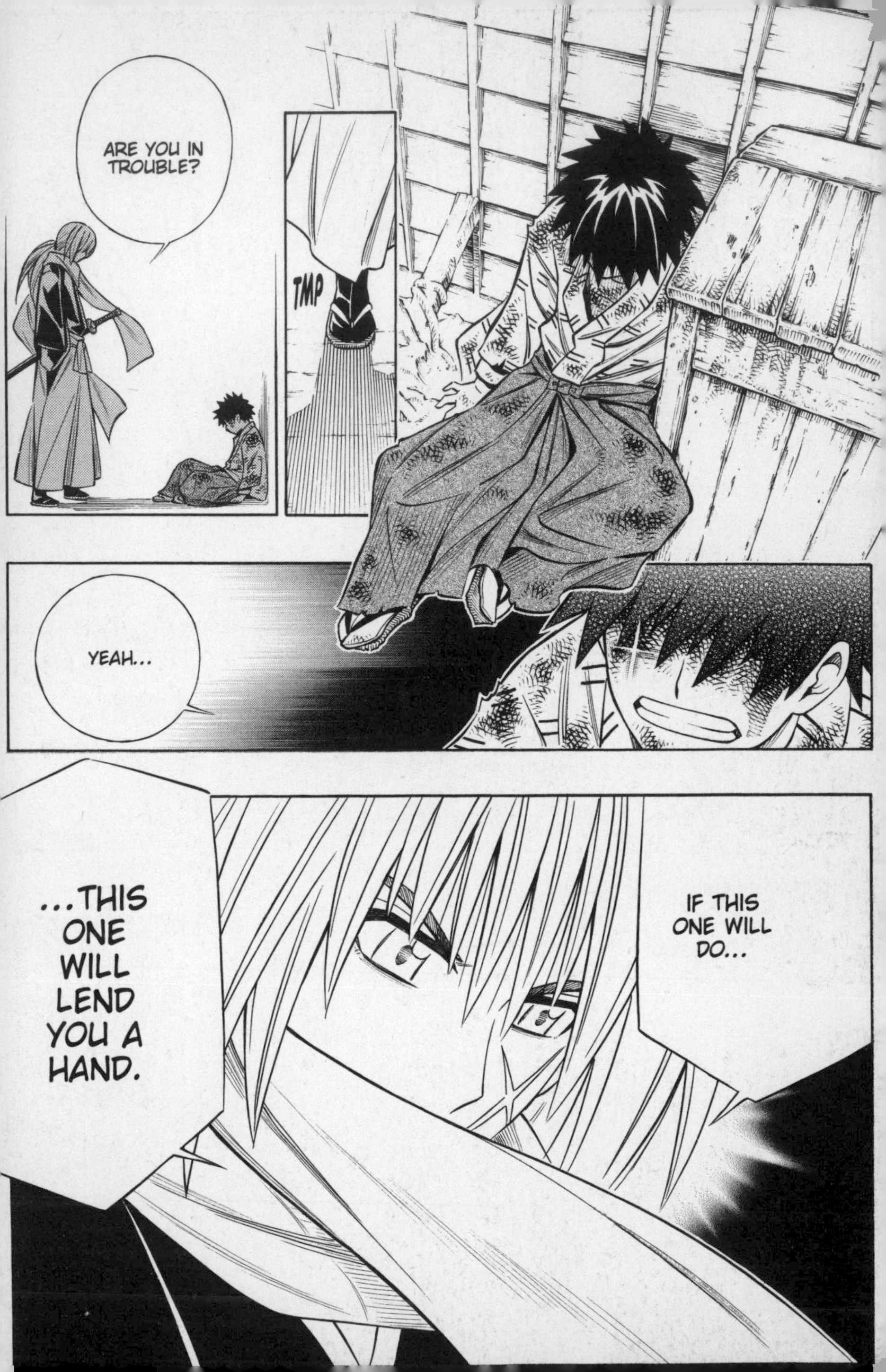
TMP
ARE YOU IN TROUBLE?
YEAH...
IF THIS ONE WILL DO...
...THIS ONE WILL LEND YOU A HAND.

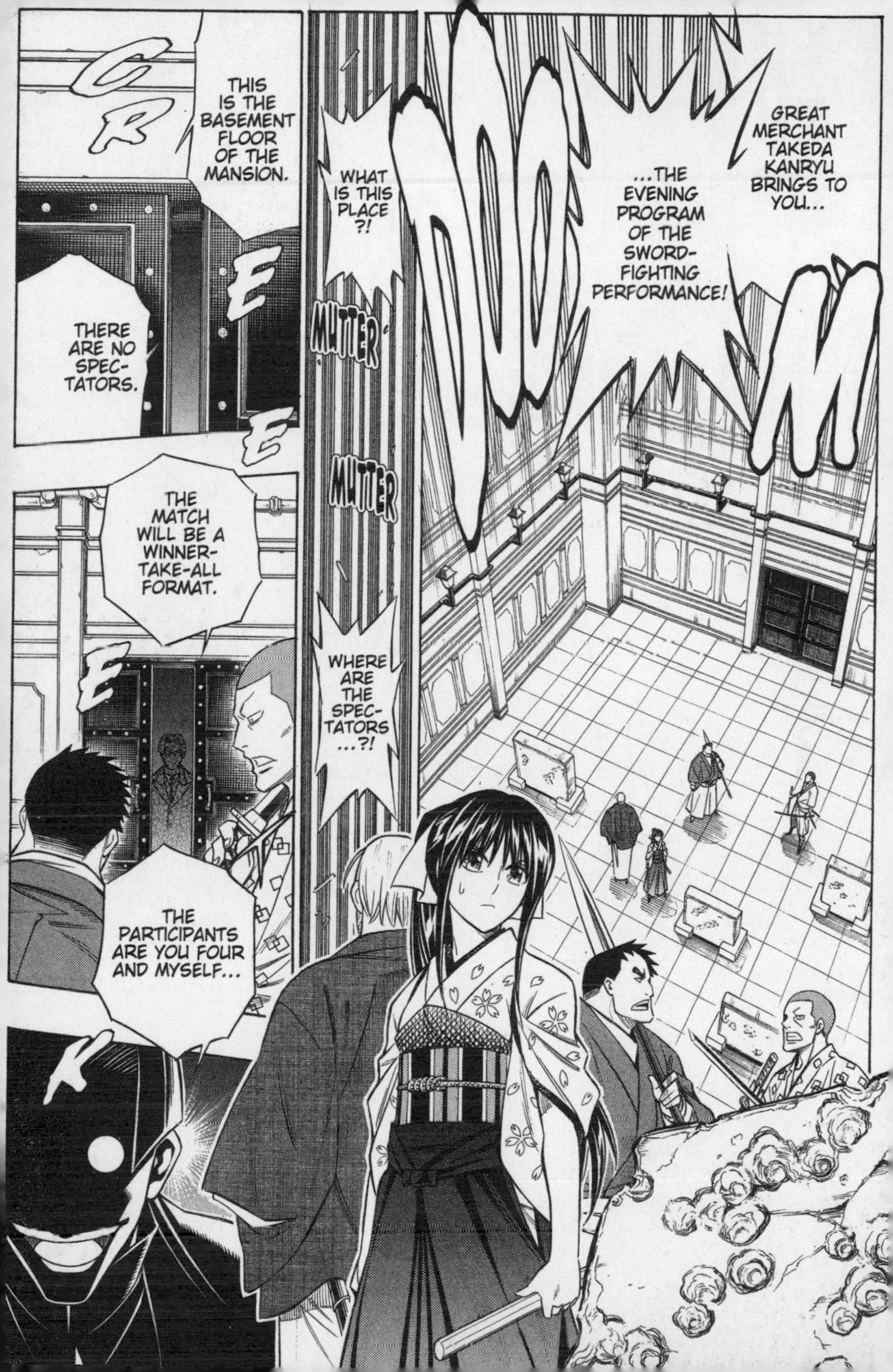
GREAT MERCHANT TAKEDA KANRYU BRINGS TO YOU...
...THE EVENING PROGRAM OF THE SWORD-FIGHTING PERFORMANCE!
DOOOM
WHAT IS THIS PLACE ?!
MUTTER
MUTTER
WHERE ARE THE SPECTATORS...?!
CR
THIS IS THE BASEMENT FLOOR OF THE MANSION.
E
THERE ARE NO SPECTATORS.
E
THE MATCH WILL BE A WINNER-TAKE-ALL FORMAT.
E
THE PARTICIPANTS ARE YOU FOUR AND MYSELF...
K

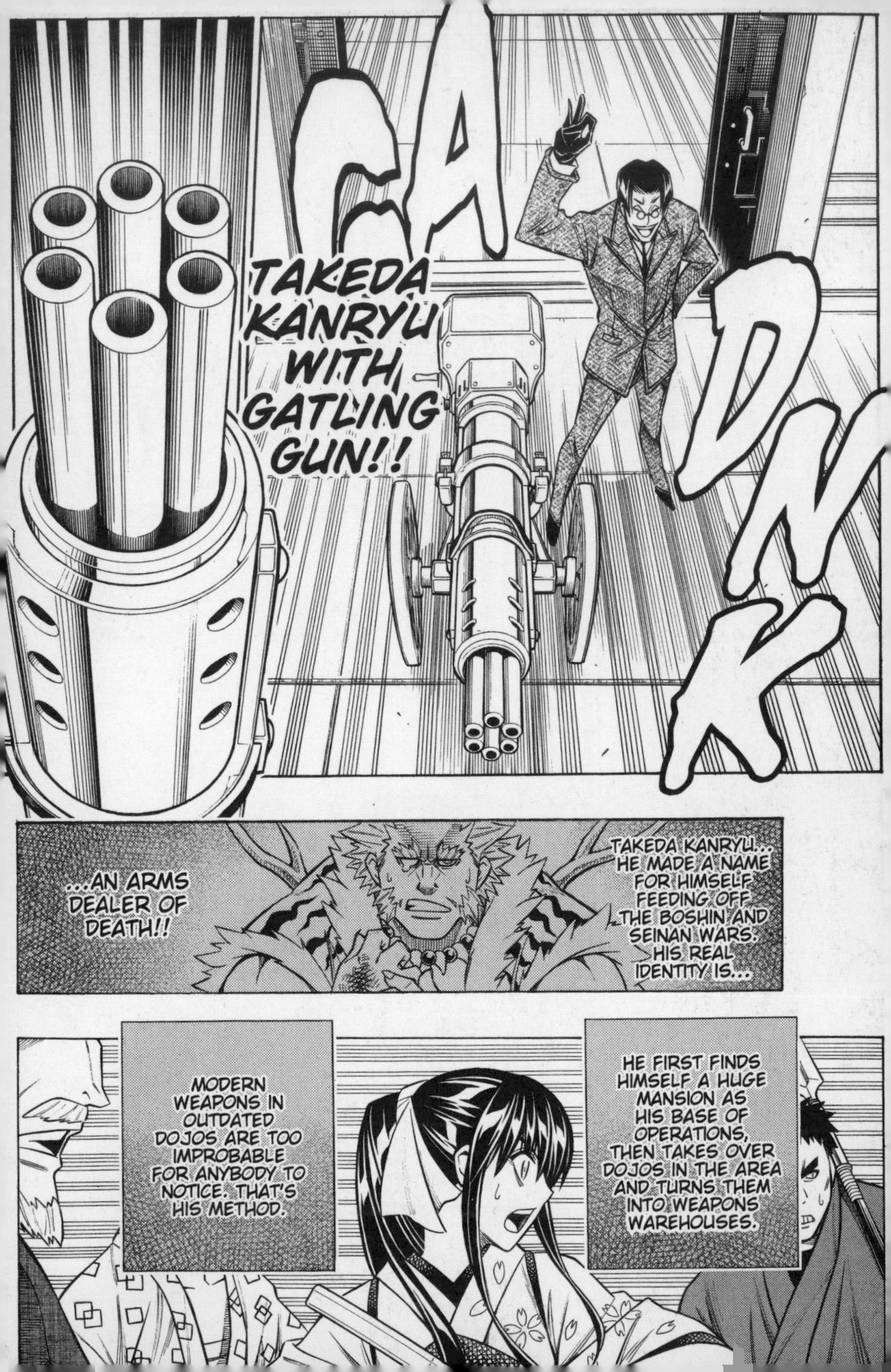
CA
DNK
TAKEDA KANRYU WITH GATLING GUN!!
TAKEDA KANRYU... HE MADE A NAME FOR HIMSELF FEEDING OFF THE BOSHIN AND SEINAN WARS. HIS REAL IDENTITY IS...
...AN ARMS DEALER OF DEATH!!
HE FIRST FINDS HIMSELF A HUGE MANSION AS HIS BASE OF OPERATIONS, THEN TAKES OVER DOJOS IN THE AREA AND TURNS THEM INTO WEAPONS WAREHOUSES.
MODERN WEAPONS IN OUTDATED DOJOS ARE TOO IMPROBABLE FOR ANYBODY TO NOTICE. THAT'S HIS METHOD.

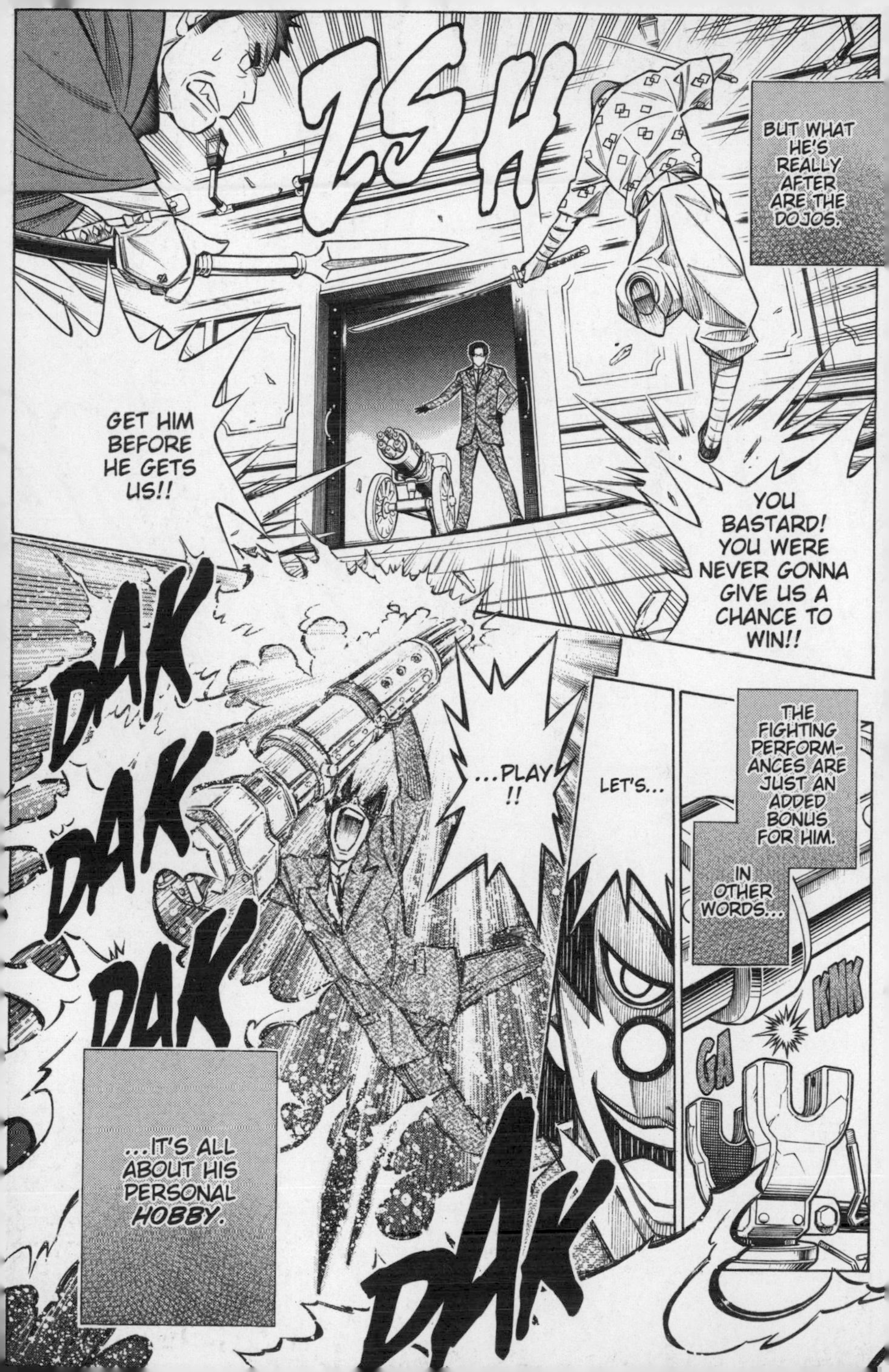
BUT WHAT HE'S REALLY AFTER ARE THE DOJOS.
ZSH
GET HIM BEFORE HE GETS US!!
YOU BASTARD! YOU WERE NEVER GONNA GIVE US A CHANCE TO WIN!!
THE FIGHTING PERFORM-ANCES ARE JUST AN ADDED BONUS FOR HIM.
IN OTHER WORDS...
KNK
GA
LET'S...
...PLAY!!
DAK
DAK
DAK
DAK
...IT'S ALL ABOUT HIS PERSONAL *HOBBY*.

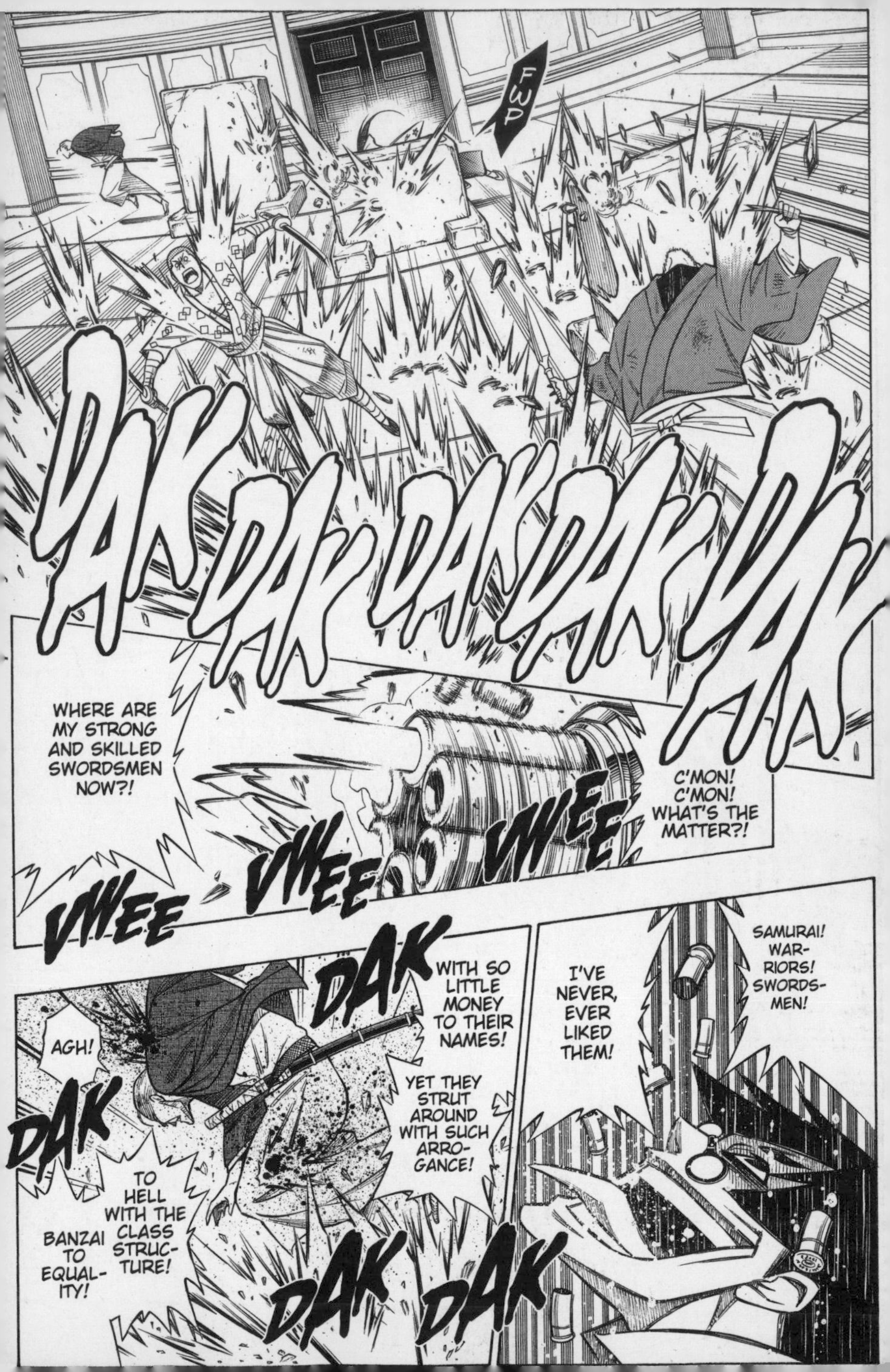
FWP
DAK DAK DAK DAK DAK
C'MON! C'MON! WHAT'S THE MATTER?!
WHERE ARE MY STRONG AND SKILLED SWORDSMEN NOW?!
VWEE
VWEE
VWEE
SAMURAI! WARRIORS! SWORDSMEN!
I'VE NEVER, EVER LIKED THEM!
DAK
WITH SO LITTLE MONEY TO THEIR NAMES!
YET THEY STRUT AROUND WITH SUCH ARROGANCE!
AGH!
DAK
TO HELL WITH THE CLASS STRUCTURE!
BANZAI TO EQUALITY!
DAK
DAK

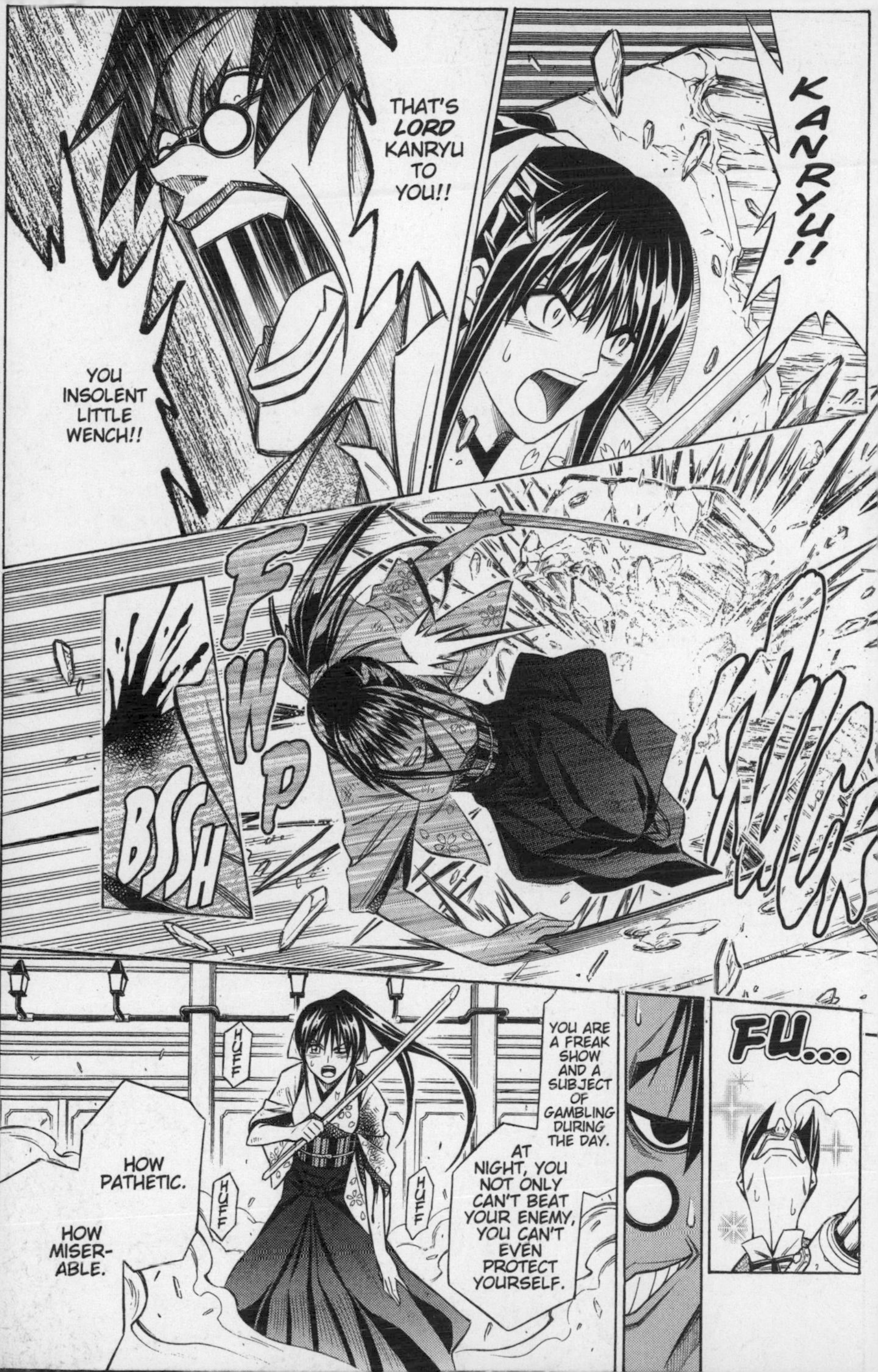
KANRYU!!
THAT'S LORD KANRYU TO YOU!!
YOU INSOLENT LITTLE WENCH!!
FWP
BSSH
FU...
YOU ARE A FREAK SHOW AND A SUBJECT OF GAMBLING DURING THE DAY.
AT NIGHT, YOU NOT ONLY CAN'T BEAT YOUR ENEMY, YOU CAN'T EVEN PROTECT YOURSELF.
HUFF
HUFF
HUFF
HOW PATHETIC.
HOW MISER-ABLE.

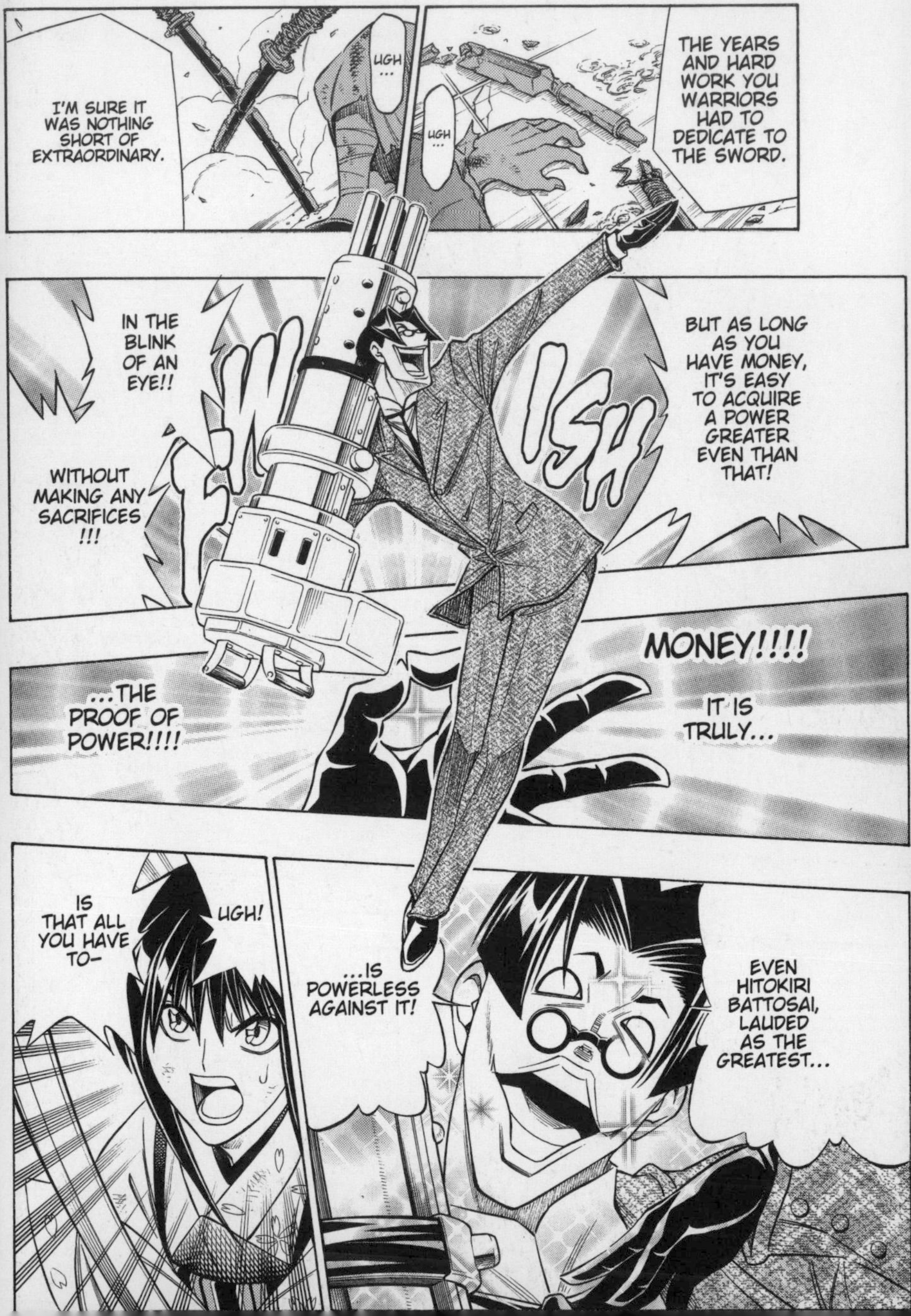

THE YEARS AND HARD WORK YOU WARRIORS HAD TO DEDICATE TO THE SWORD.
UGH...
UGH...
I'M SURE IT WAS NOTHING SHORT OF EXTRAORDINARY.
BUT AS LONG AS YOU HAVE MONEY, IT'S EASY TO ACQUIRE A POWER GREATER EVEN THAN THAT!
WISH
IN THE BLINK OF AN EYE!!
WITHOUT MAKING ANY SACRIFICES!!!
IT IS TRULY...
MONEY!!!!!
...THE PROOF OF POWER!!!!
EVEN HITOKIRI BATTOSAI, LAUDED AS THE GREATEST...
...IS POWERLESS AGAINST IT!
UGH!
IS THAT ALL YOU HAVE TO-

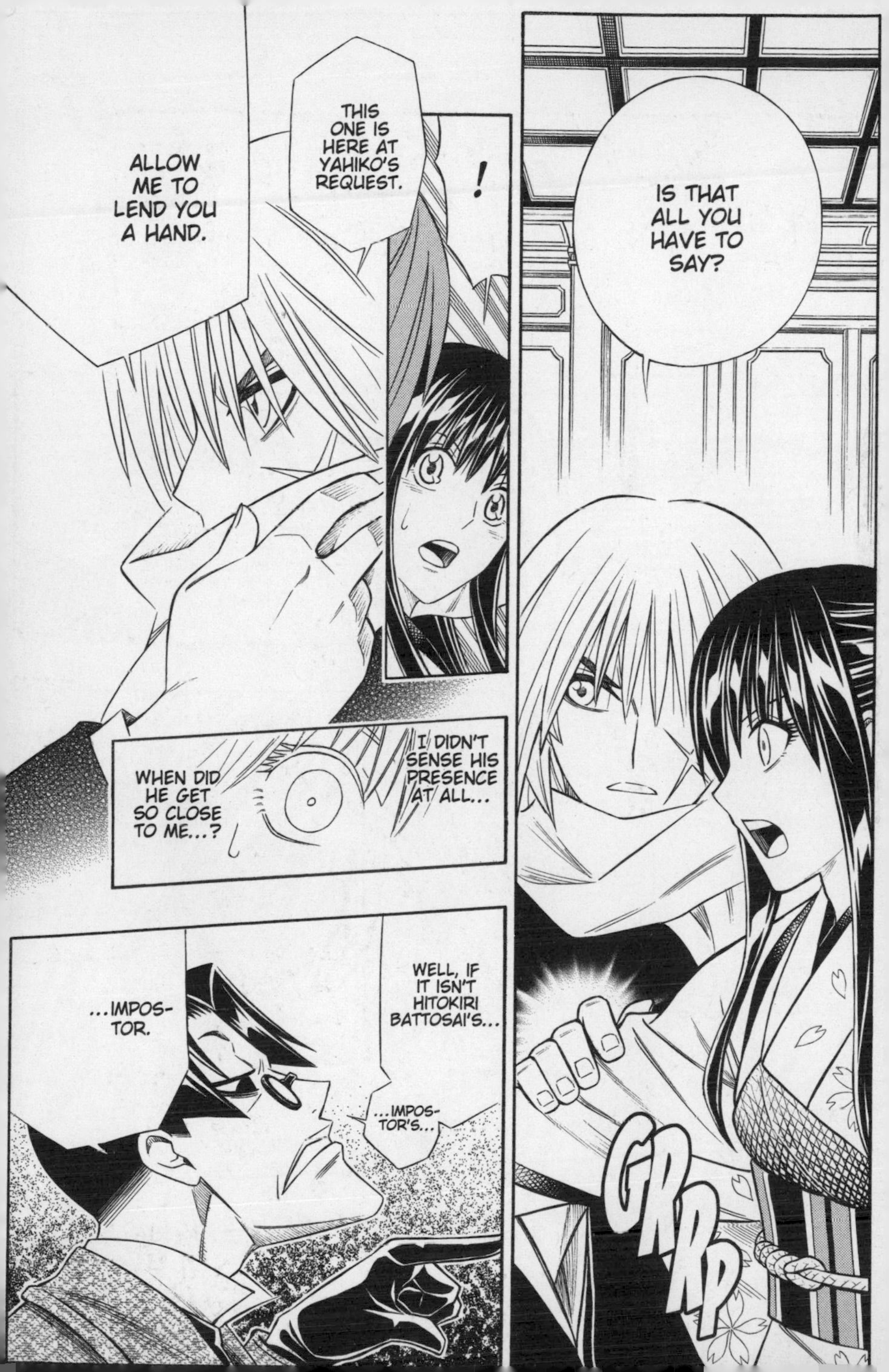
IS THAT ALL YOU HAVE TO SAY?
GRRRP
THIS ONE IS HERE AT YAHIKO'S REQUEST.
!
ALLOW ME TO LEND YOU A HAND.
I DIDN'T SENSE HIS PRESENCE AT ALL...
WHEN DID HE GET SO CLOSE TO ME...?
WELL, IF IT ISN'T HITOKIRI BATTOSAI'S...
...IMPOS-TOR'S...
...IMPOS-TOR.

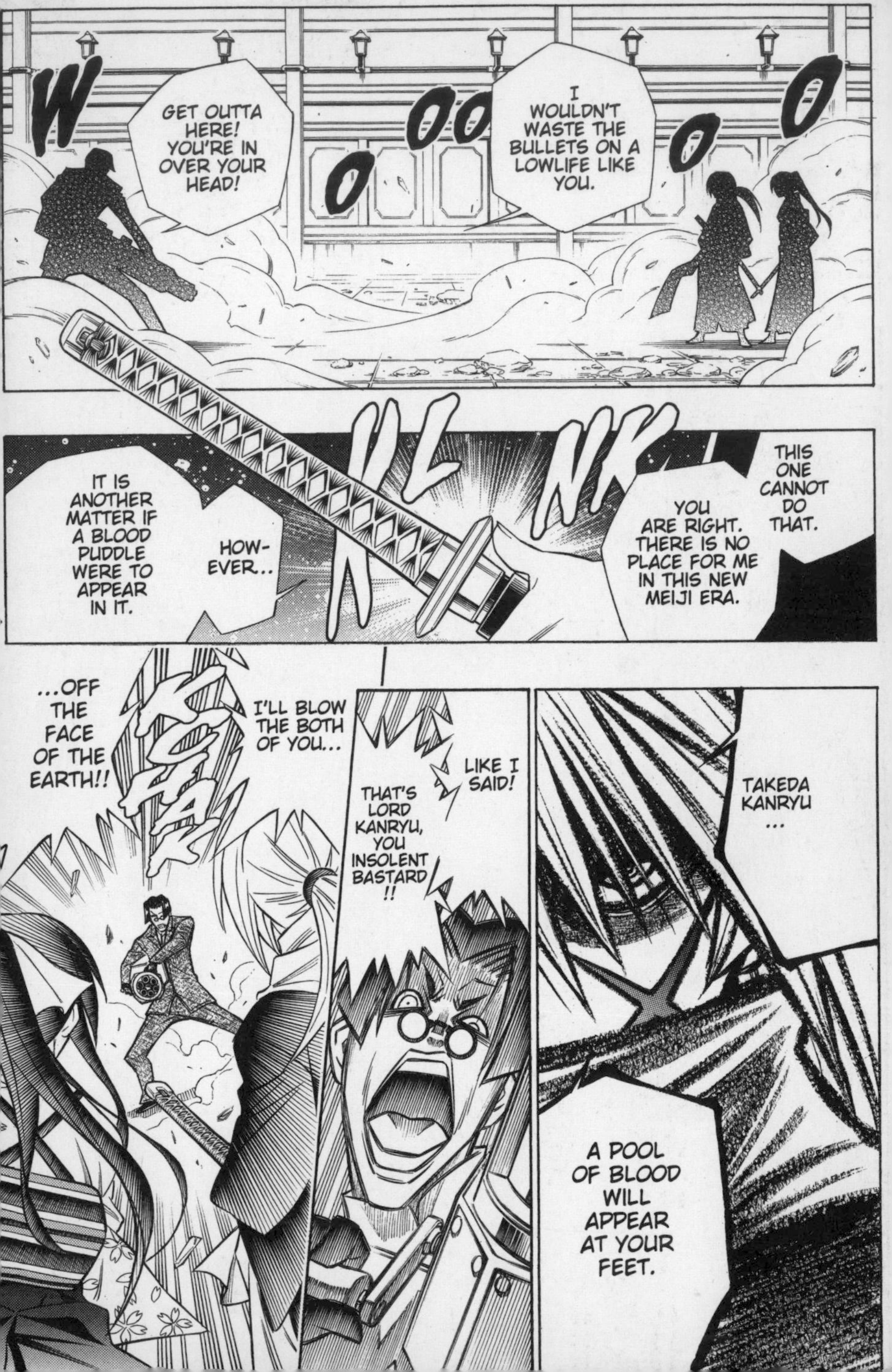
I WOULDN'T WASTE THE BULLETS ON A LOWLIFE LIKE YOU.
GET OUTTA HERE! YOU'RE IN OVER YOUR HEAD!
THIS ONE CANNOT DO THAT.
YOU ARE RIGHT. THERE IS NO PLACE FOR ME IN THIS NEW MEIJI ERA.
HOW-EVER...
IT IS ANOTHER MATTER IF A BLOOD PUDDLE WERE TO APPEAR IN IT.
TAKEDA KANRYU ...
A POOL OF BLOOD WILL APPEAR AT YOUR FEET.
LIKE I SAID!
THAT'S LORD KANRYU, YOU INSOLENT BASTARD !!
I'LL BLOW THE BOTH OF YOU...
...OFF THE FACE OF THE EARTH!!

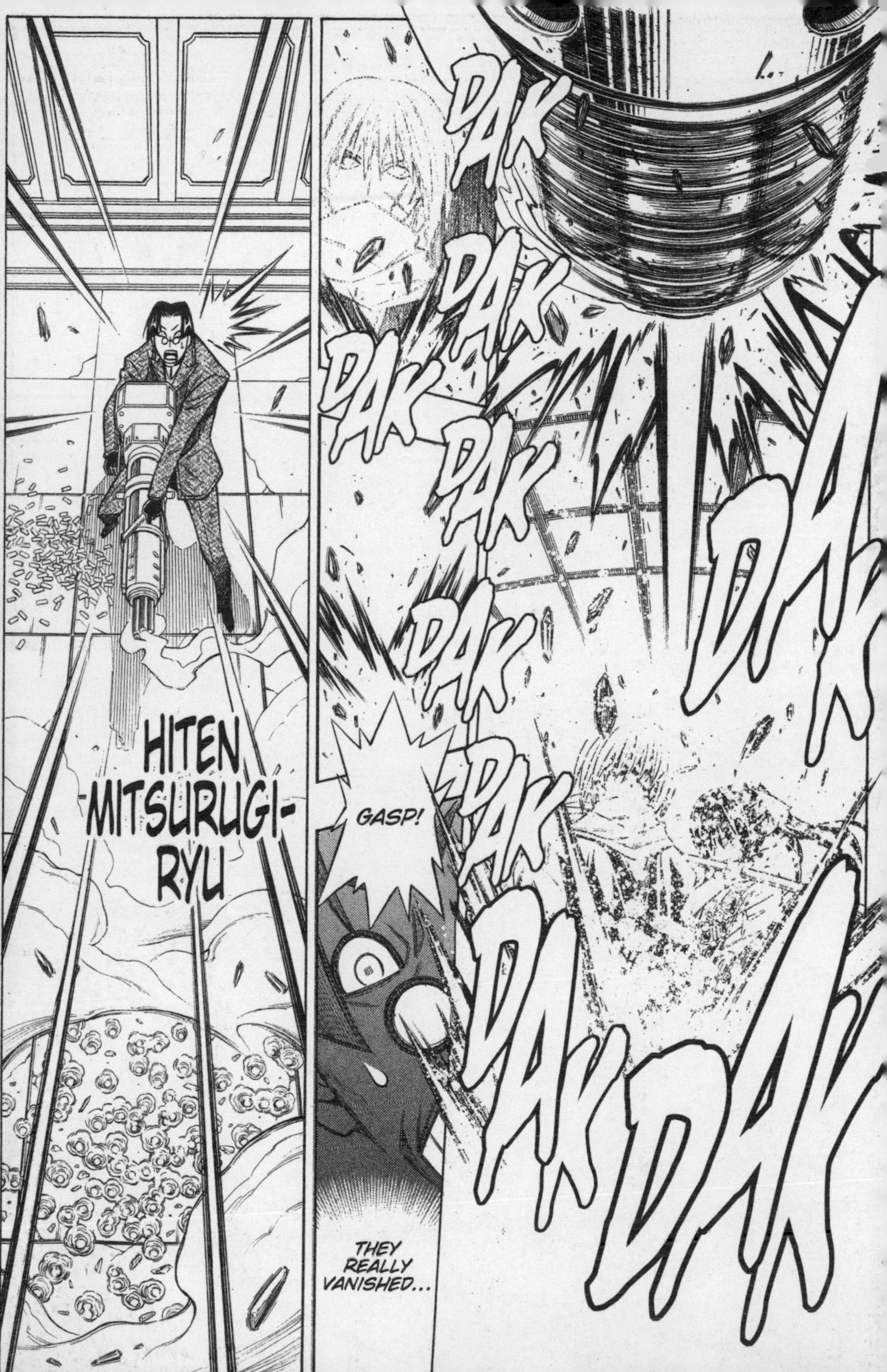
DAK
DAK
DAK
DAK
DAK
DAK
DAK
DAK
DAK
DAK
GASP!
THEY REALLY VANISHED...
HITEN MITSURUGI-RYU

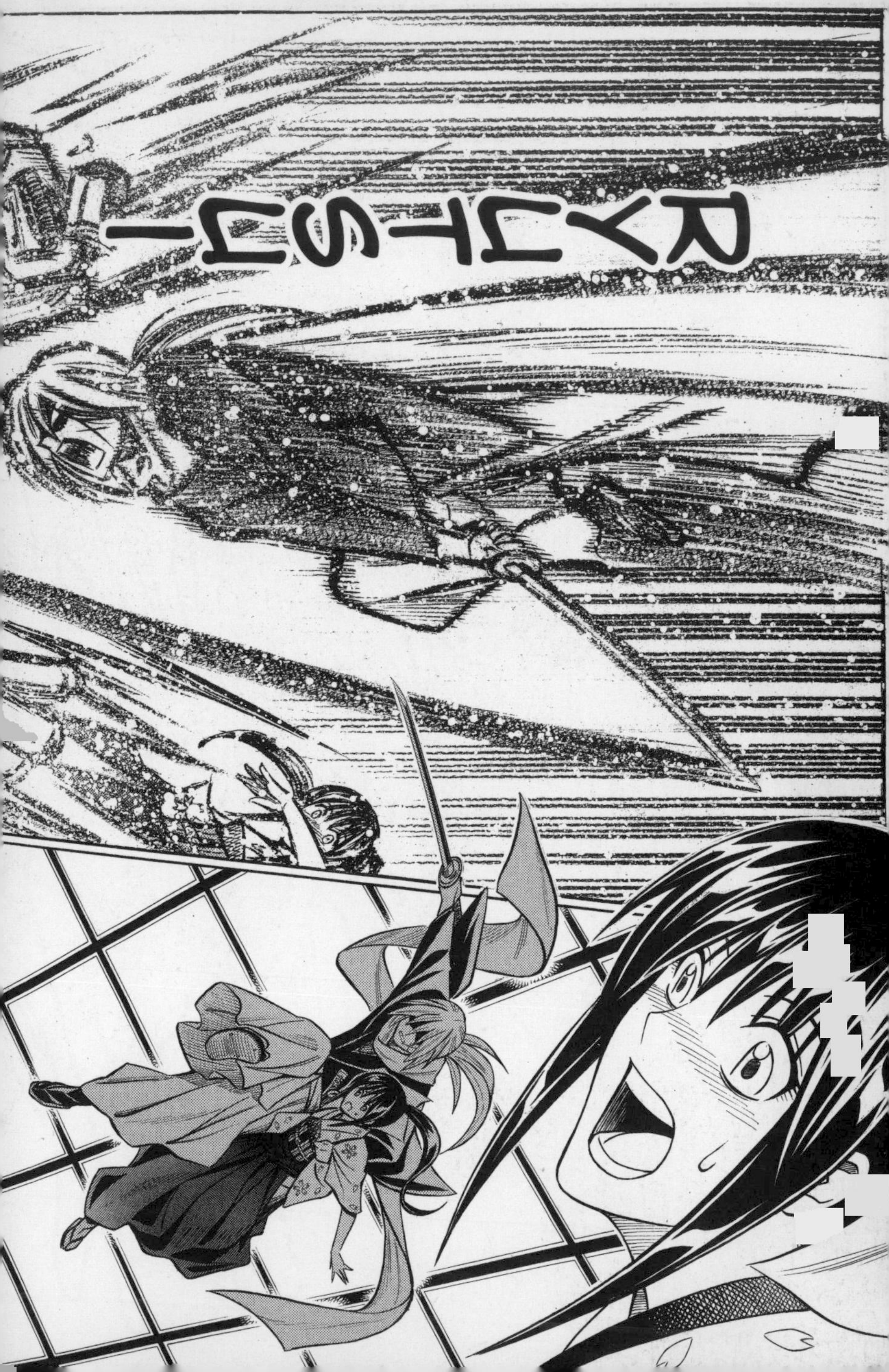

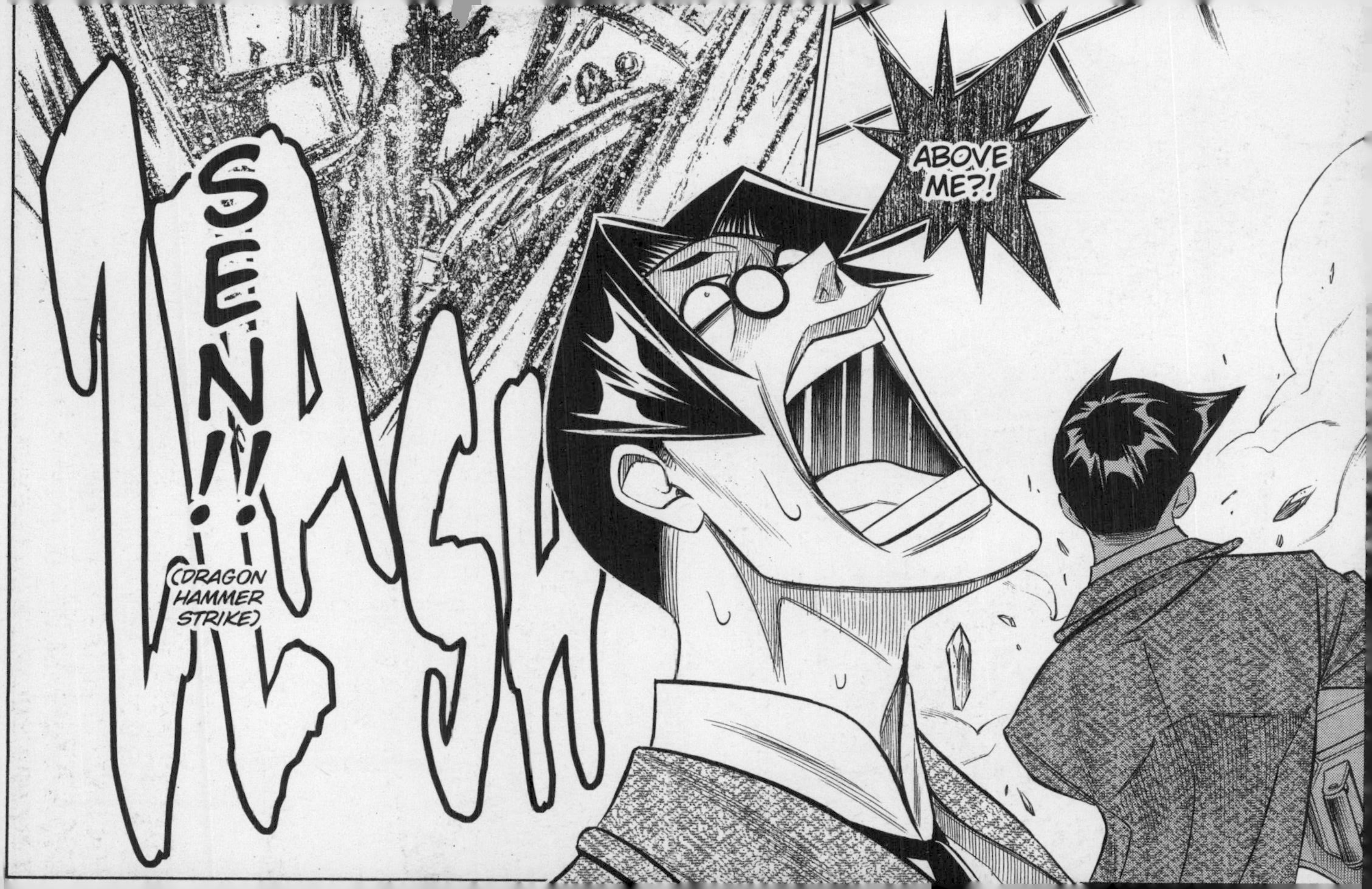
ABOVE ME?!
SEN!!
(DRAGON HAMMER STRIKE)

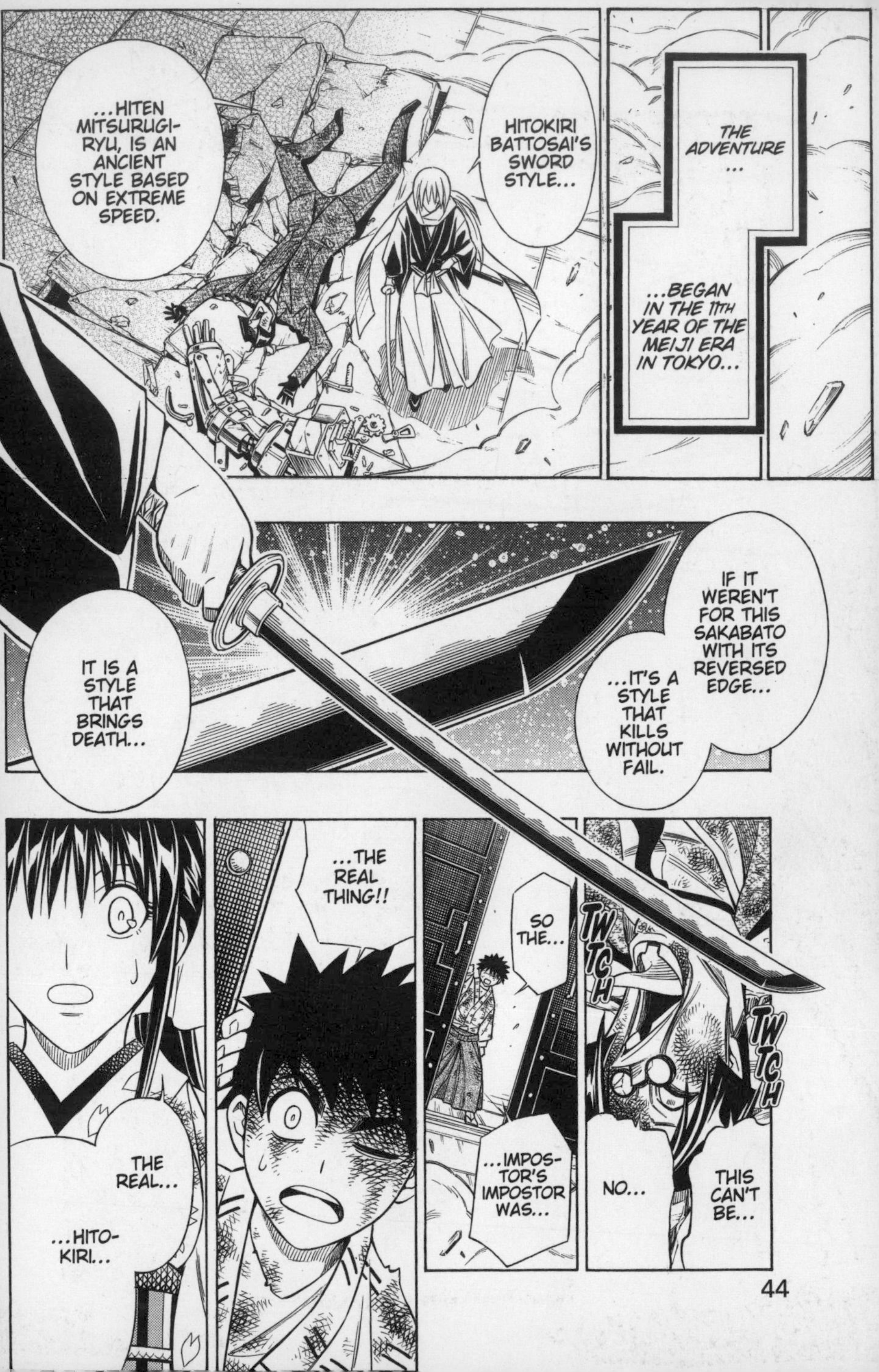
THE ADVENTURE ...
...BEGAN IN THE 11TH YEAR OF THE MEIJI ERA IN TOKYO...
HITOKIRI BATTOSAI'S SWORD STYLE...
...HITEN MITSURUGI-RYU, IS AN ANCIENT STYLE BASED ON EXTREME SPEED.
IF IT WEREN'T FOR THIS SAKABATO WITH ITS REVERSED EDGE...
...IT'S A STYLE THAT KILLS WITHOUT FAIL.
IT IS A STYLE THAT BRINGS DEATH...
TWTCH
TWTCH
THIS CAN'T BE...
NO...
SO THE...
...IMPOSTOR'S IMPOSTOR WAS...
...THE REAL THING!!
THE REAL...
...HITO-KIRI...

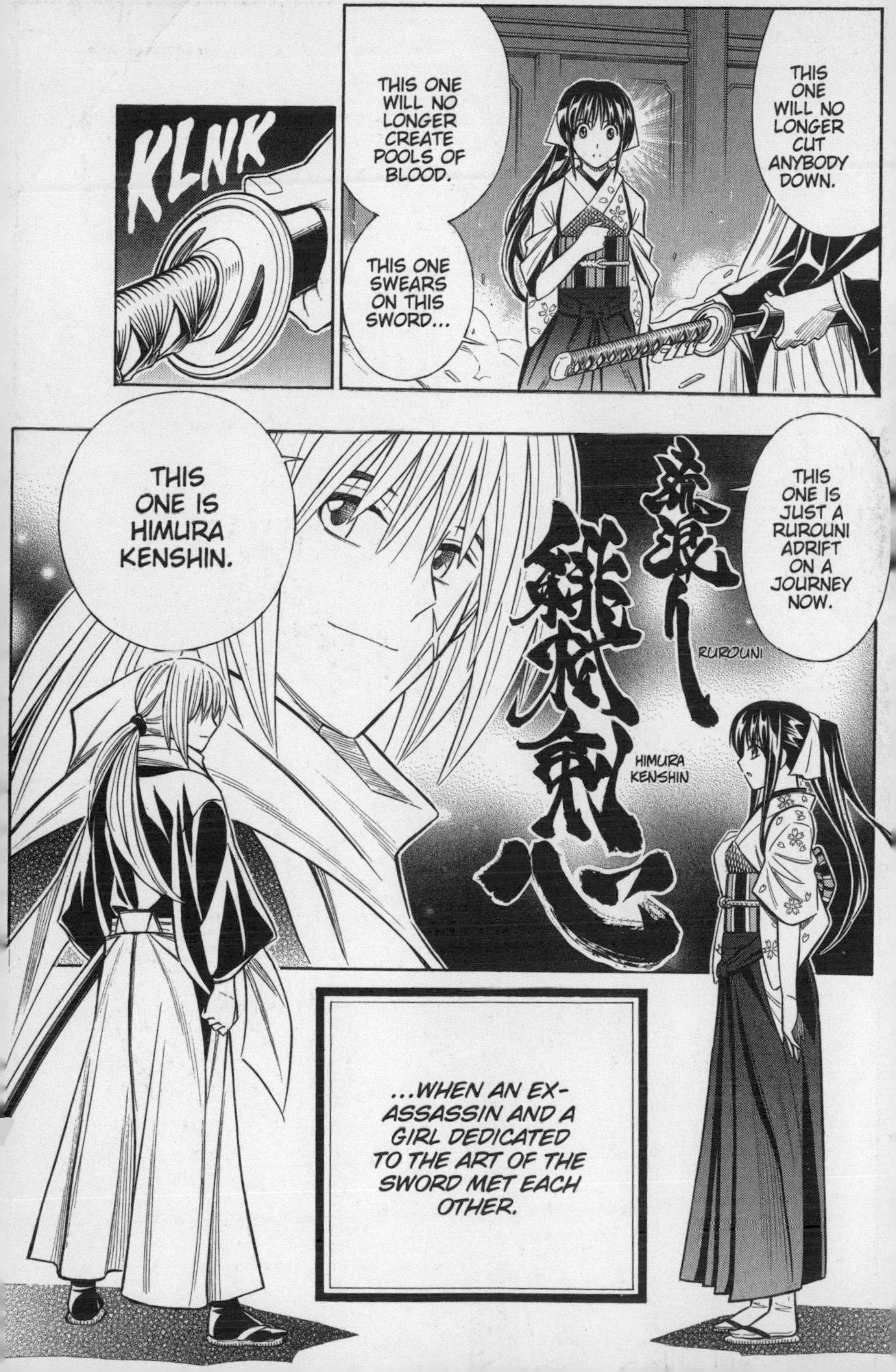

THIS ONE WILL NO LONGER CUT ANYBODY DOWN.
THIS ONE WILL NO LONGER CREATE POOLS OF BLOOD.
THIS ONE SWEARS ON THIS SWORD...
KLNK
THIS ONE IS JUST A RUROUNI ADRIFT ON A JOURNEY NOW.
RUROUNI
HIMURA KENSHIN
THIS ONE IS HIMURA KENSHIN.
...WHEN AN EX-ASSASSIN AND A GIRL DEDICATED TO THE ART OF THE SWORD MET EACH OTHER.

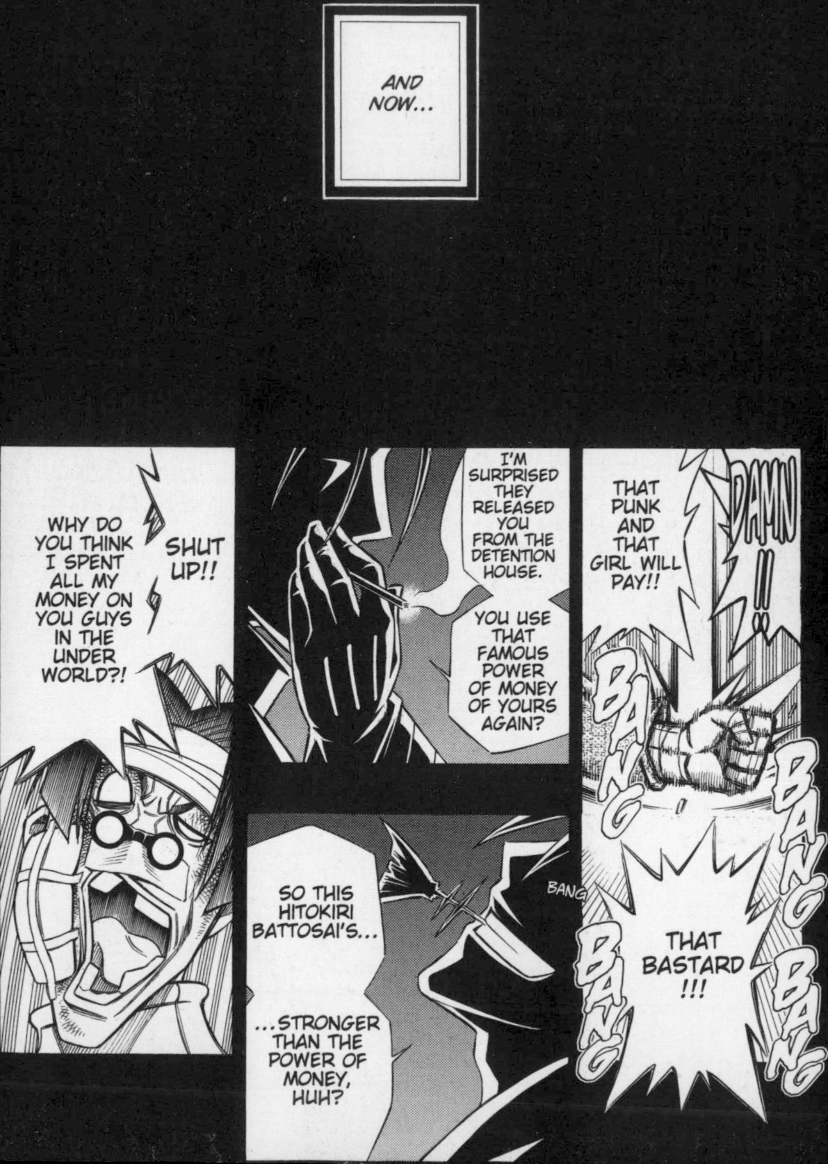
AND NOW...
DAMN!!
THAT PUNK AND THAT GIRL WILL PAY!!
BANG
BANG
BANG
BANG
THAT BASTARD!!!
I'M SURPRISED THEY RELEASED YOU FROM THE DETENTION HOUSE.
YOU USE THAT FAMOUS POWER OF MONEY OF YOURS AGAIN?
BANG
SO THIS HITOKIRI BATTOSAI'S...
...STRONGER THAN THE POWER OF MONEY, HUH?
SHUT UP!!
WHY DO YOU THINK I SPENT ALL MY MONEY ON YOU GUYS IN THE UNDER WORLD?!

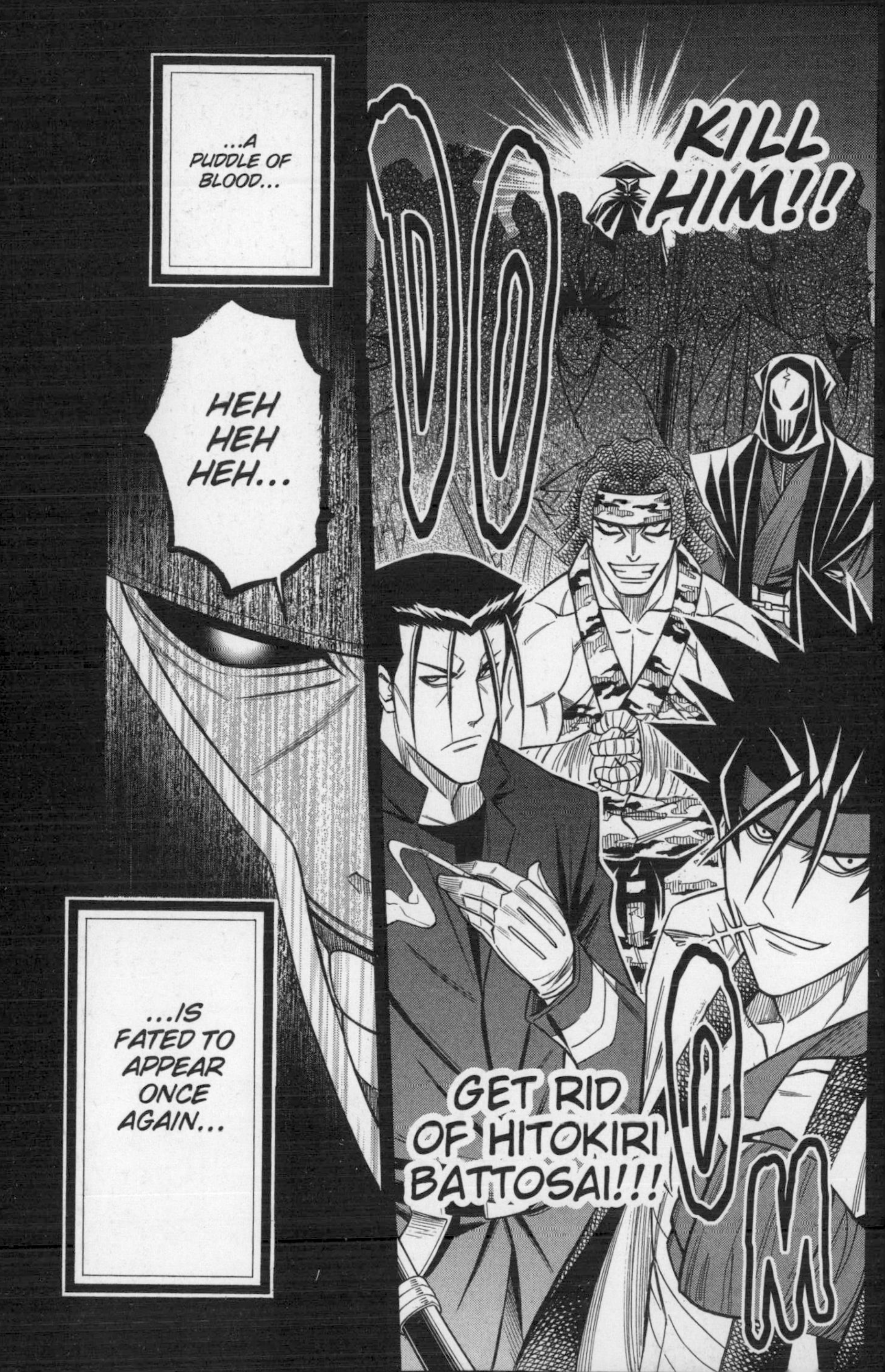
DO
KILL HIM!!
GET RID OF HITOKIRI BATTOSAI!!!
OM
...A PUDDLE OF BLOOD...
HEH HEH HEH...
...IS FATED TO APPEAR ONCE AGAIN...

Rurouni Kenshin

—RESTORATION—

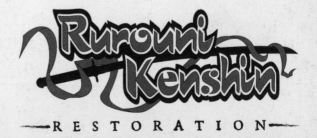

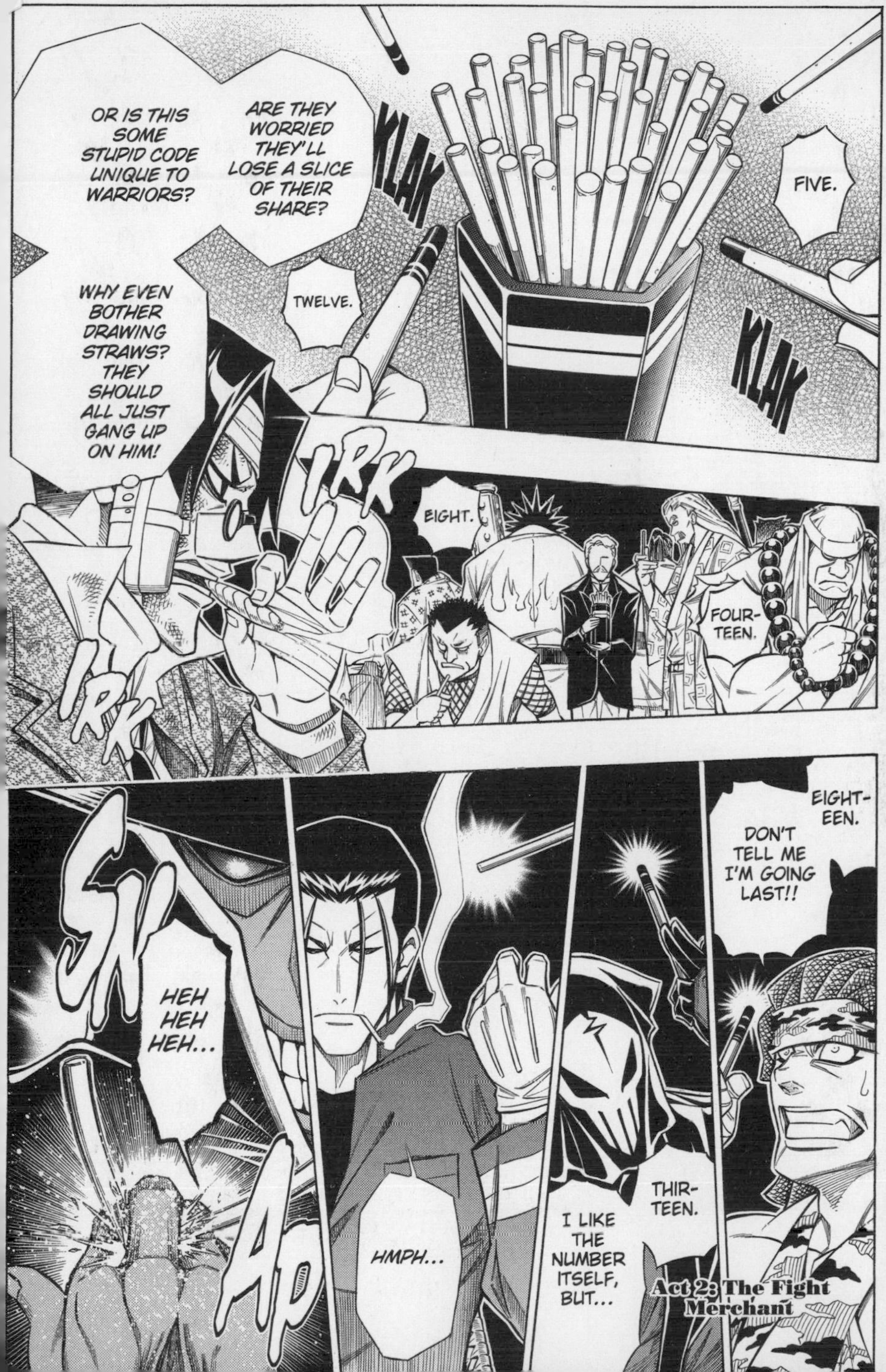
FIVE.
KLAK
KLAK
ARE THEY WORRIED THEY'LL LOSE A SLICE OF THEIR SHARE?
OR IS THIS SOME STUPID CODE UNIQUE TO WARRIORS?
TWELVE.
WHY EVEN BOTHER DRAWING STRAWS? THEY SHOULD ALL JUST GANG UP ON HIM!
FOUR-TEEN.
EIGHT.
IRK
IRK
EIGHT-EEN.
DON'T TELL ME I'M GOING LAST!!
Act 2: The Fight Merchant
THIR-TEEN.
I LIKE THE NUMBER ITSELF, BUT...
HMPH...
SNAP
HEH HEH HEH...

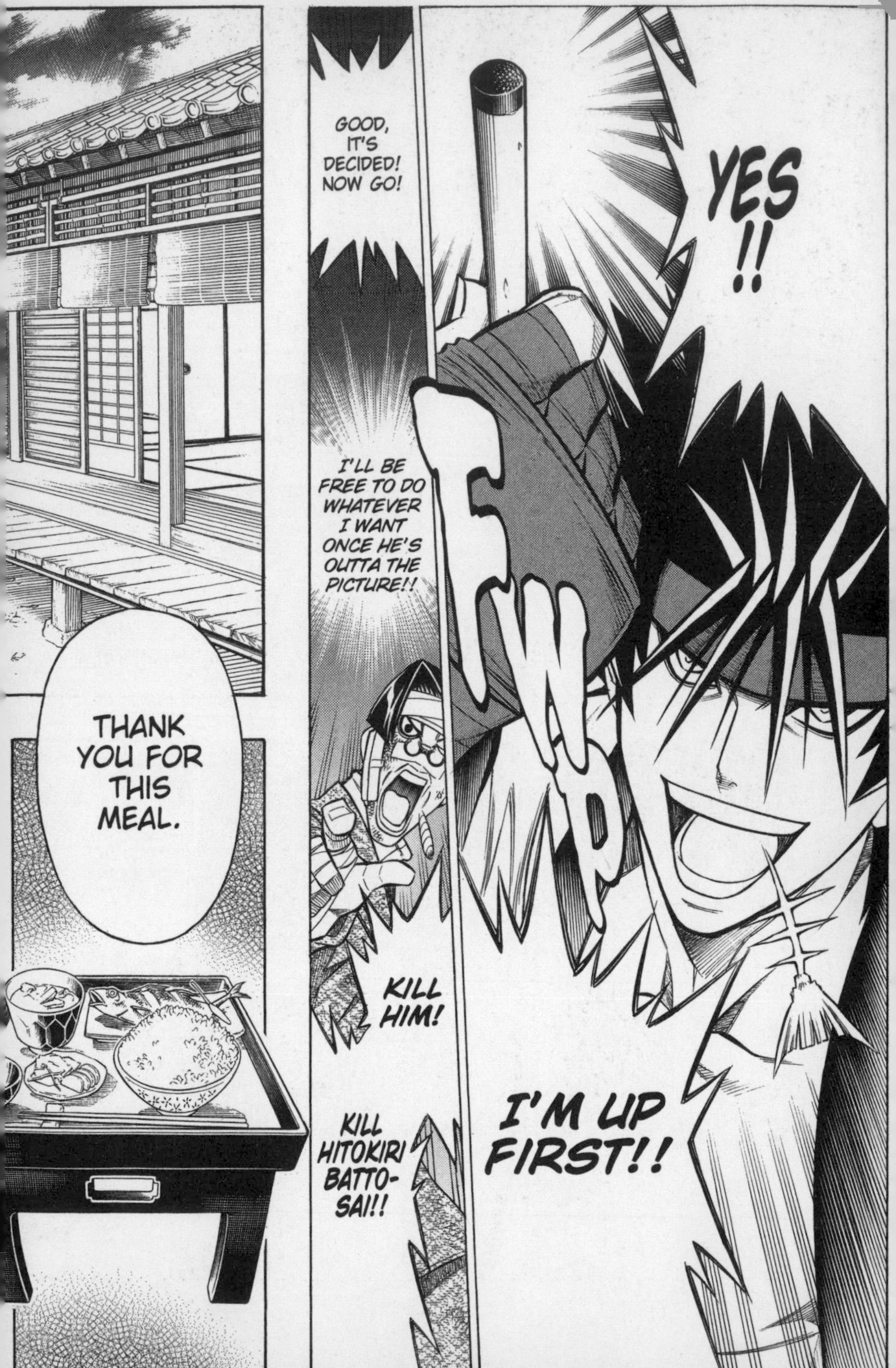
YES!!
FWIP
I'M UP FIRST!!
GOOD, IT'S DECIDED! NOW GO!
I'LL BE FREE TO DO WHATEVER I WANT ONCE HE'S OUTTA THE PICTURE!!
KILL HIM!
KILL HITOKIRI BATTO-SAI!!
THANK YOU FOR THIS MEAL.

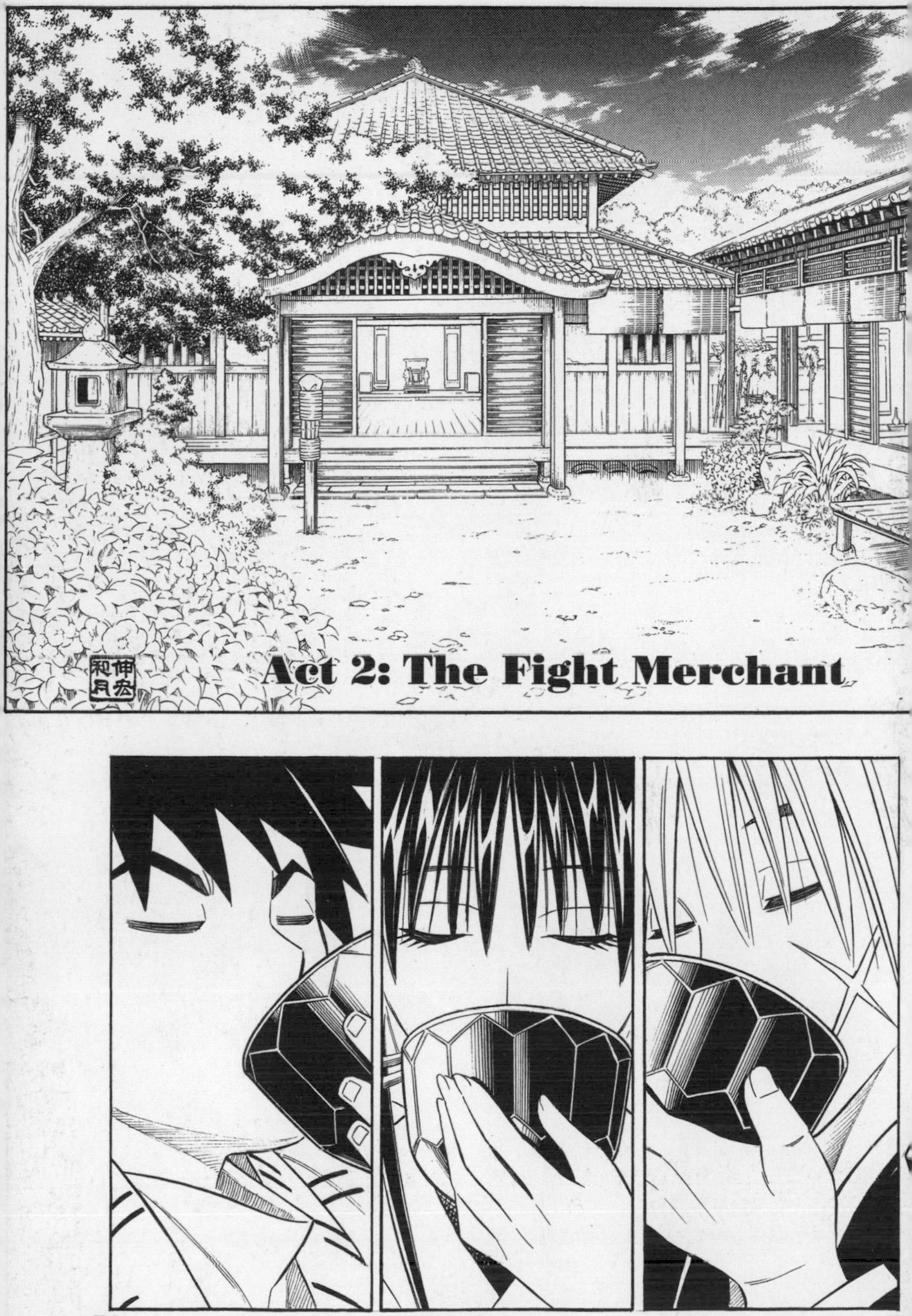
Act 2: The Fight Merchant

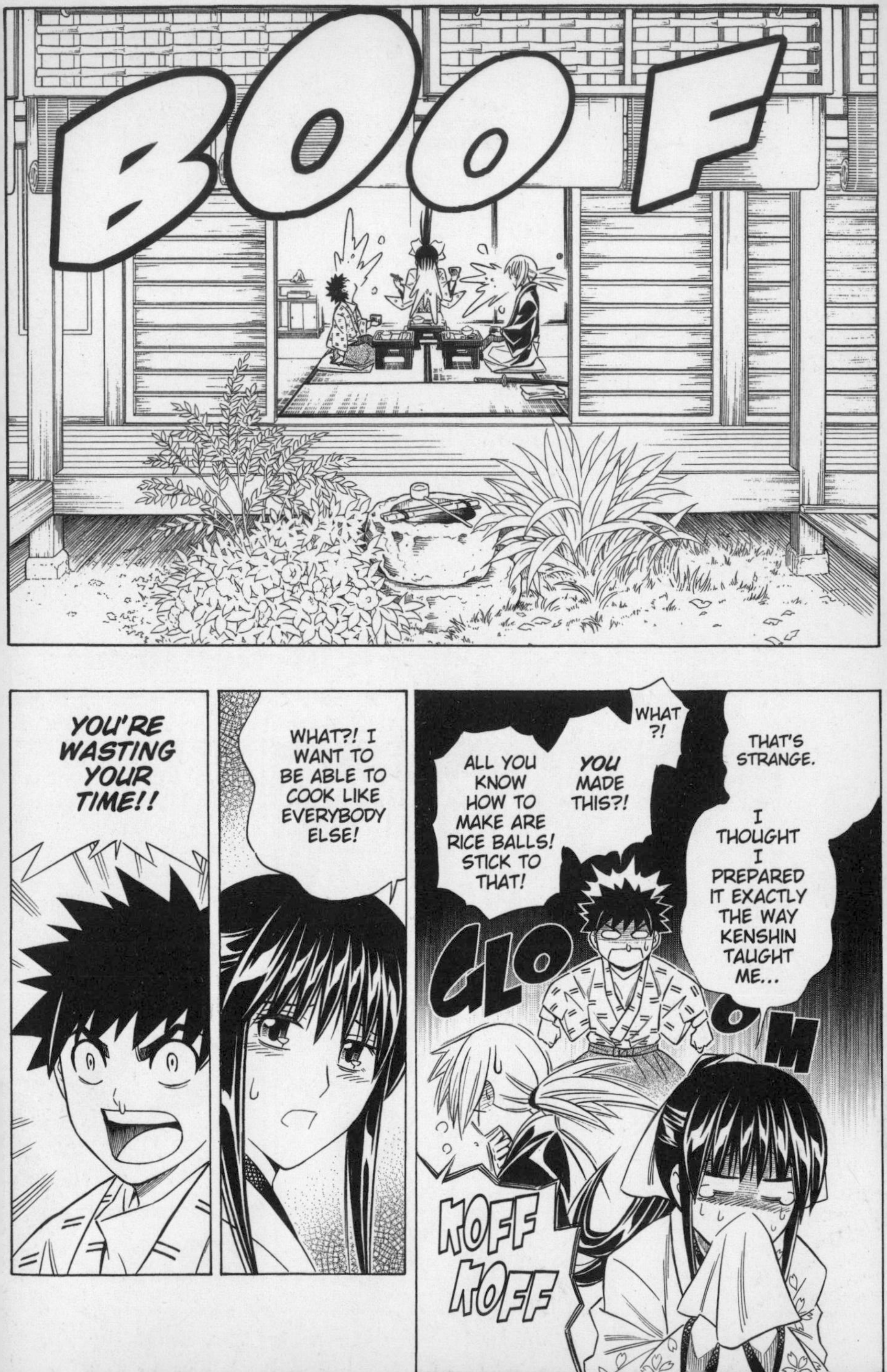
BOOF
WHAT?!
THAT'S STRANGE.
I THOUGHT I PREPARED IT EXACTLY THE WAY KENSHIN TAUGHT ME...
YOU MADE THIS?!
ALL YOU KNOW HOW TO MAKE ARE RICE BALLS! STICK TO THAT!
GLOOM
KOFF KOFF
WHAT?! I WANT TO BE ABLE TO COOK LIKE EVERYBODY ELSE!
YOU'RE WASTING YOUR TIME!!

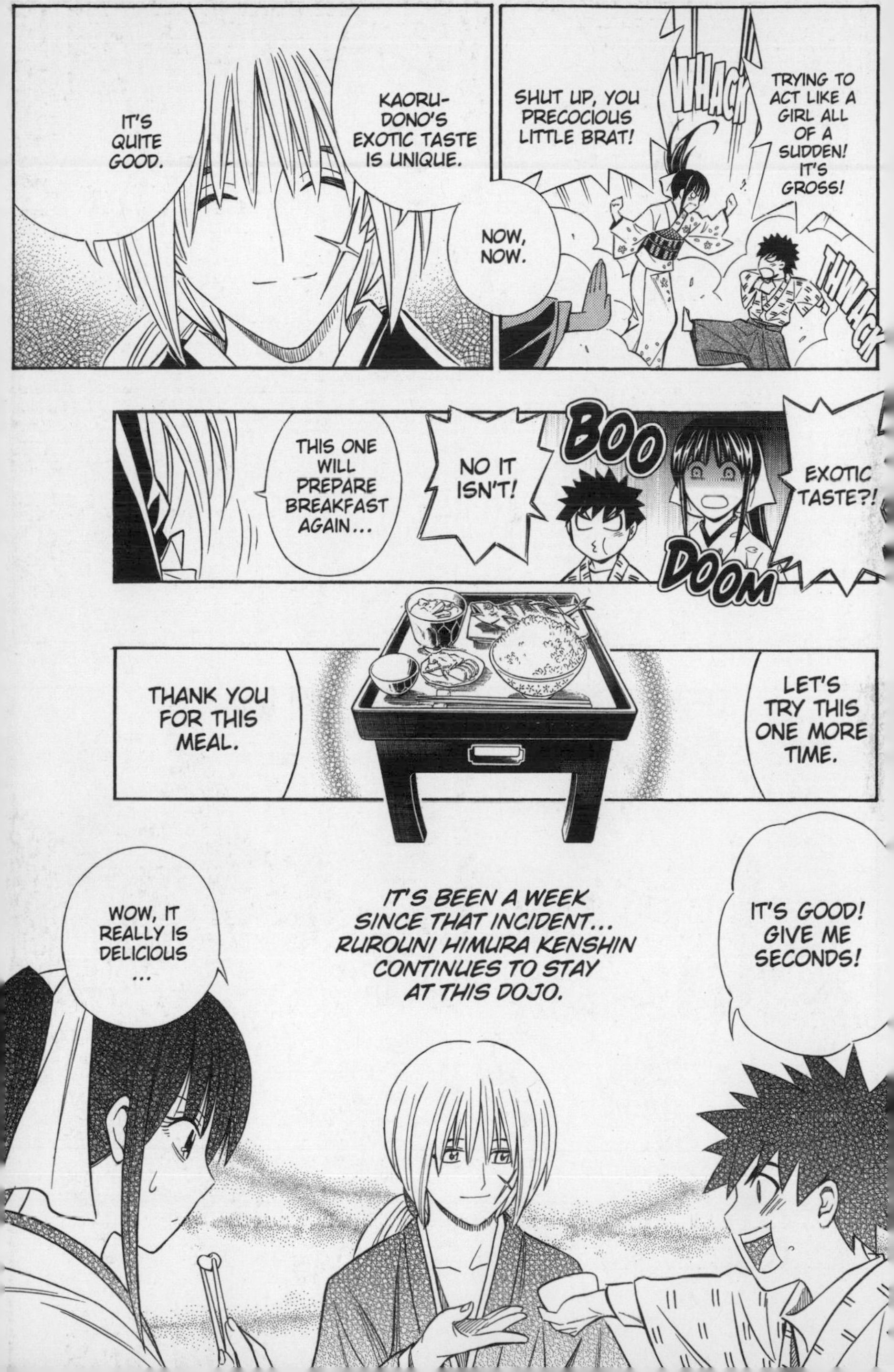
TRYING TO ACT LIKE A GIRL ALL OF A SUDDEN! IT'S GROSS!
WHACK
SHUT UP, YOU PRECOCIOUS LITTLE BRAT!
THWACK
NOW, NOW.
KAORU-DONO'S EXOTIC TASTE IS UNIQUE.
IT'S QUITE GOOD.
EXOTIC TASTE?!
BOO
DOOM
NO IT ISN'T!
THIS ONE WILL PREPARE BREAKFAST AGAIN...
LET'S TRY THIS ONE MORE TIME.
THANK YOU FOR THIS MEAL.
IT'S GOOD! GIVE ME SECONDS!
IT'S BEEN A WEEK SINCE THAT INCIDENT... RUROUNI HIMURA KENSHIN CONTINUES TO STAY AT THIS DOJO.
WOW, IT REALLY IS DELICIOUS...

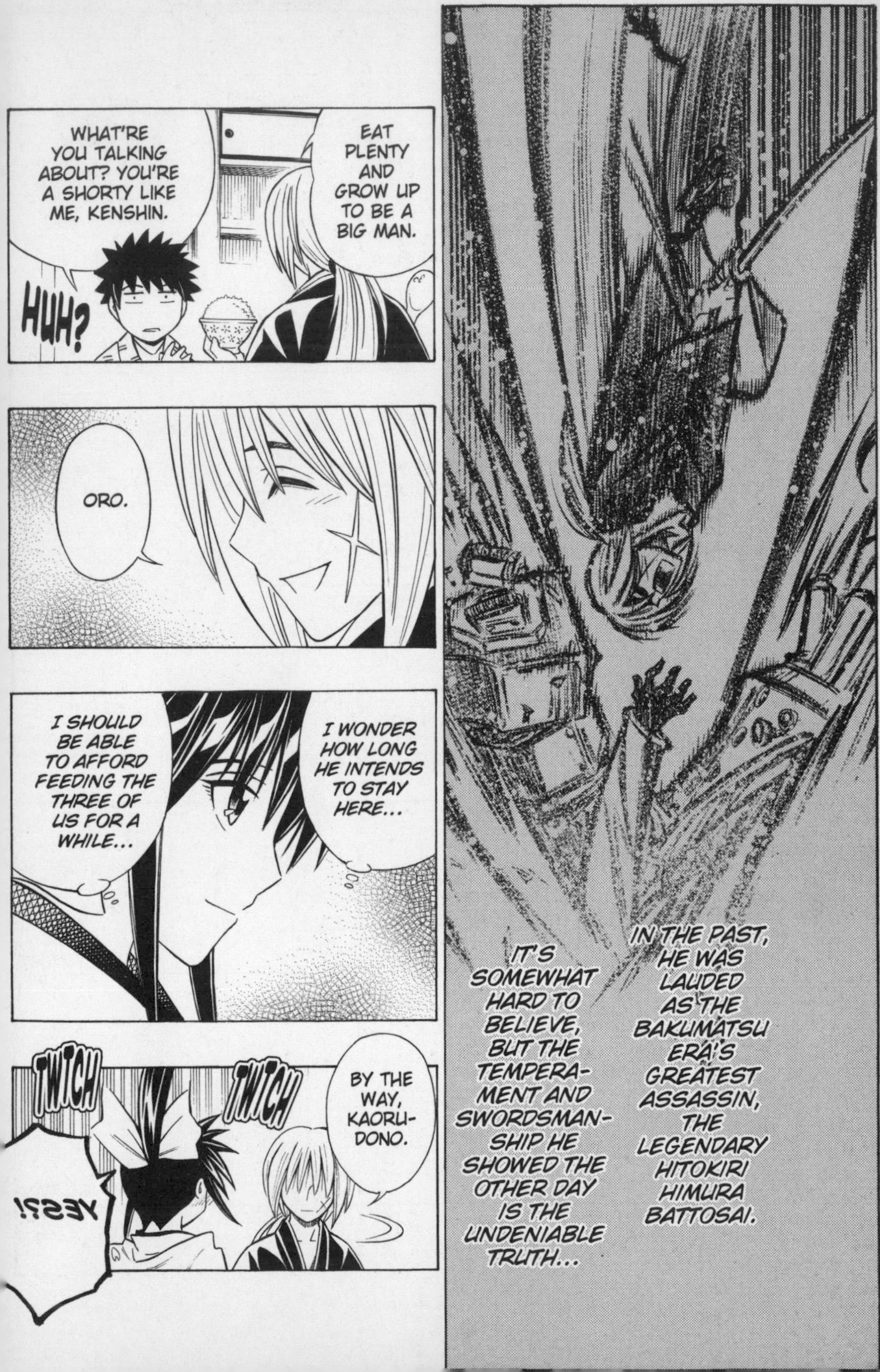
IN THE PAST, HE WAS LAUDED AS THE BAKUMATSU ERA'S GREATEST ASSASSIN, THE LEGENDARY HITOKIRI HIMURA BATTOSAI.
IT'S SOMEWHAT HARD TO BELIEVE, BUT THE TEMPERAMENT AND SWORDSMANSHIP HE SHOWED THE OTHER DAY IS THE UNDENIABLE TRUTH...
EAT PLENTY AND GROW UP TO BE A BIG MAN.
WHAT'RE YOU TALKING ABOUT? YOU'RE A SHORTY LIKE ME, KENSHIN.
HUH?
ORO.
I WONDER HOW LONG HE INTENDS TO STAY HERE...
I SHOULD BE ABLE TO AFFORD FEEDING THE THREE OF US FOR A WHILE...
BY THE WAY, KAORU-DONO.
TWITCH
TWITCH
YES?!

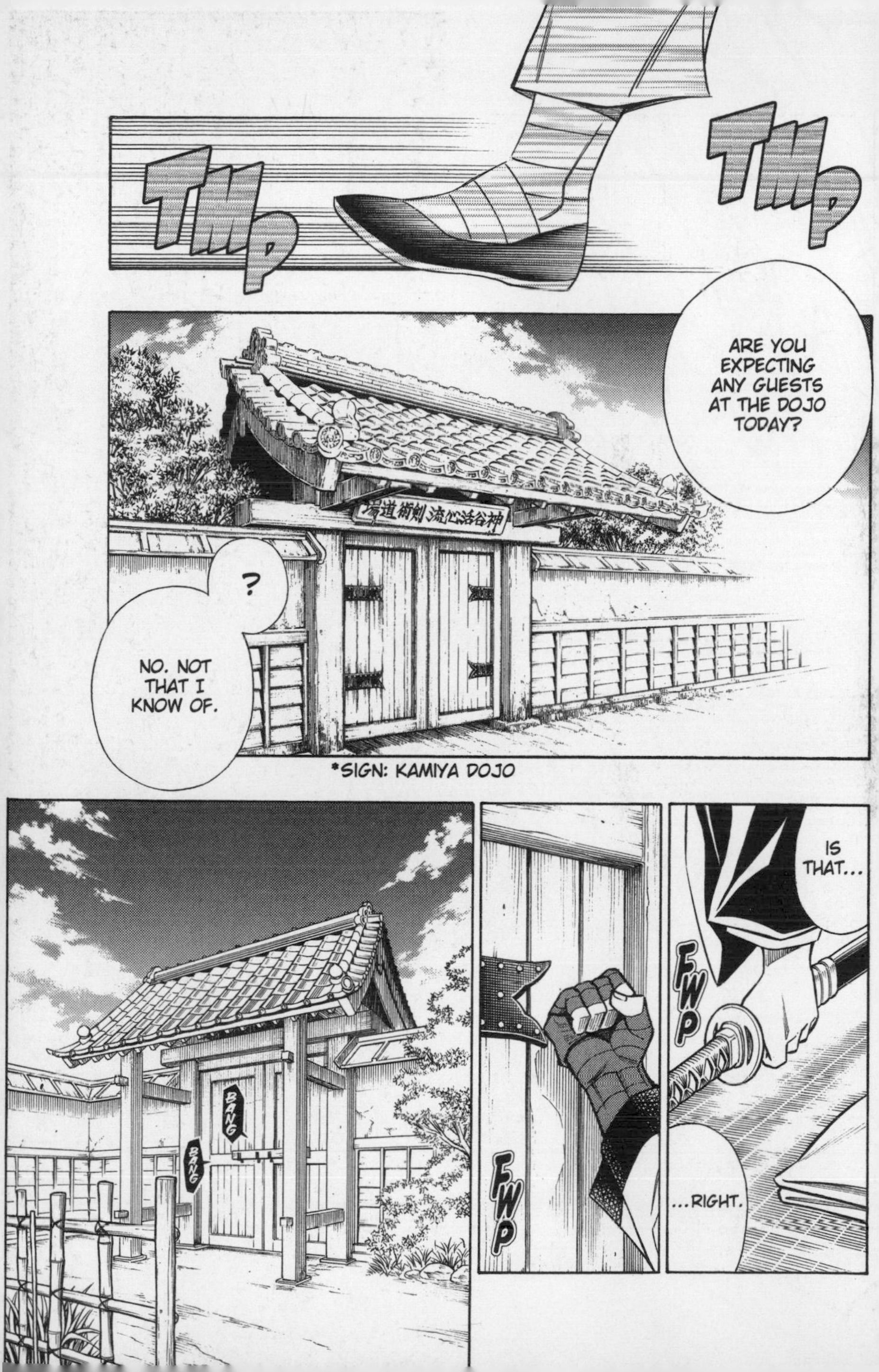
TMP
TMP
ARE YOU EXPECTING ANY GUESTS AT THE DOJO TODAY?
神谷活心流 剣術道場
?
NO. NOT THAT I KNOW OF.
*SIGN: KAMIYA DOJO
IS THAT...
FWP
...RIGHT.
FWP
BANG
BANG

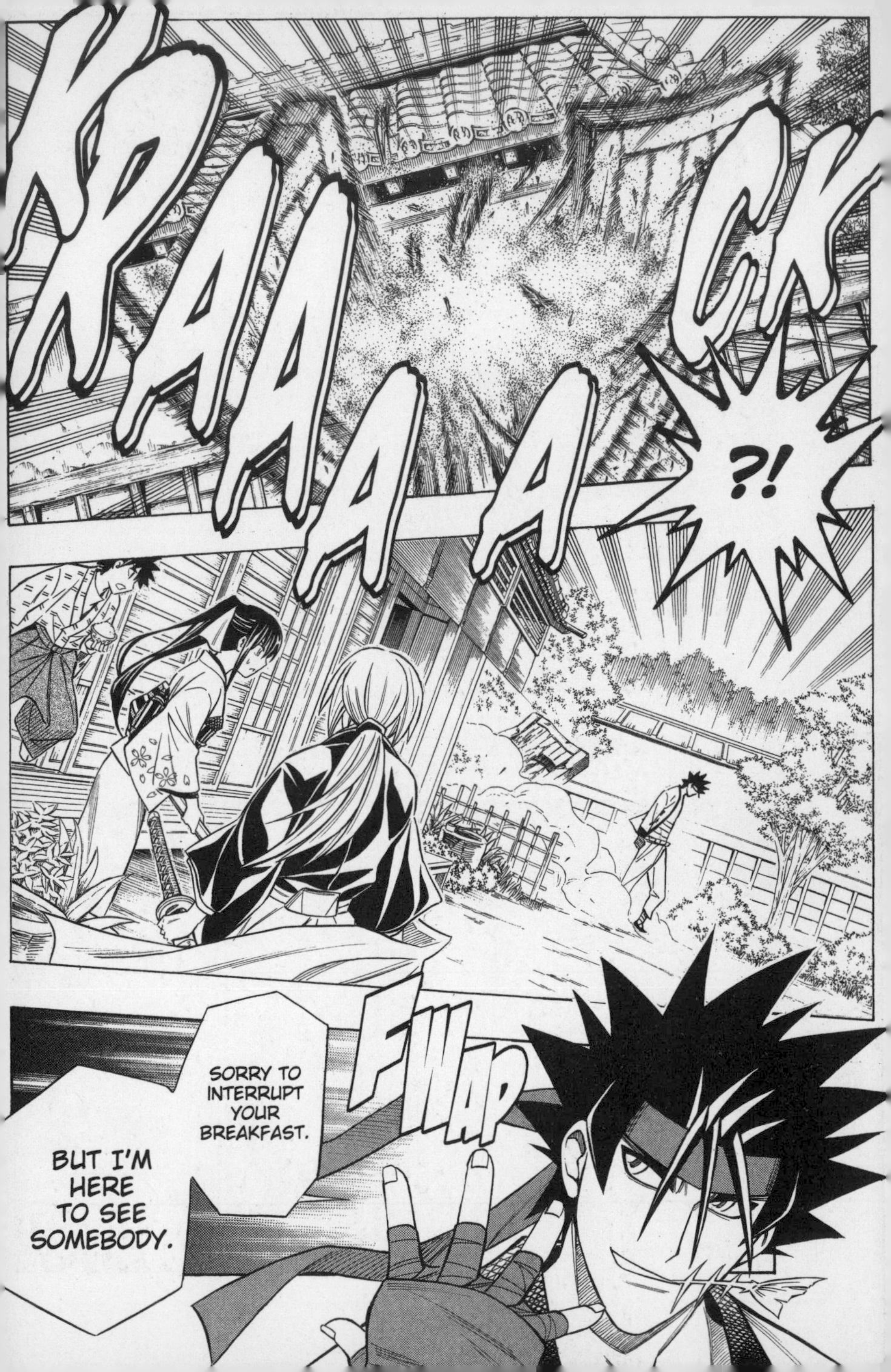
KRAAAACK
?!
FWAP
SORRY TO INTERRUPT YOUR BREAKFAST.
BUT I'M HERE TO SEE SOMEBODY.

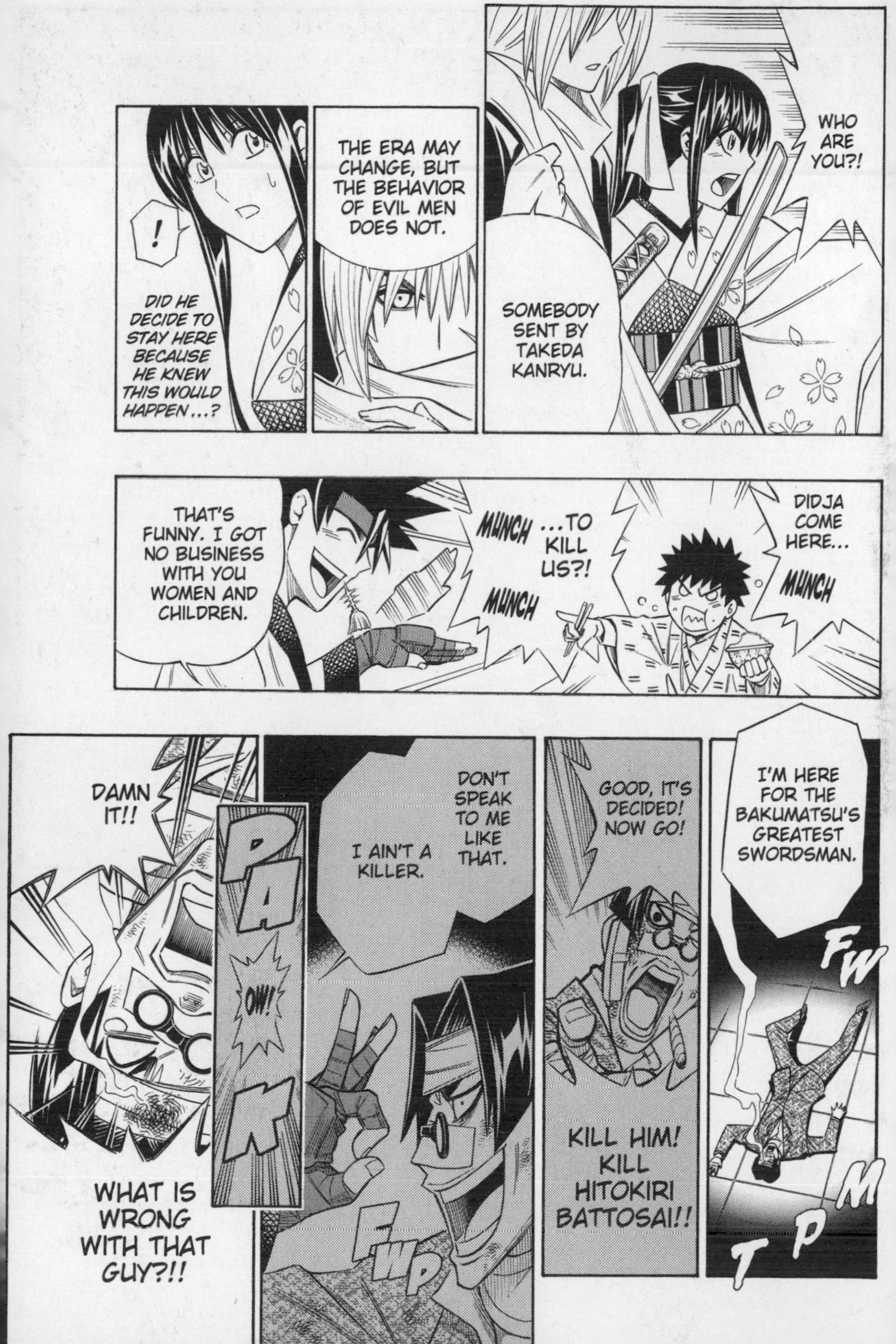
WHO ARE YOU?!
SOMEBODY SENT BY TAKEDA KANRYU.
THE ERA MAY CHANGE, BUT THE BEHAVIOR OF EVIL MEN DOES NOT.
!
DID HE DECIDE TO STAY HERE BECAUSE HE KNEW THIS WOULD HAPPEN...?
DIDJA COME HERE...
MUNCH
...TO KILL US?!
MUNCH
MUNCH
THAT'S FUNNY. I GOT NO BUSINESS WITH YOU WOMEN AND CHILDREN.
I'M HERE FOR THE BAKUMATSU'S GREATEST SWORDSMAN.
FW
T P M
GOOD, IT'S DECIDED! NOW GO!
KILL HIM! KILL HITOKIRI BATTOSAI!!
DON'T SPEAK TO ME LIKE THAT.
I AIN'T A KILLER.
FWP
PA
OW!
K
DAMN IT!!
WHAT IS WRONG WITH THAT GUY?!!

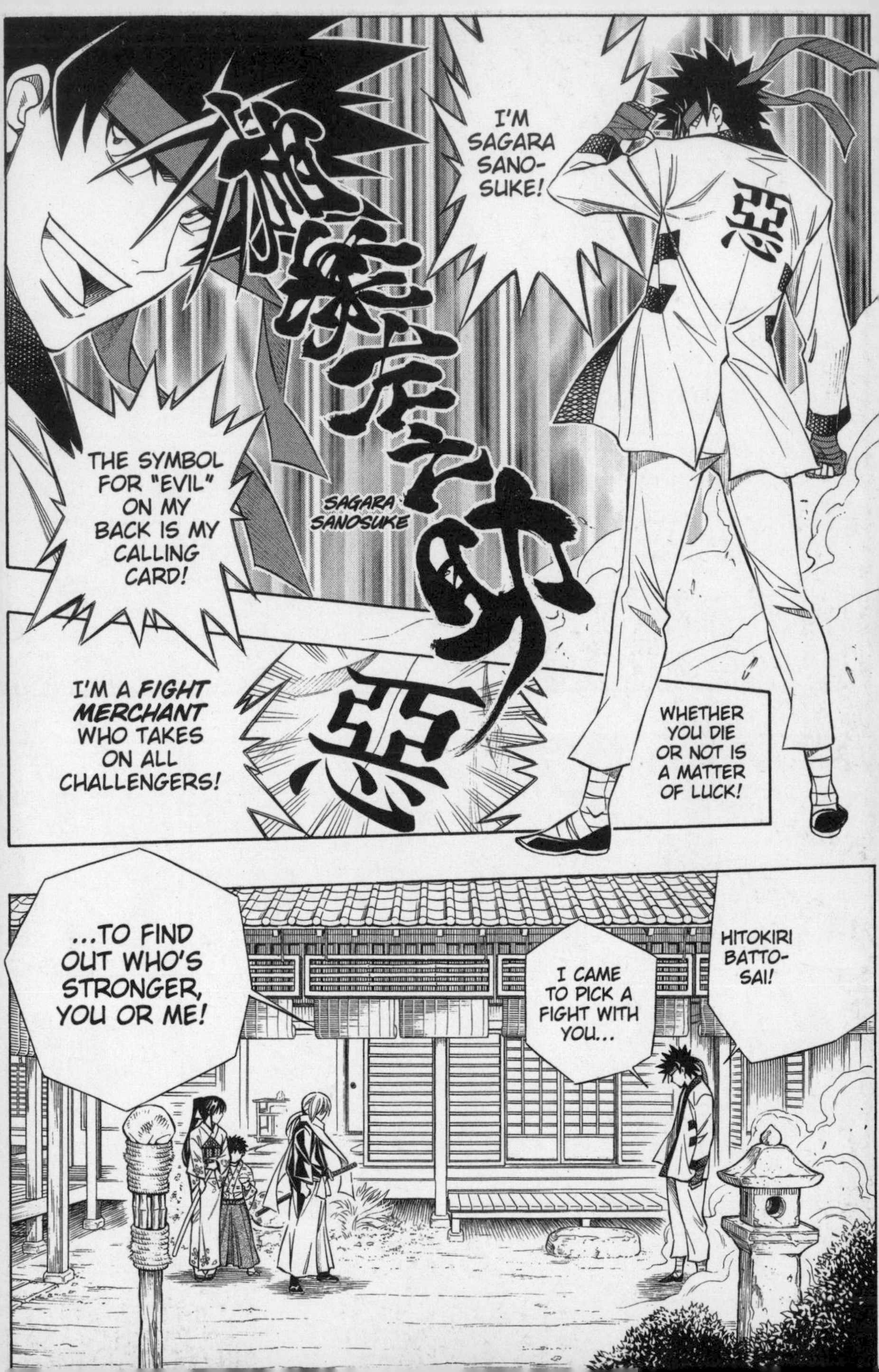
I'M SAGARA SANO-SUKE!
SAGARA SANOSUKE
THE SYMBOL FOR "EVIL" ON MY BACK IS MY CALLING CARD!
WHETHER YOU DIE OR NOT IS A MATTER OF LUCK!
I'M A *FIGHT MERCHANT* WHO TAKES ON ALL CHALLENGERS!
HITOKIRI BATTO-SAI!
I CAME TO PICK A FIGHT WITH YOU...
...TO FIND OUT WHO'S STRONGER, YOU OR ME!

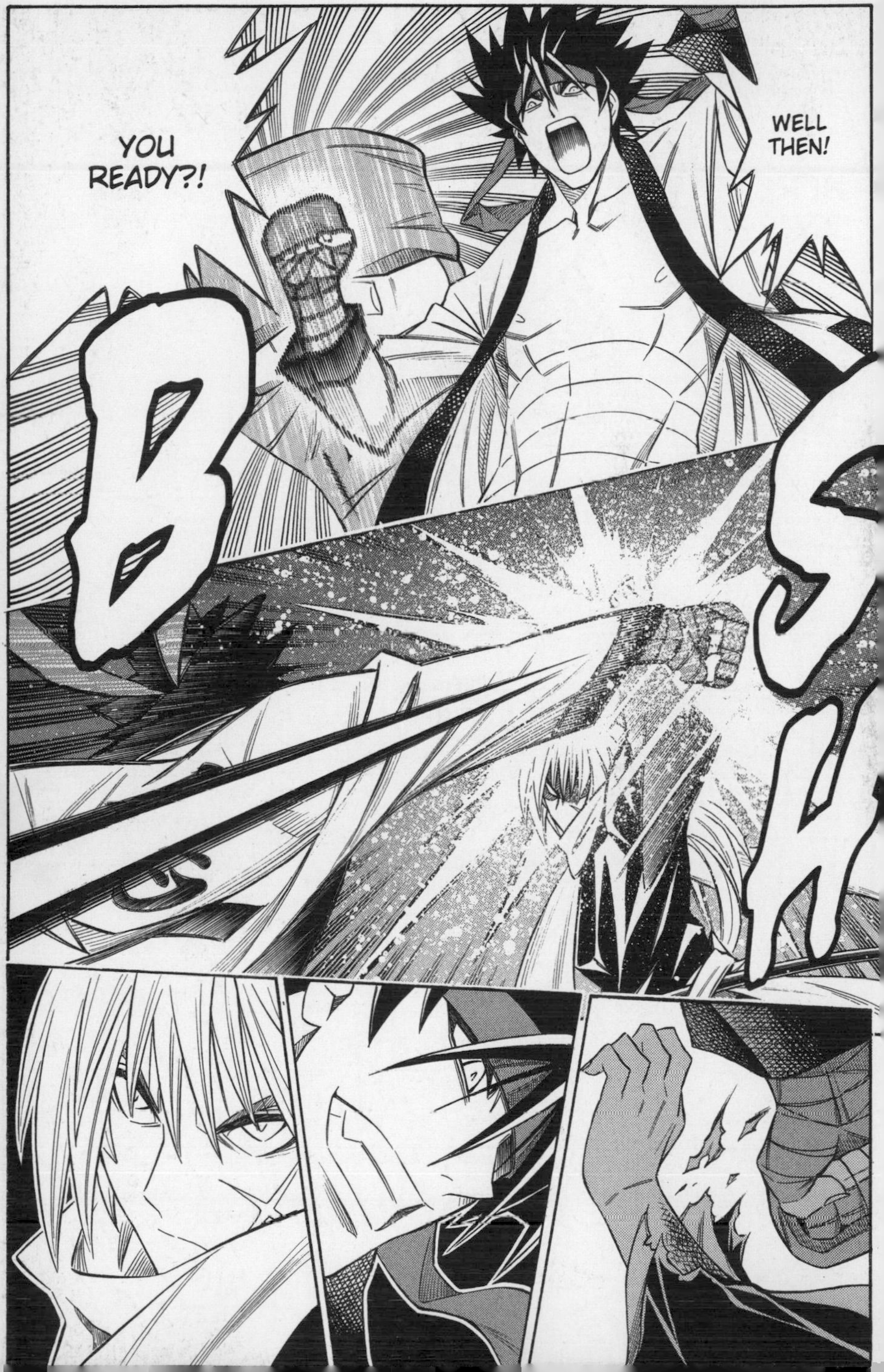
WELL THEN!
YOU READY?!

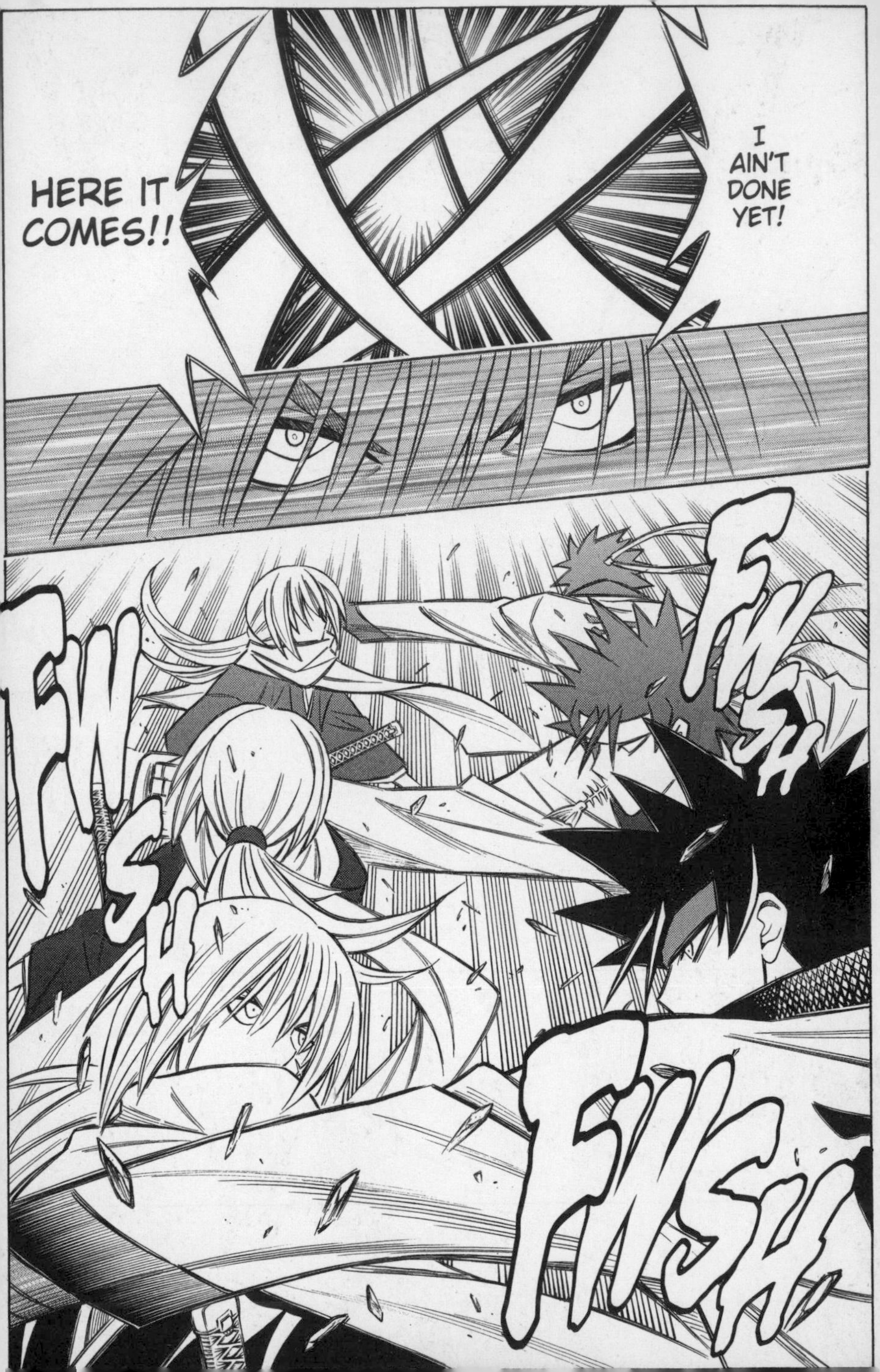
I AIN'T DONE YET!
HERE IT COMES!!
FWSH
FWSH
FWSH

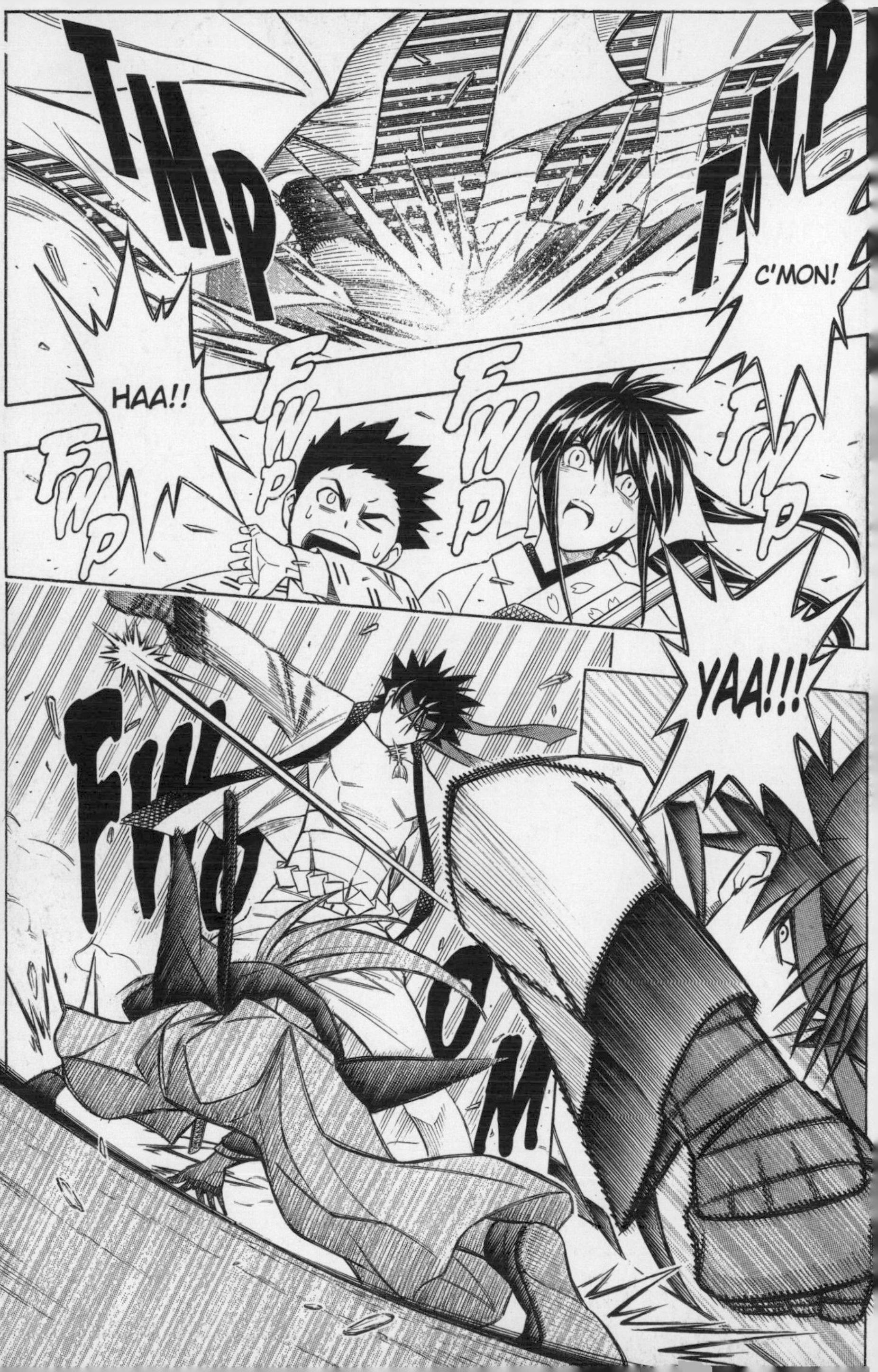
TMP
C'MON!
TMP
HAA!!
FWP
FWP
FWP
FWP
YAA!!!
FWOOM

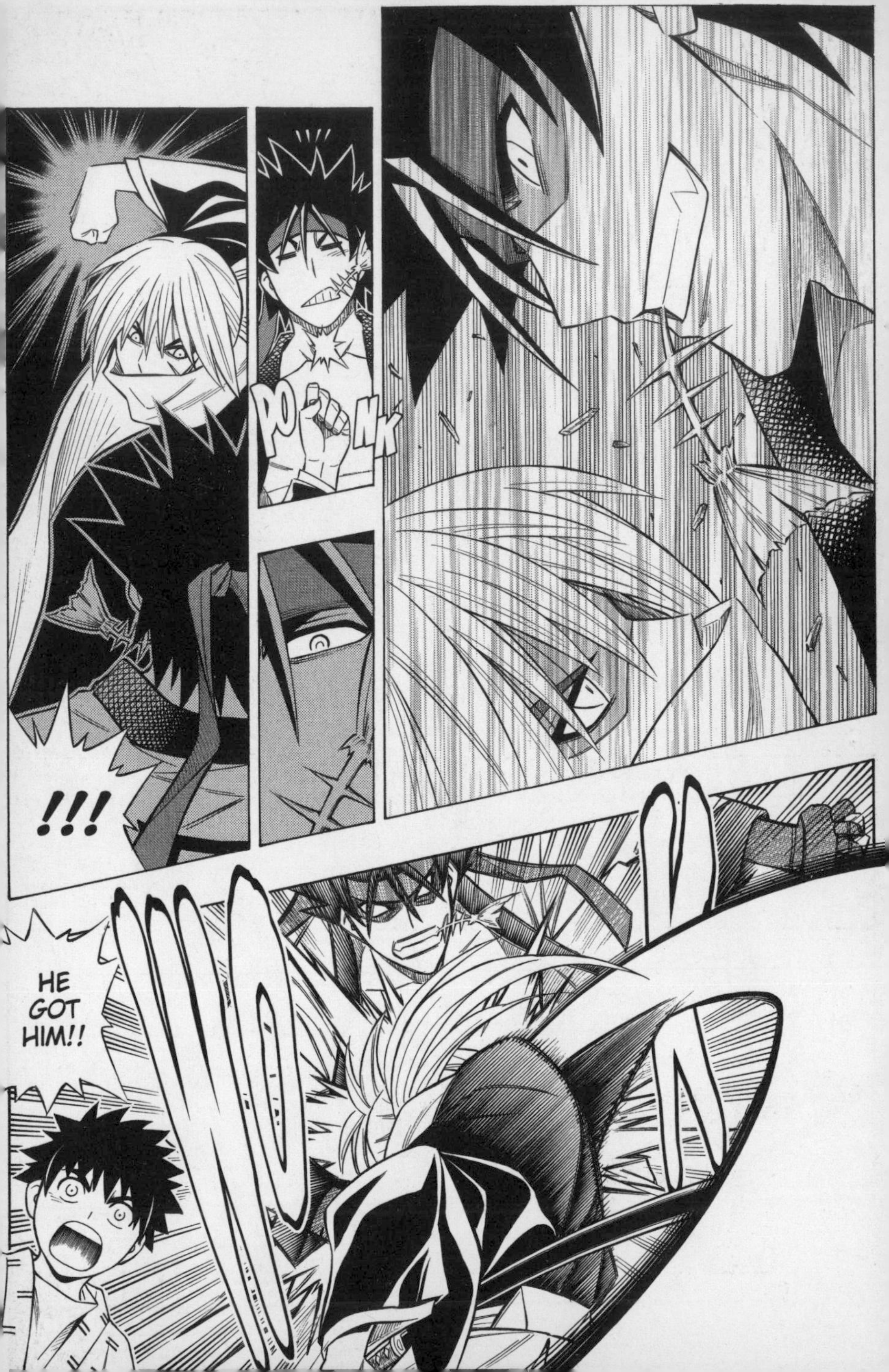
PONK
!!!
HE GOT HIM!!

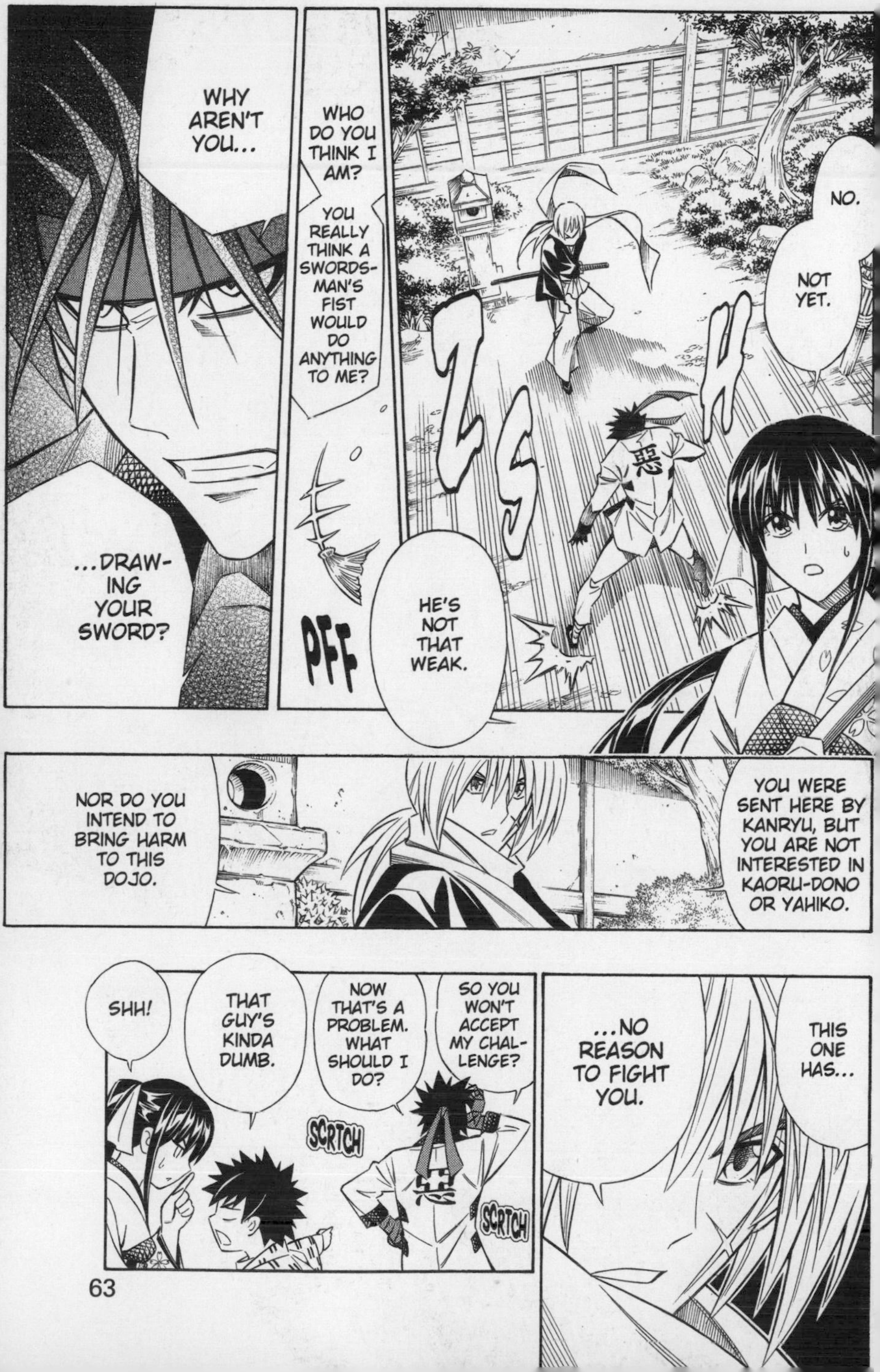
NO.
NOT YET.
ZSH
HE'S NOT THAT WEAK.
WHO DO YOU THINK I AM?
YOU REALLY THINK A SWORDS-MAN'S FIST WOULD DO ANYTHING TO ME?
PFF
WHY AREN'T YOU...
...DRAWING YOUR SWORD?
YOU WERE SENT HERE BY KANRYU, BUT YOU ARE NOT INTERESTED IN KAORU-DONO OR YAHIKO.
NOR DO YOU INTEND TO BRING HARM TO THIS DOJO.
THIS ONE HAS...
...NO REASON TO FIGHT YOU.
SO YOU WON'T ACCEPT MY CHAL-LENGE?
NOW THAT'S A PROBLEM. WHAT SHOULD I DO?
SCRTCH
SCRTCH
THAT GUY'S KINDA DUMB.
SHH!

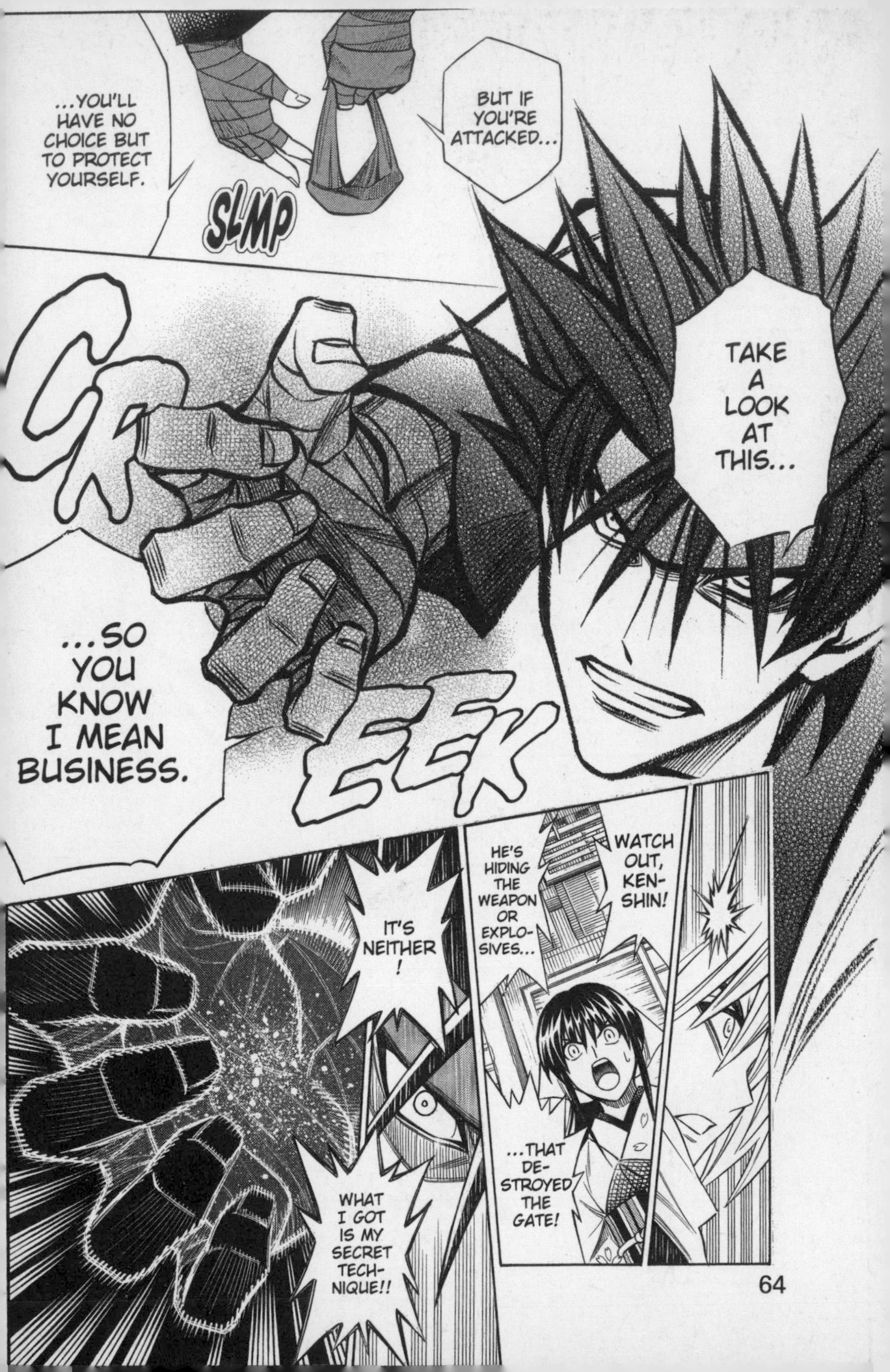
BUT IF YOU'RE ATTACKED...
...YOU'LL HAVE NO CHOICE BUT TO PROTECT YOURSELF.
SLMP
TAKE A LOOK AT THIS...
...SO YOU KNOW I MEAN BUSINESS.
CREEK
WATCH OUT, KEN-SHIN!
HE'S HIDING THE WEAPON OR EXPLO-SIVES...
...THAT DE-STROYED THE GATE!
IT'S NEITHER!
WHAT I GOT IS MY SECRET TECH-NIQUE!!

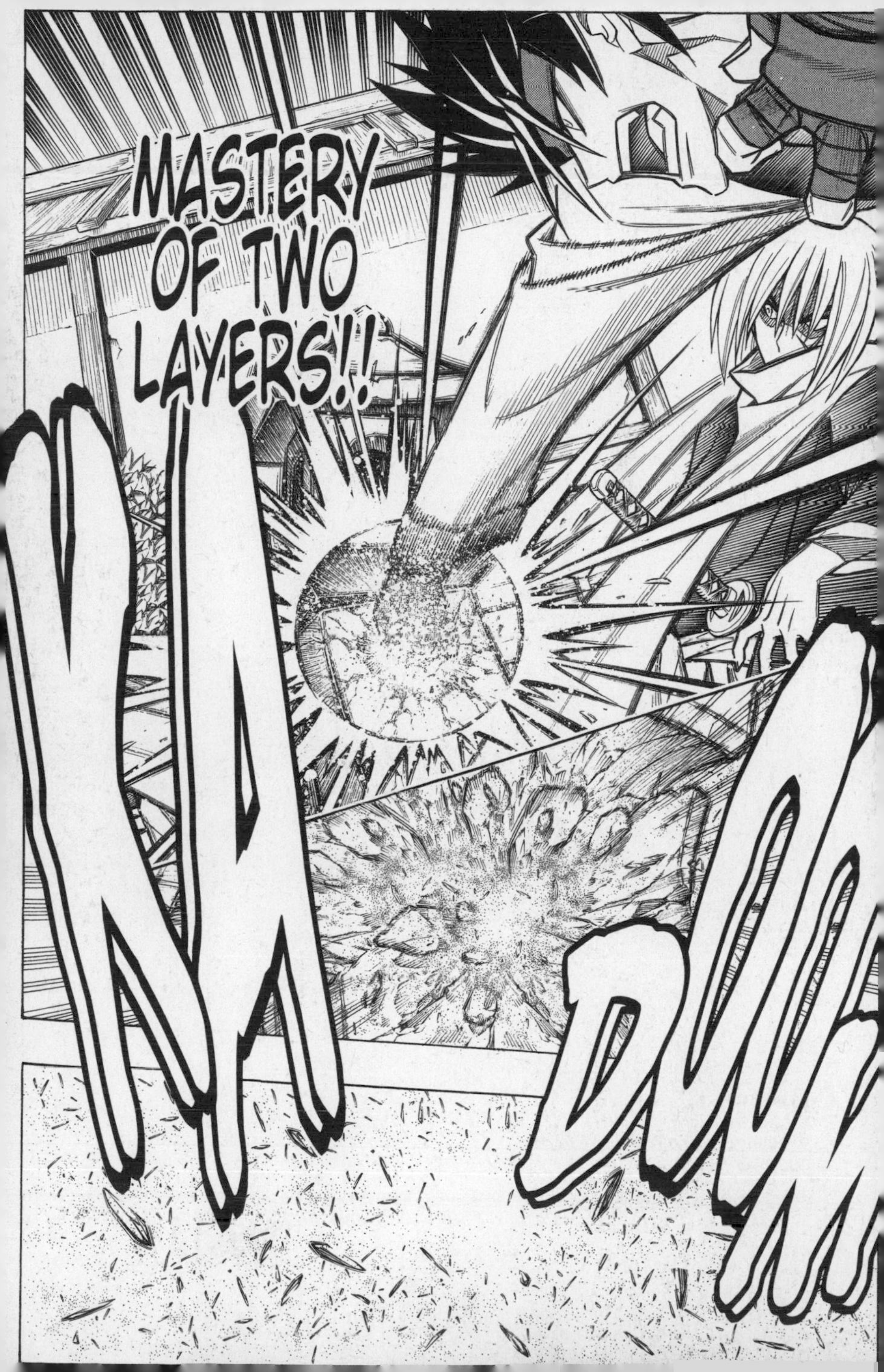
MASTERY OF TWO LAYERS!!

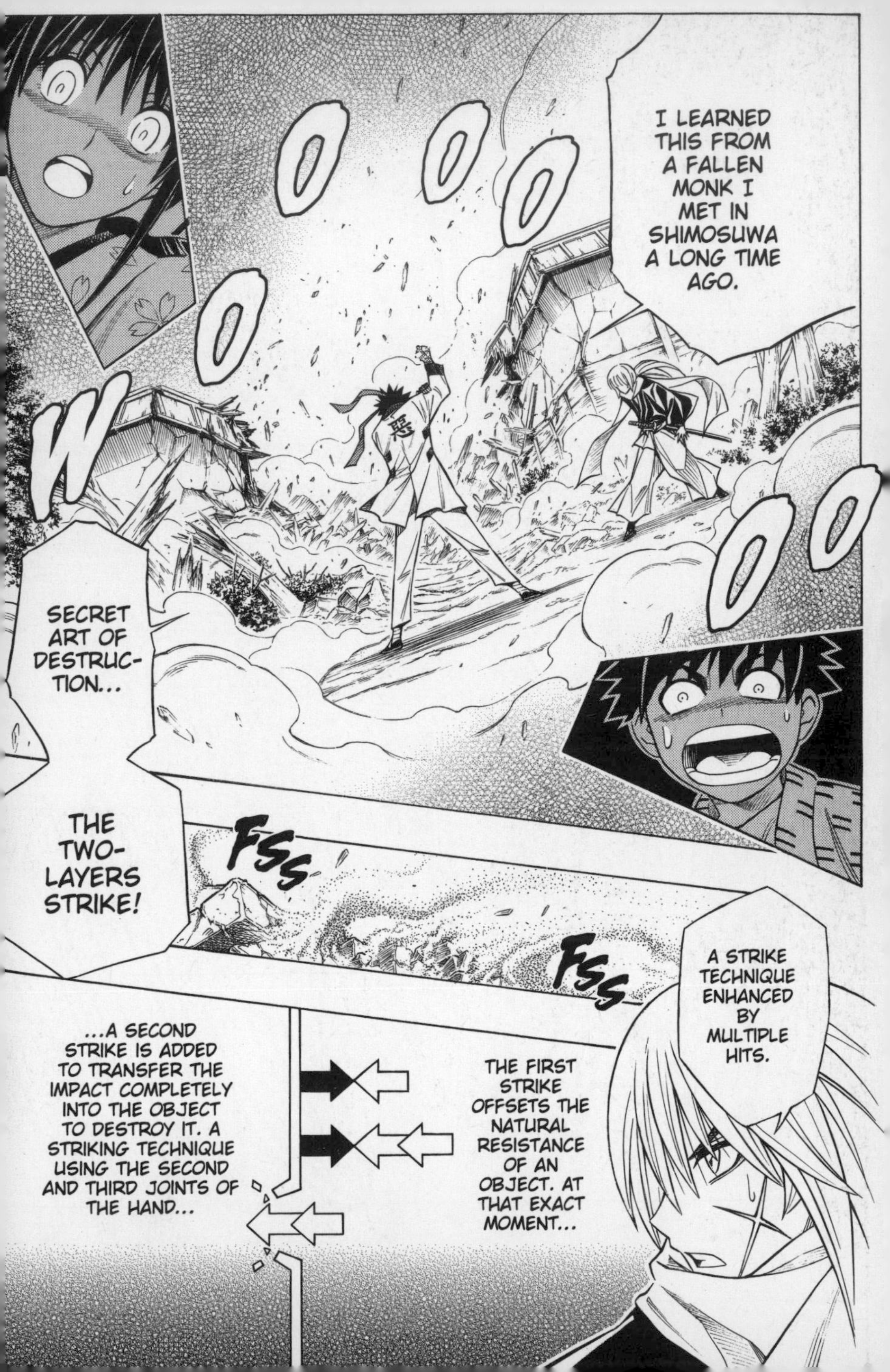
I LEARNED THIS FROM A FALLEN MONK I MET IN SHIMOSUWA A LONG TIME AGO.
WOOOOOOOO
SECRET ART OF DESTRUC-TION...
THE TWO-LAYERS STRIKE!
FSS
FSS
A STRIKE TECHNIQUE ENHANCED BY MULTIPLE HITS.
THE FIRST STRIKE OFFSETS THE NATURAL RESISTANCE OF AN OBJECT. AT THAT EXACT MOMENT...
...A SECOND STRIKE IS ADDED TO TRANSFER THE IMPACT COMPLETELY INTO THE OBJECT TO DESTROY IT. A STRIKING TECHNIQUE USING THE SECOND AND THIRD JOINTS OF THE HAND...

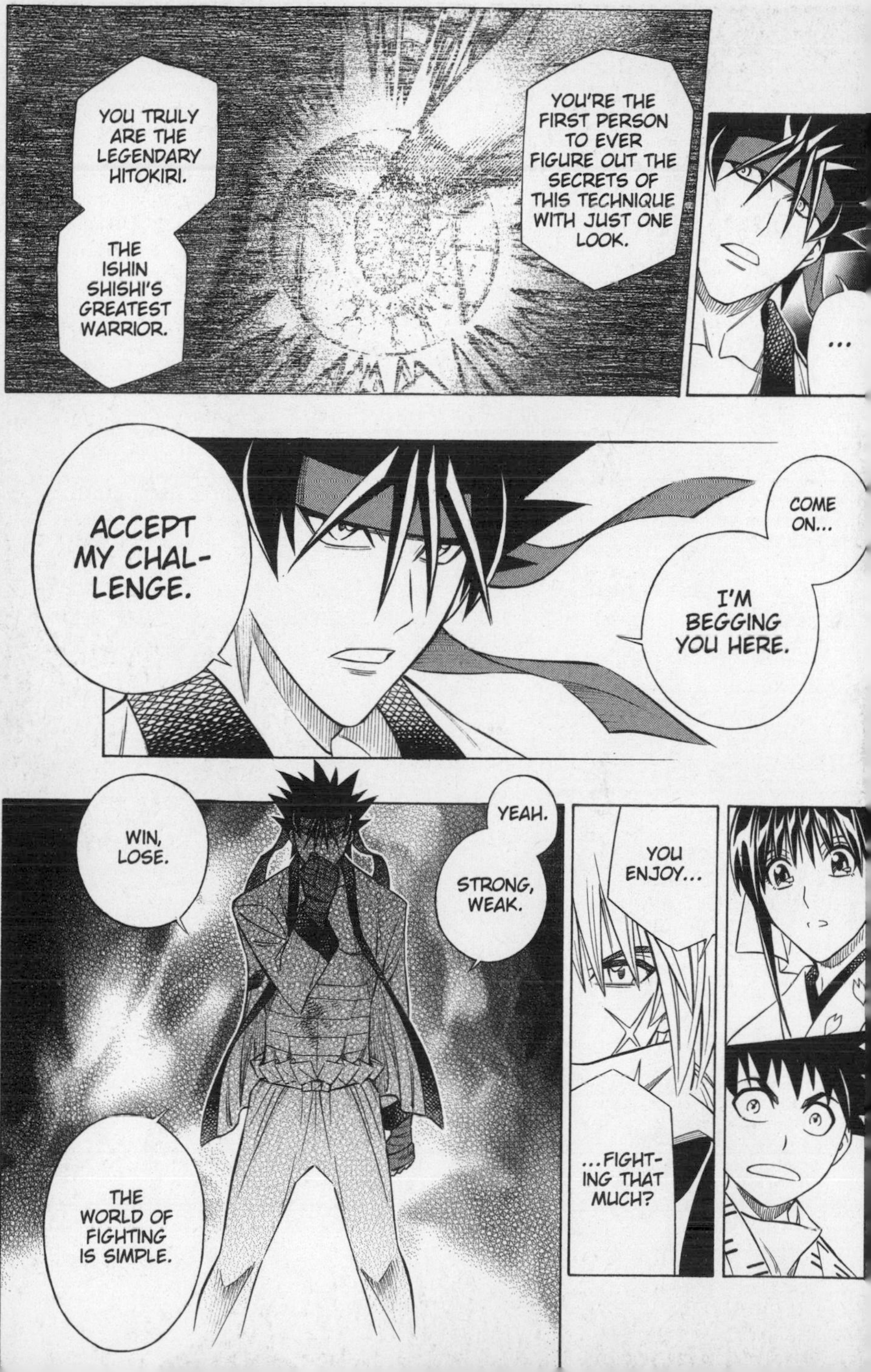
...
YOU'RE THE FIRST PERSON TO EVER FIGURE OUT THE SECRETS OF THIS TECHNIQUE WITH JUST ONE LOOK.
YOU TRULY ARE THE LEGENDARY HITOKIRI.
THE ISHIN SHISHI'S GREATEST WARRIOR.
COME ON...
I'M BEGGING YOU HERE.
ACCEPT MY CHAL-LENGE.
YOU ENJOY...
...FIGHT-ING THAT MUCH?
YEAH.
STRONG, WEAK.
WIN, LOSE.
THE WORLD OF FIGHTING IS SIMPLE.

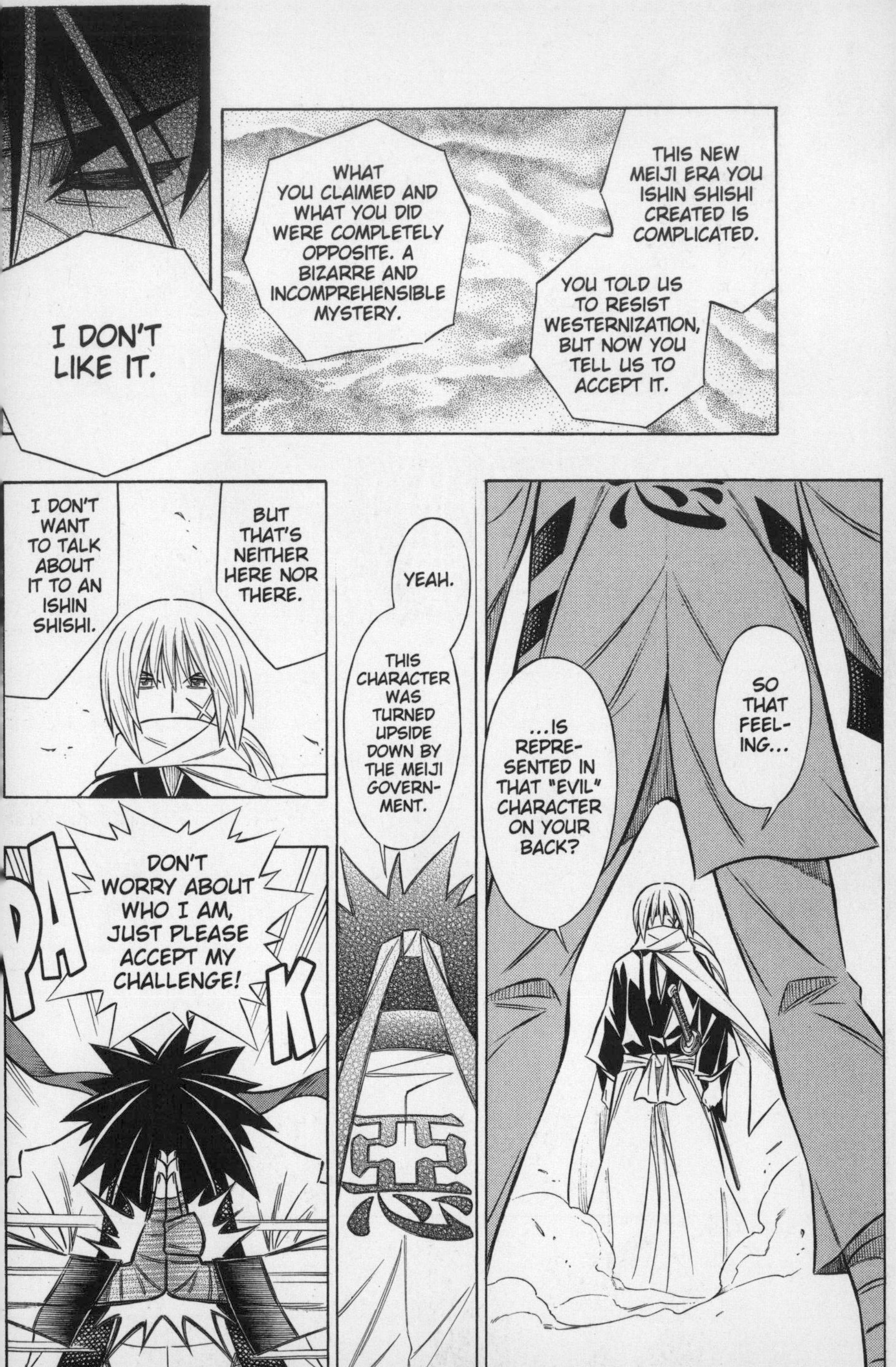
THIS NEW MEIJI ERA YOU ISHIN SHISHI CREATED IS COMPLICATED.
YOU TOLD US TO RESIST WESTERNIZATION, BUT NOW YOU TELL US TO ACCEPT IT.
WHAT YOU CLAIMED AND WHAT YOU DID WERE COMPLETELY OPPOSITE. A BIZARRE AND INCOMPREHENSIBLE MYSTERY.
I DON'T LIKE IT.
SO THAT FEEL-ING...
...IS REPRE-SENTED IN THAT "EVIL" CHARACTER ON YOUR BACK?
YEAH.
THIS CHARACTER WAS TURNED UPSIDE DOWN BY THE MEIJI GOVERN-MENT.
BUT THAT'S NEITHER HERE NOR THERE.
I DON'T WANT TO TALK ABOUT IT TO AN ISHIN SHISHI.
DON'T WORRY ABOUT WHO I AM, JUST PLEASE ACCEPT MY CHALLENGE!
PA
K

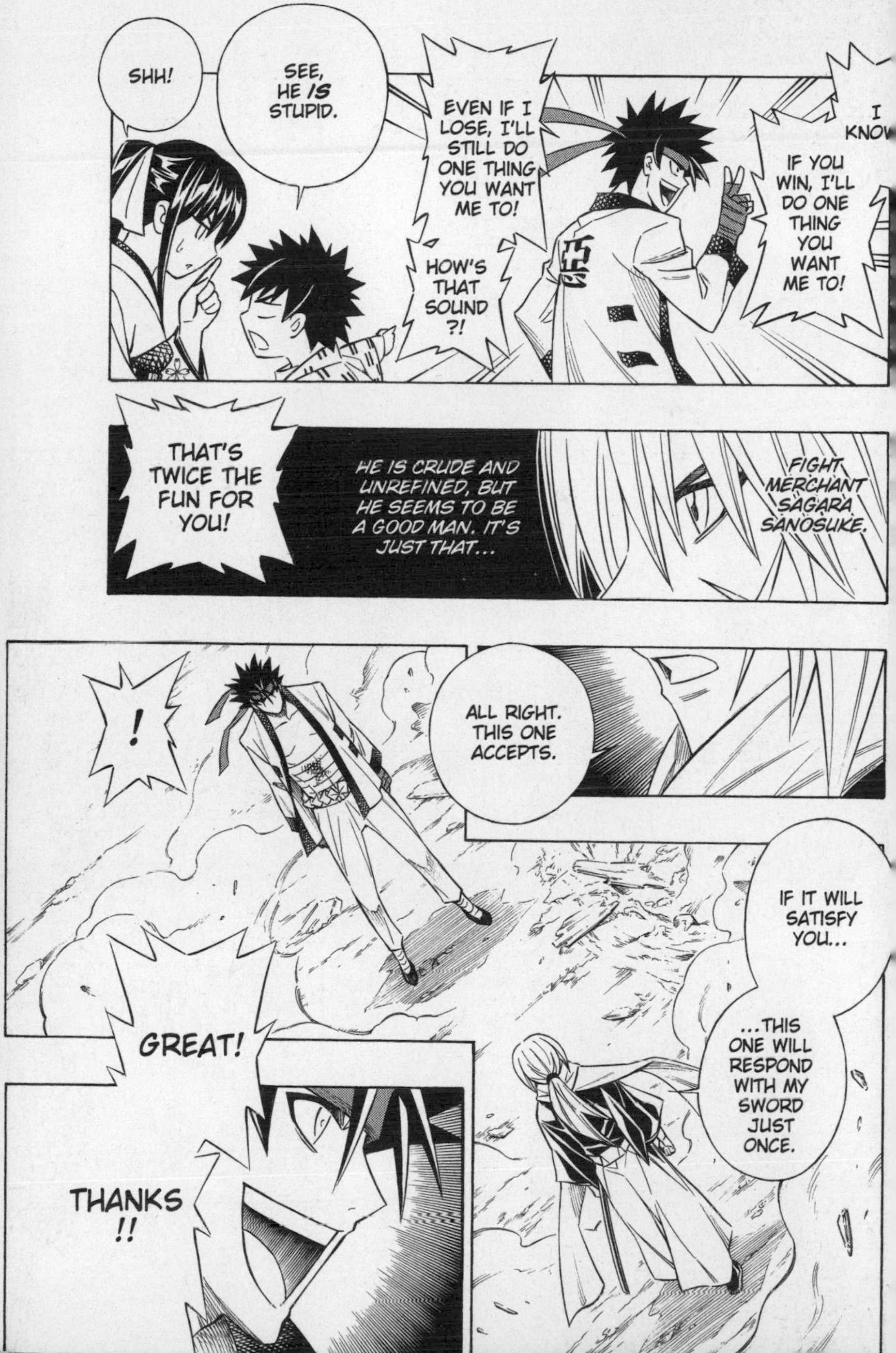

I KNO
IF YOU WIN, I'LL DO ONE THING YOU WANT ME TO!
EVEN IF I LOSE, I'LL STILL DO ONE THING YOU WANT ME TO!
HOW'S THAT SOUND ?!
SEE, HE *IS* STUPID.
SHH!
FIGHT MERCHANT SAGARA SANOSUKE.
HE IS CRUDE AND UNREFINED, BUT HE SEEMS TO BE A GOOD MAN. IT'S JUST THAT...
THAT'S TWICE THE FUN FOR YOU!
ALL RIGHT. THIS ONE ACCEPTS.
!
IF IT WILL SATISFY YOU...
...THIS ONE WILL RESPOND WITH MY SWORD JUST ONCE.
GREAT!
THANKS !!

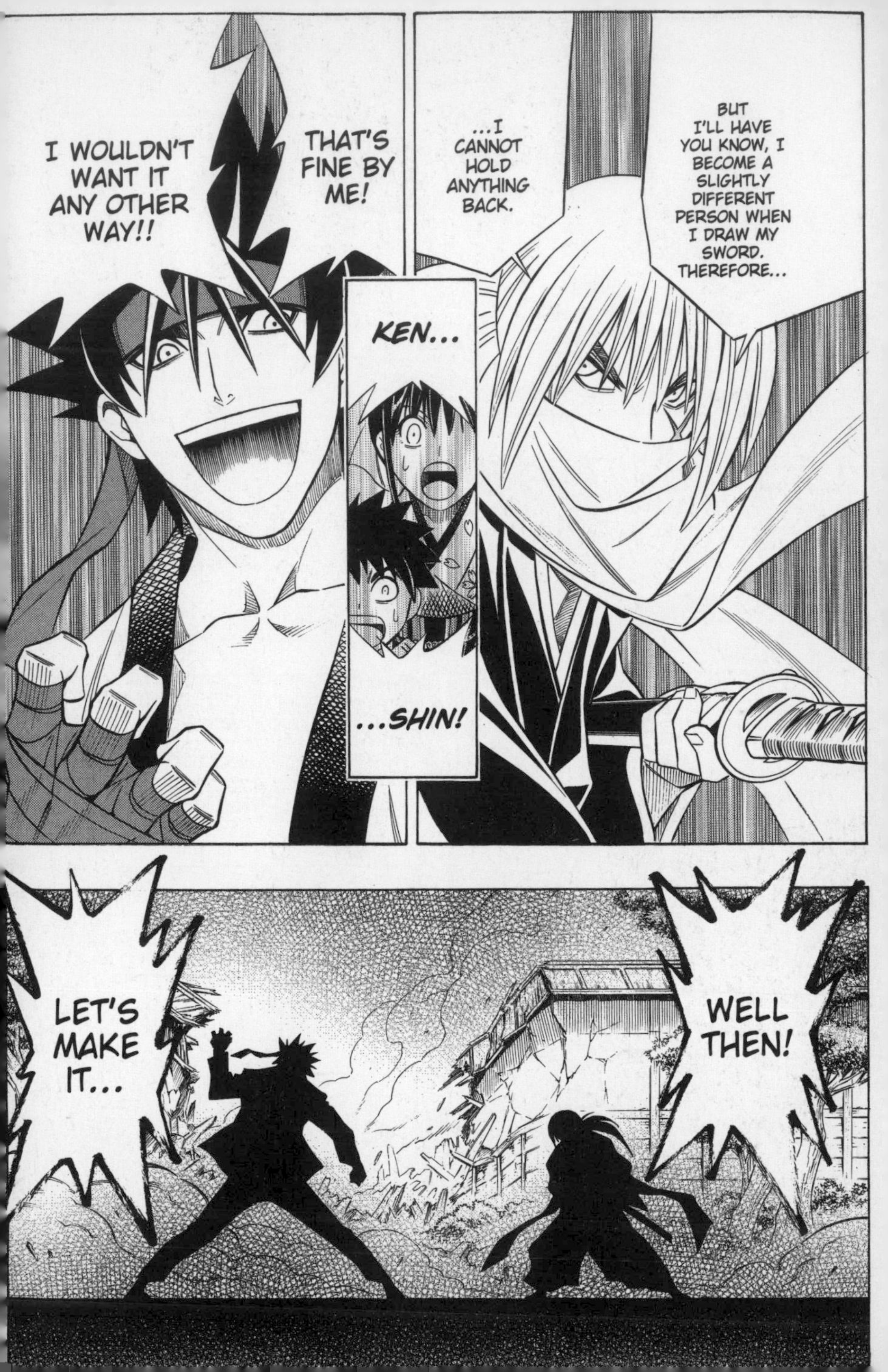
BUT I'LL HAVE YOU KNOW, I BECOME A SLIGHTLY DIFFERENT PERSON WHEN I DRAW MY SWORD. THEREFORE...
...I CANNOT HOLD ANYTHING BACK.
KEN...
...SHIN!
THAT'S FINE BY ME!
I WOULDN'T WANT IT ANY OTHER WAY!!
WELL THEN!
LET'S MAKE IT...

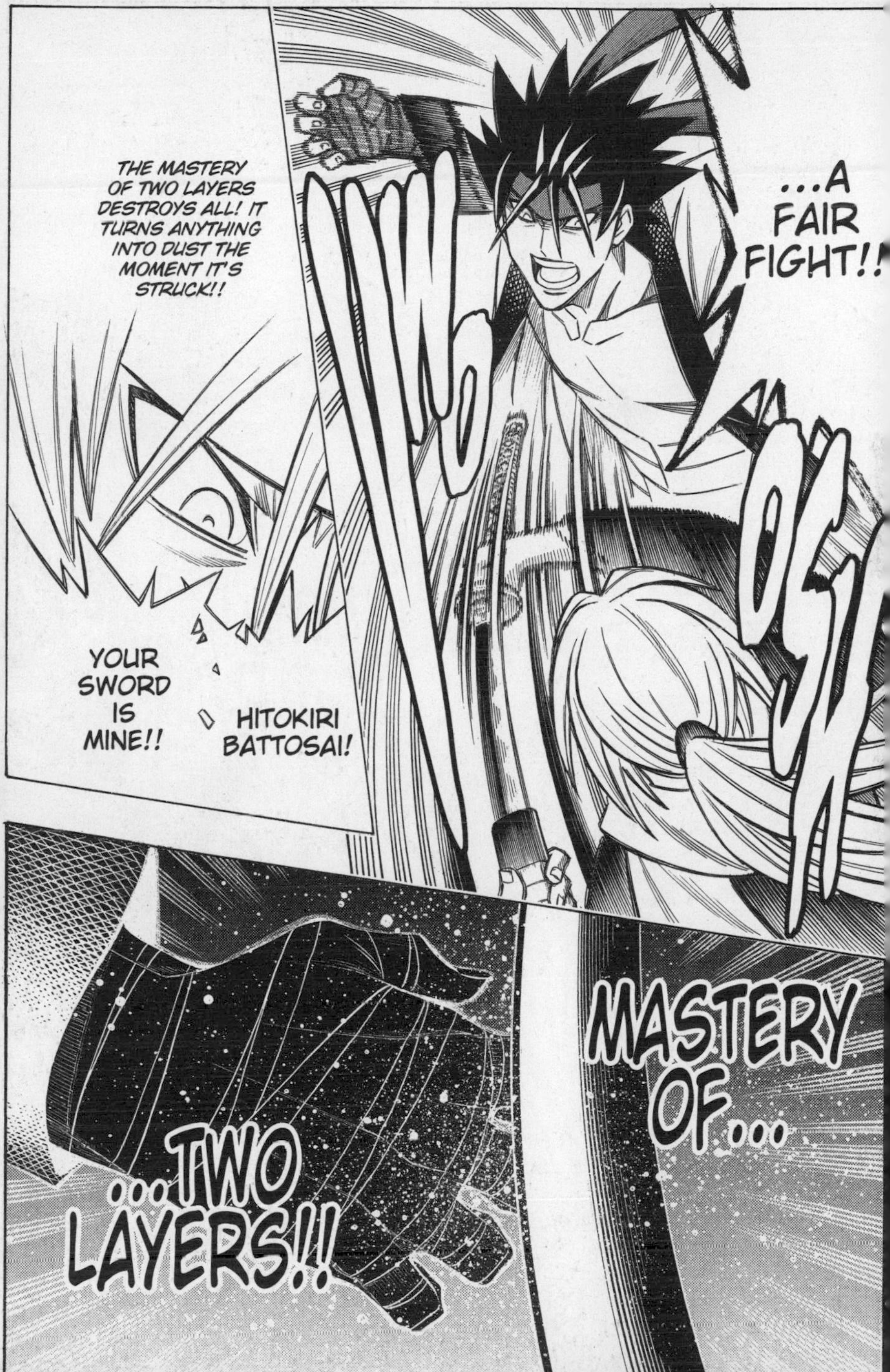
...A FAIR FIGHT!!
THE MASTERY OF TWO LAYERS DESTROYS ALL! IT TURNS ANYTHING INTO DUST THE MOMENT IT'S STRUCK!!
HITOKIRI BATTOSAI!
YOUR SWORD IS MINE!!
MASTERY OF...
...TWO LAYERS!!

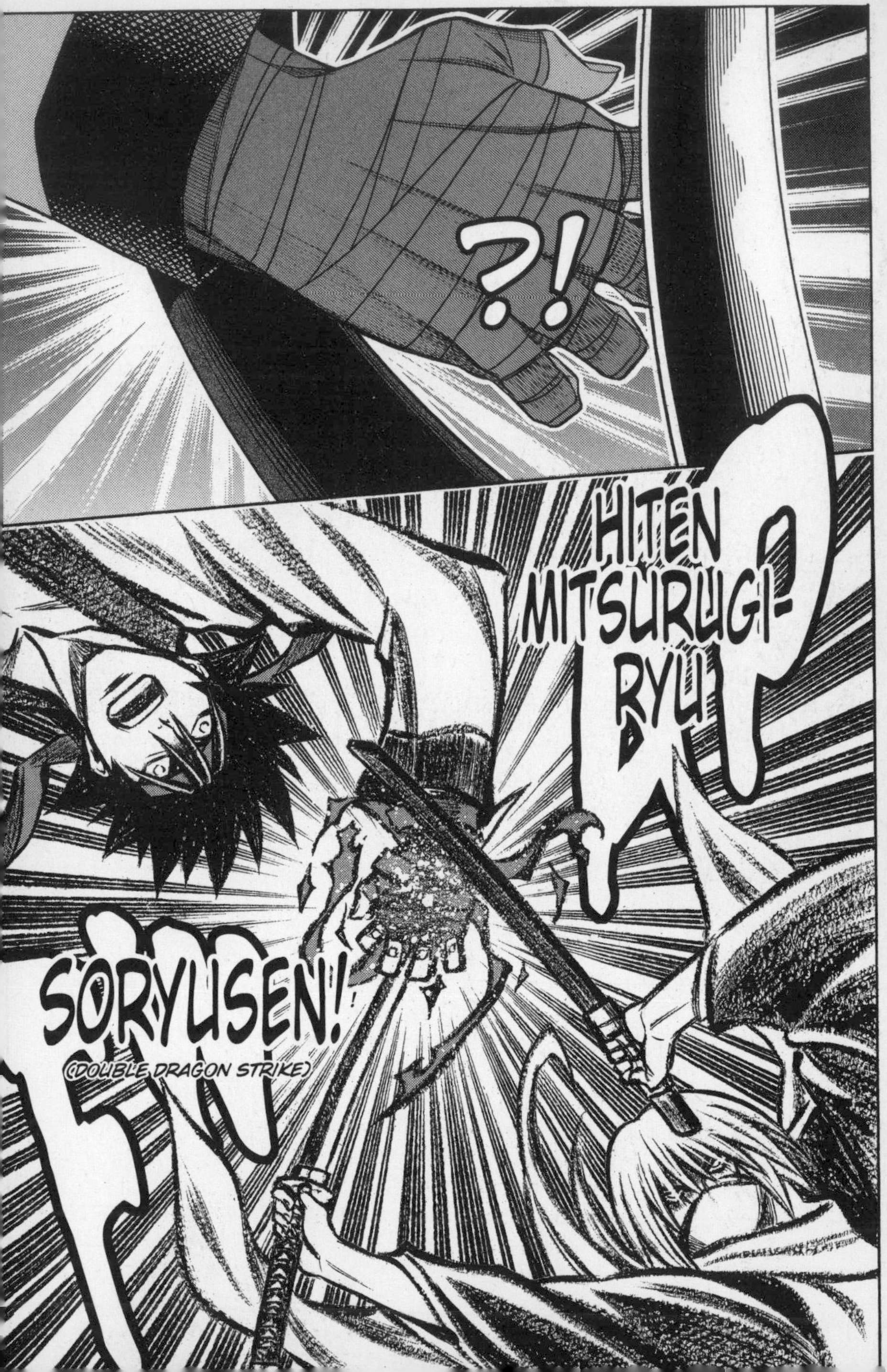
?!
HITEN MITSURUGI-RYU
SORYUSEN!
(DOUBLE DRAGON STRIKE)

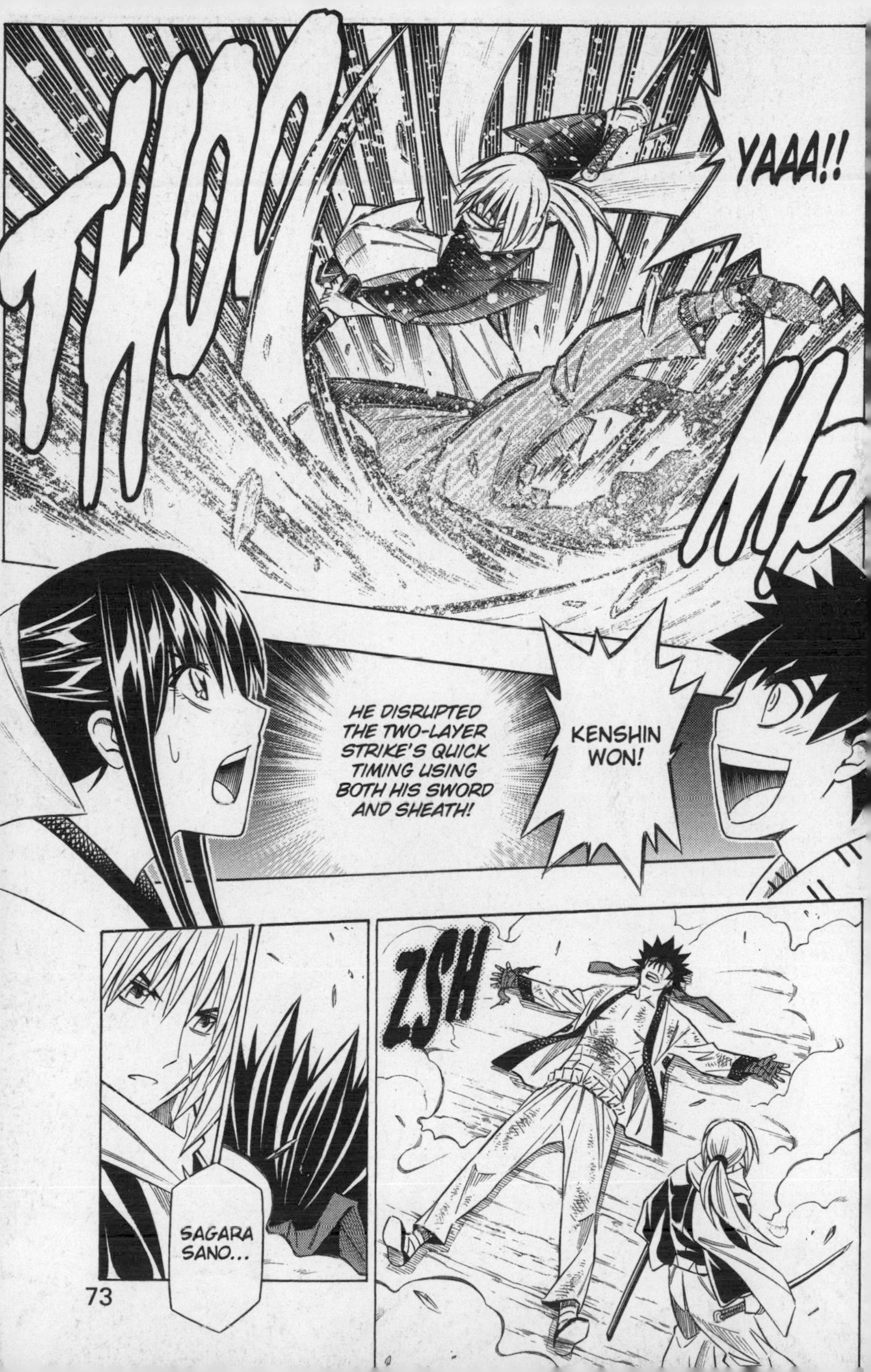
YAAA!!
KENSHIN WON!
HE DISRUPTED THE TWO-LAYER STRIKE'S QUICK TIMING USING BOTH HIS SWORD AND SHEATH!
ZSH
SAGARA SANO...

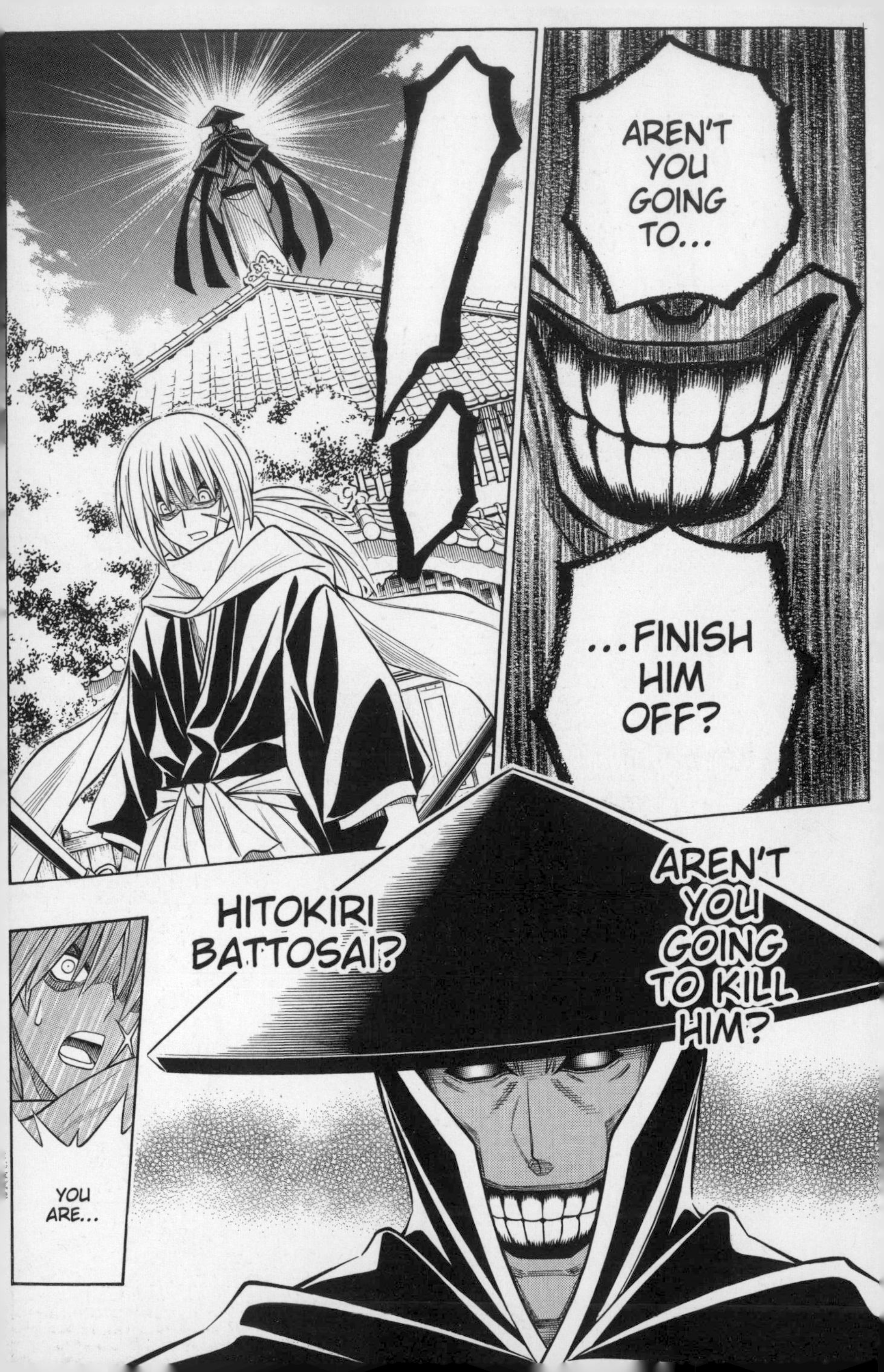
AREN'T YOU GOING TO...
...FINISH HIM OFF?
!
AREN'T YOU GOING TO KILL HIM?
HITOKIRI BATTOSAI?
YOU ARE...

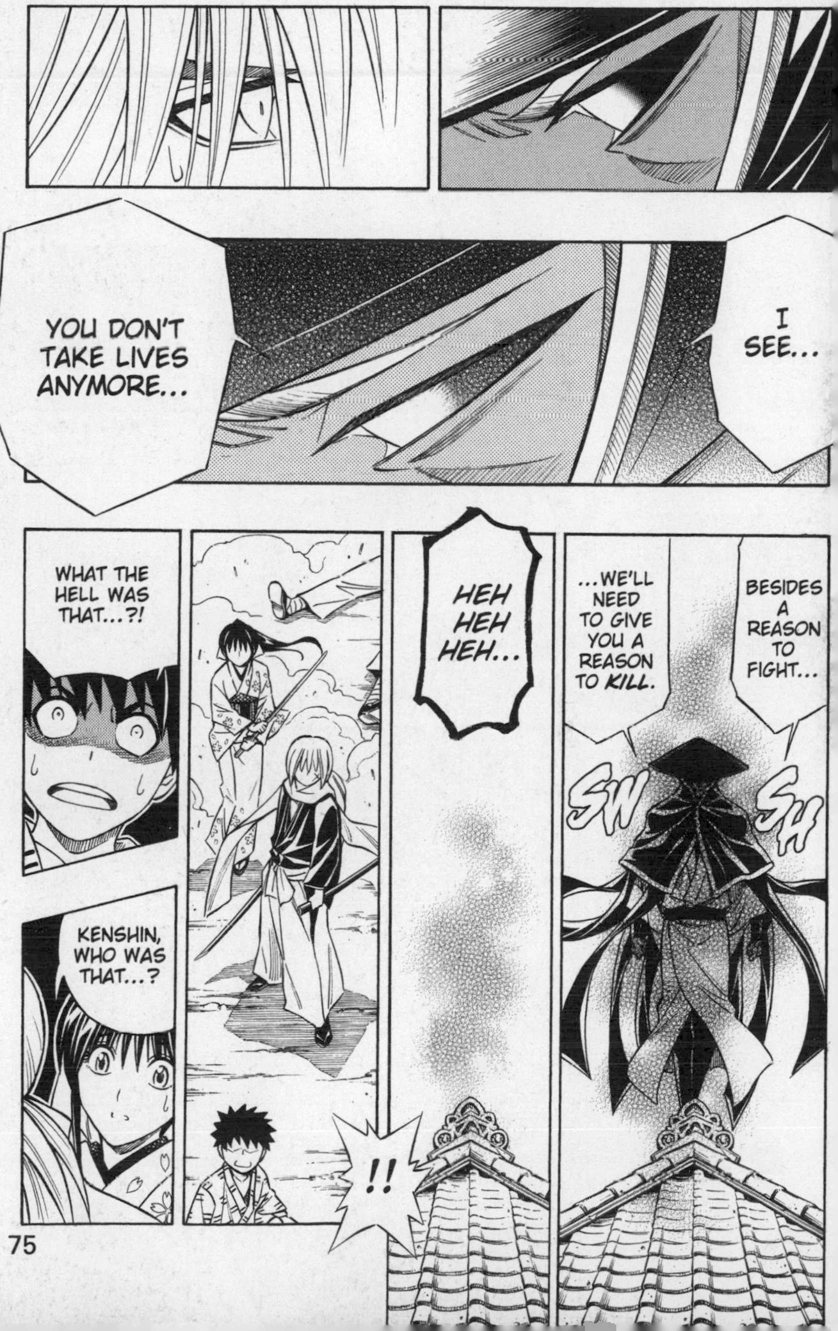
I SEE...
YOU DON'T TAKE LIVES ANYMORE...
BESIDES A REASON TO FIGHT...
...WE'LL NEED TO GIVE YOU A REASON TO *KILL*.
SW
SH
HEH HEH HEH...
!!
WHAT THE HELL WAS THAT...?!
KENSHIN, WHO WAS THAT...?

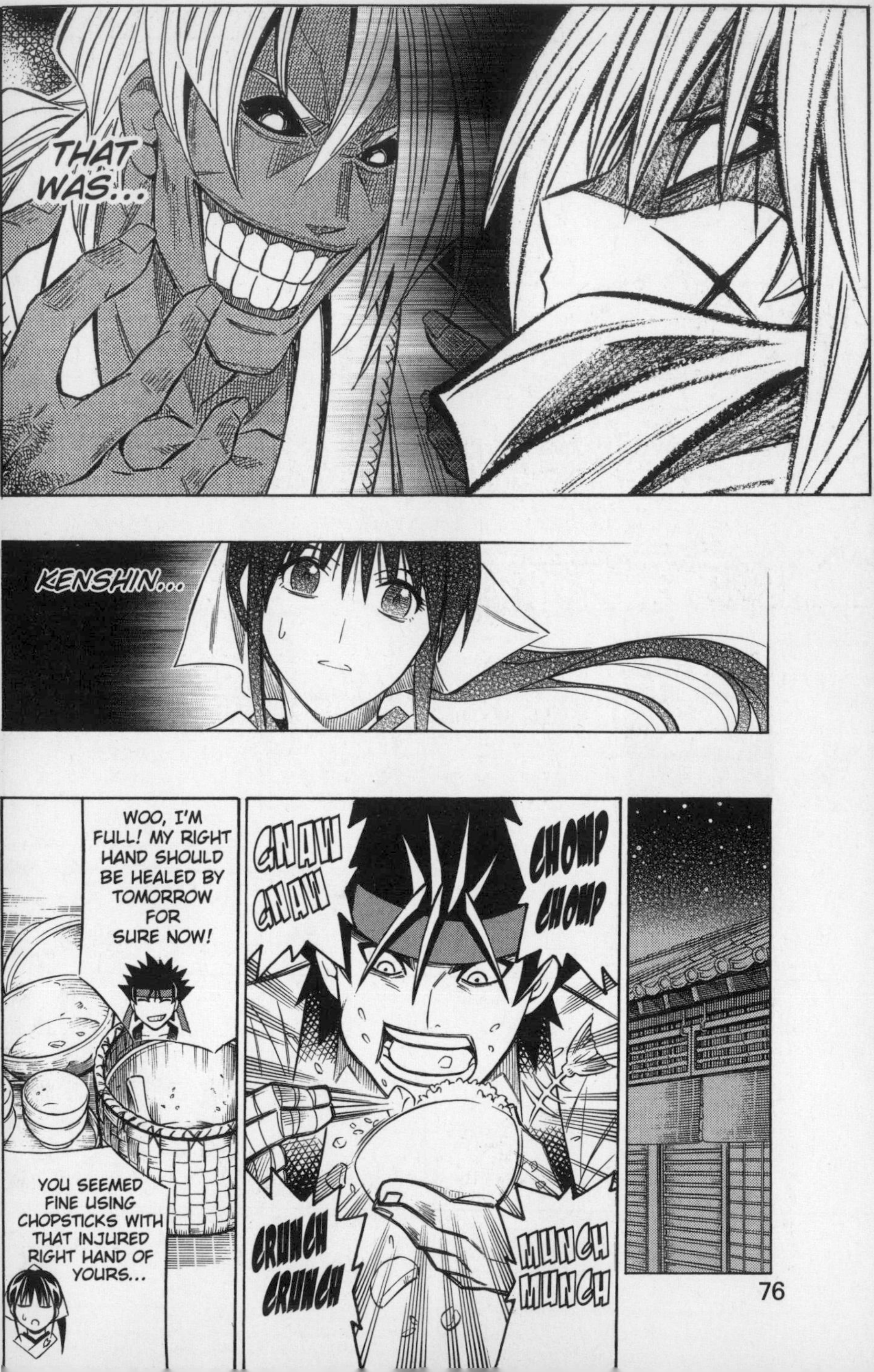
THAT WAS...
KENSHIN...
CHOMP CHOMP
GNAW GNAW
MUNCH MUNCH
CRUNCH CRUNCH
WOO, I'M FULL! MY RIGHT HAND SHOULD BE HEALED BY TOMORROW FOR SURE NOW!
YOU SEEMED FINE USING CHOPSTICKS WITH THAT INJURED RIGHT HAND OF YOURS...

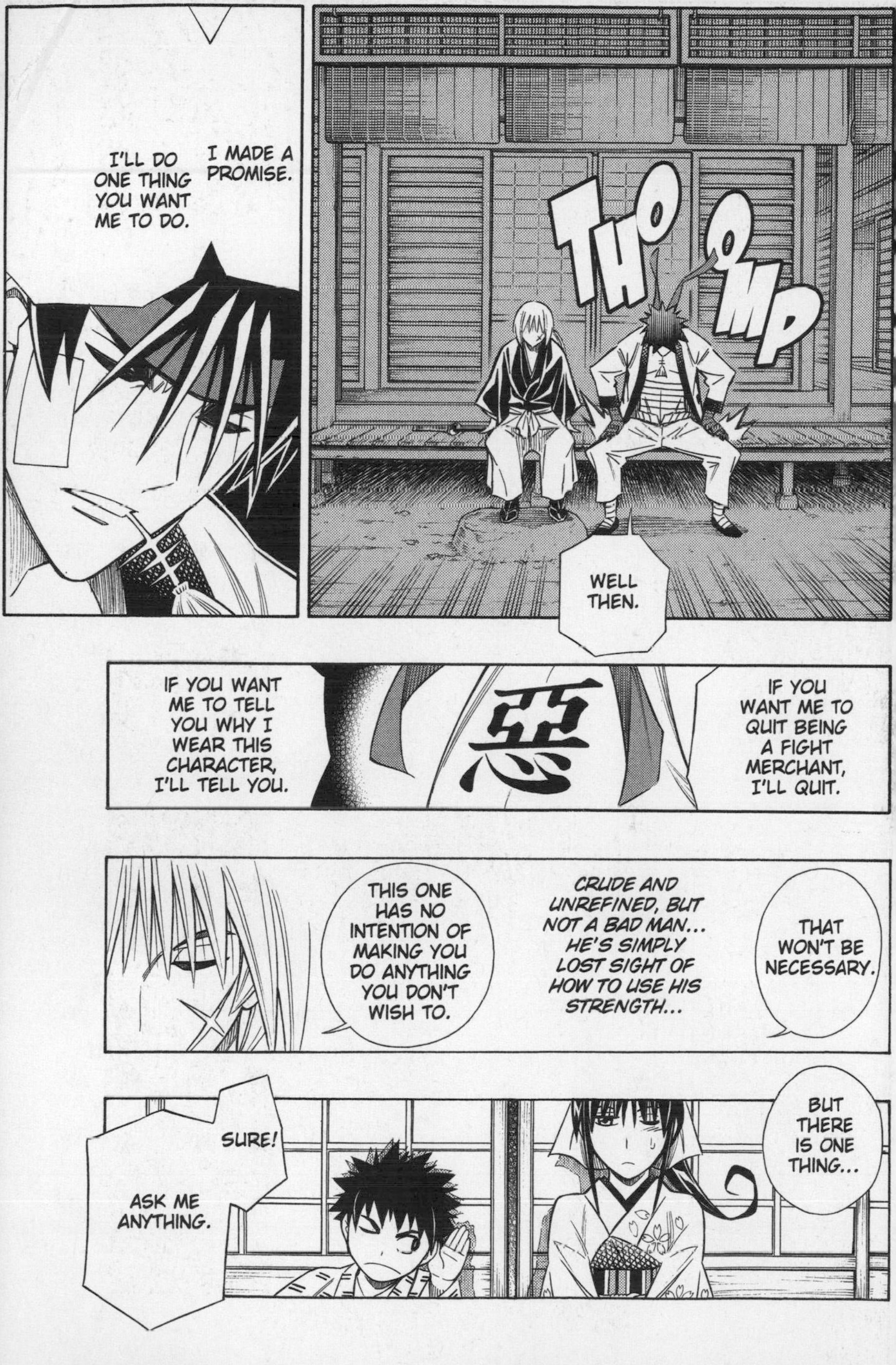
THOOMP
WELL THEN.
I MADE A PROMISE.
I'LL DO ONE THING YOU WANT ME TO DO.
IF YOU WANT ME TO QUIT BEING A FIGHT MERCHANT, I'LL QUIT.
悪
IF YOU WANT ME TO TELL YOU WHY I WEAR THIS CHARACTER, I'LL TELL YOU.
THAT WON'T BE NECESSARY.
CRUDE AND UNREFINED, BUT NOT A BAD MAN... HE'S SIMPLY LOST SIGHT OF HOW TO USE HIS STRENGTH...
THIS ONE HAS NO INTENTION OF MAKING YOU DO ANYTHING YOU DON'T WISH TO.
BUT THERE IS ONE THING...
SURE!
ASK ME ANYTHING.

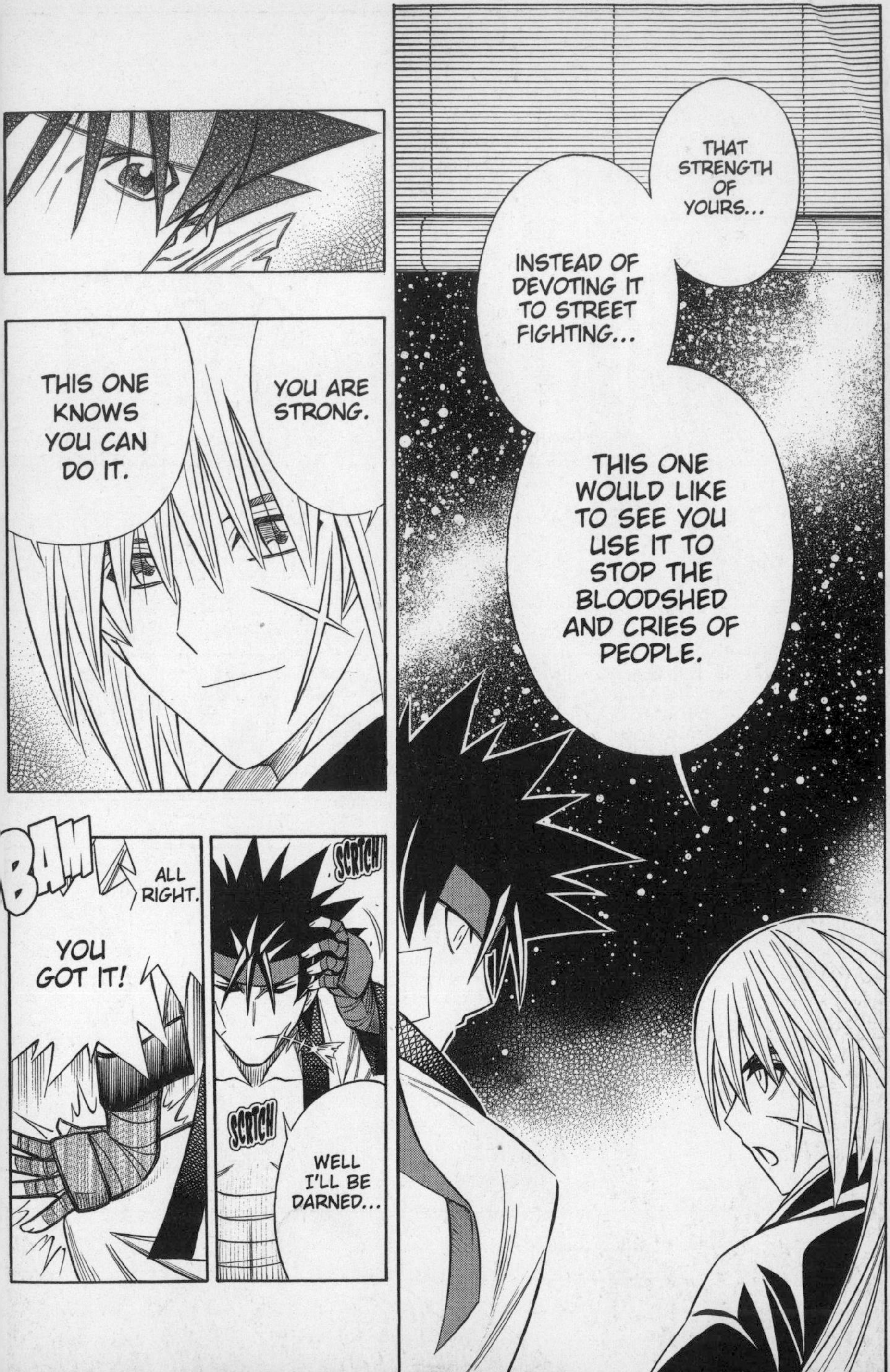
THAT STRENGTH OF YOURS...
INSTEAD OF DEVOTING IT TO STREET FIGHTING...
THIS ONE WOULD LIKE TO SEE YOU USE IT TO STOP THE BLOODSHED AND CRIES OF PEOPLE.
YOU ARE STRONG.
THIS ONE KNOWS YOU CAN DO IT.
SCRITCH
SCRITCH
WELL I'LL BE DARNED...
BAM
ALL RIGHT.
YOU GOT IT!

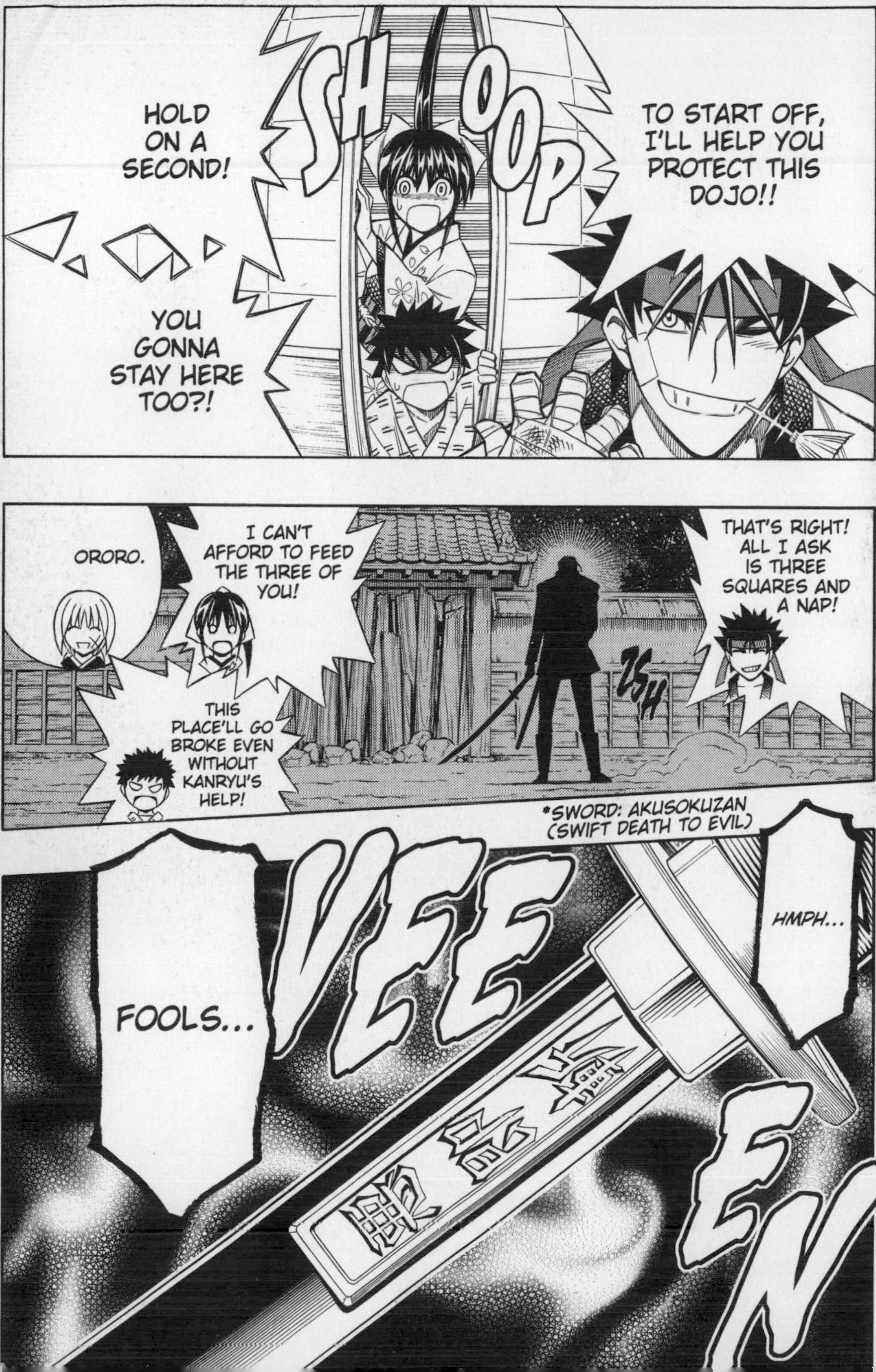
TO START OFF, I'LL HELP YOU PROTECT THIS DOJO!!
SHOOOP
HOLD ON A SECOND!
YOU GONNA STAY HERE TOO?!
THAT'S RIGHT! ALL I ASK IS THREE SQUARES AND A NAP!
ZSH
I CAN'T AFFORD TO FEED THE THREE OF YOU!
ORORO.
THIS PLACE'LL GO BROKE EVEN WITHOUT KANRYU'S HELP!
*SWORD: AKUSOKUZAN (SWIFT DEATH TO EVIL)
HMPH...
VEEEN
FOOLS...

Rurouni Kenshin

RESTORATION

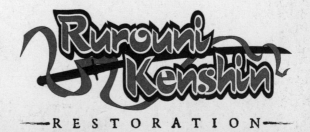

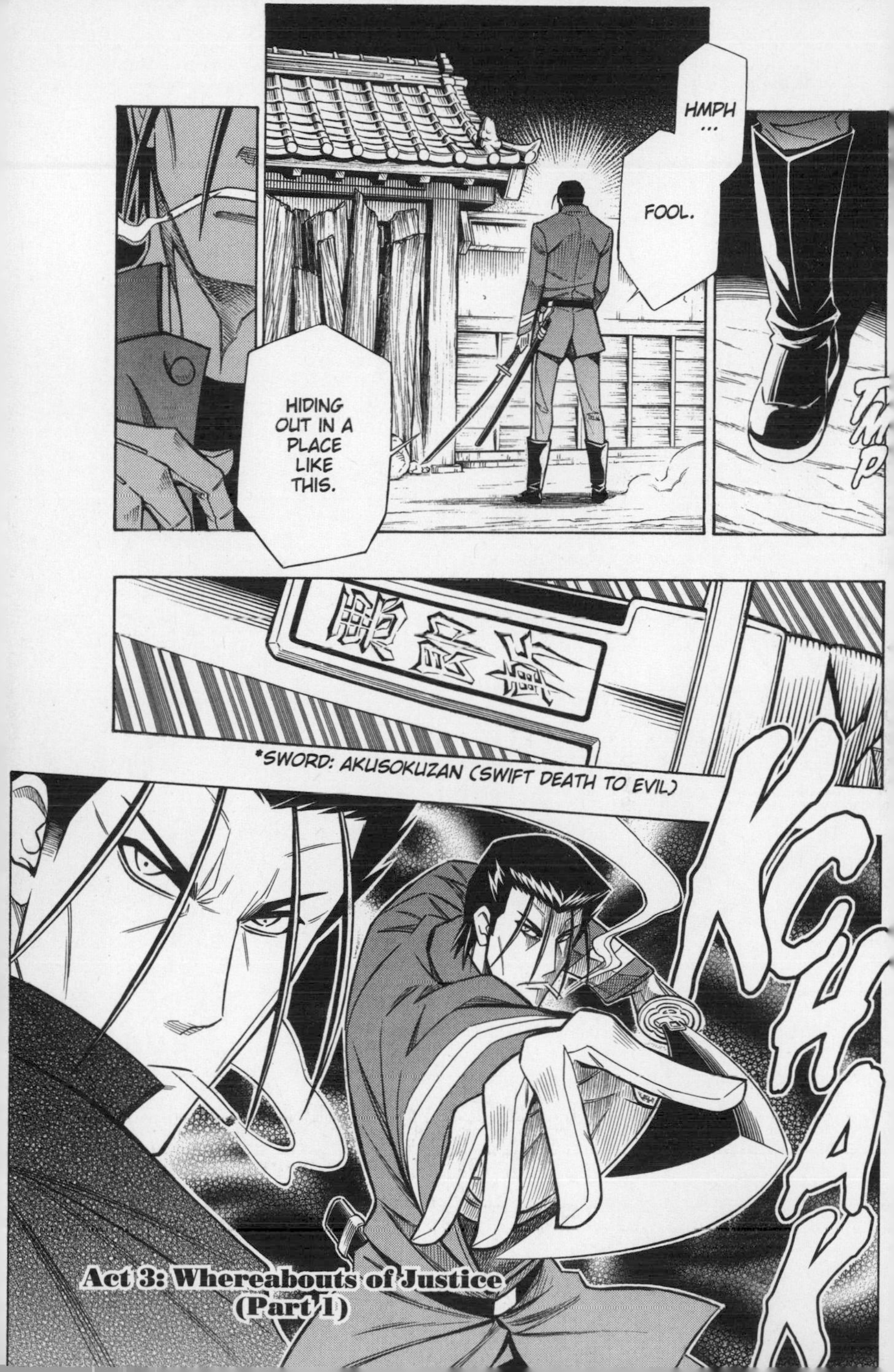
HMPH ...
FOOL.
HIDING OUT IN A PLACE LIKE THIS.
*SWORD: AKUSOKUZAN (SWIFT DEATH TO EVIL)
KCHAK

Act 3: Whereabouts of Justice (Part 1)

Act 3: Whereabouts of Justice (Part 1)

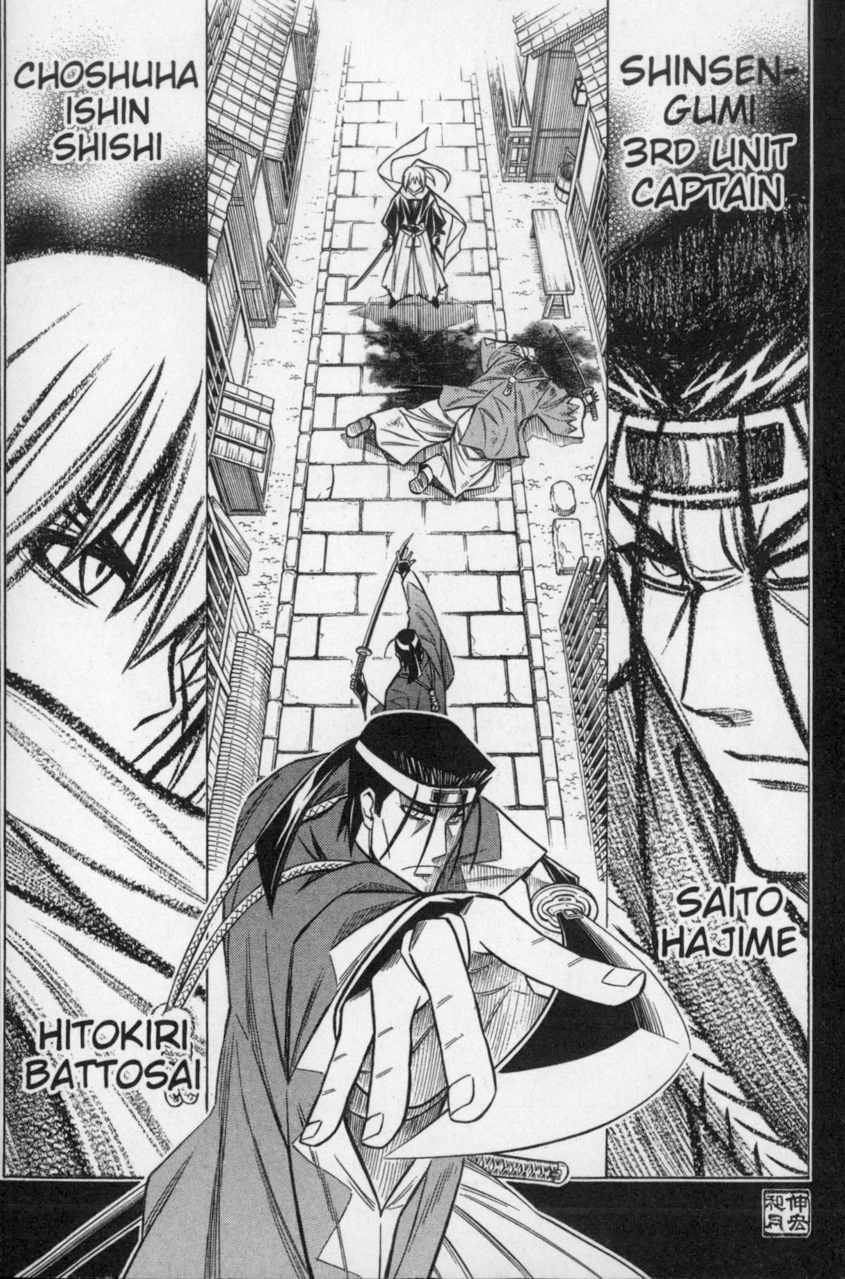
SHINSEN-GUMI 3RD UNIT CAPTAIN
SAITO HAJIME
CHOSHUHA ISHIN SHISHI
HITOKIRI BATTOSAI

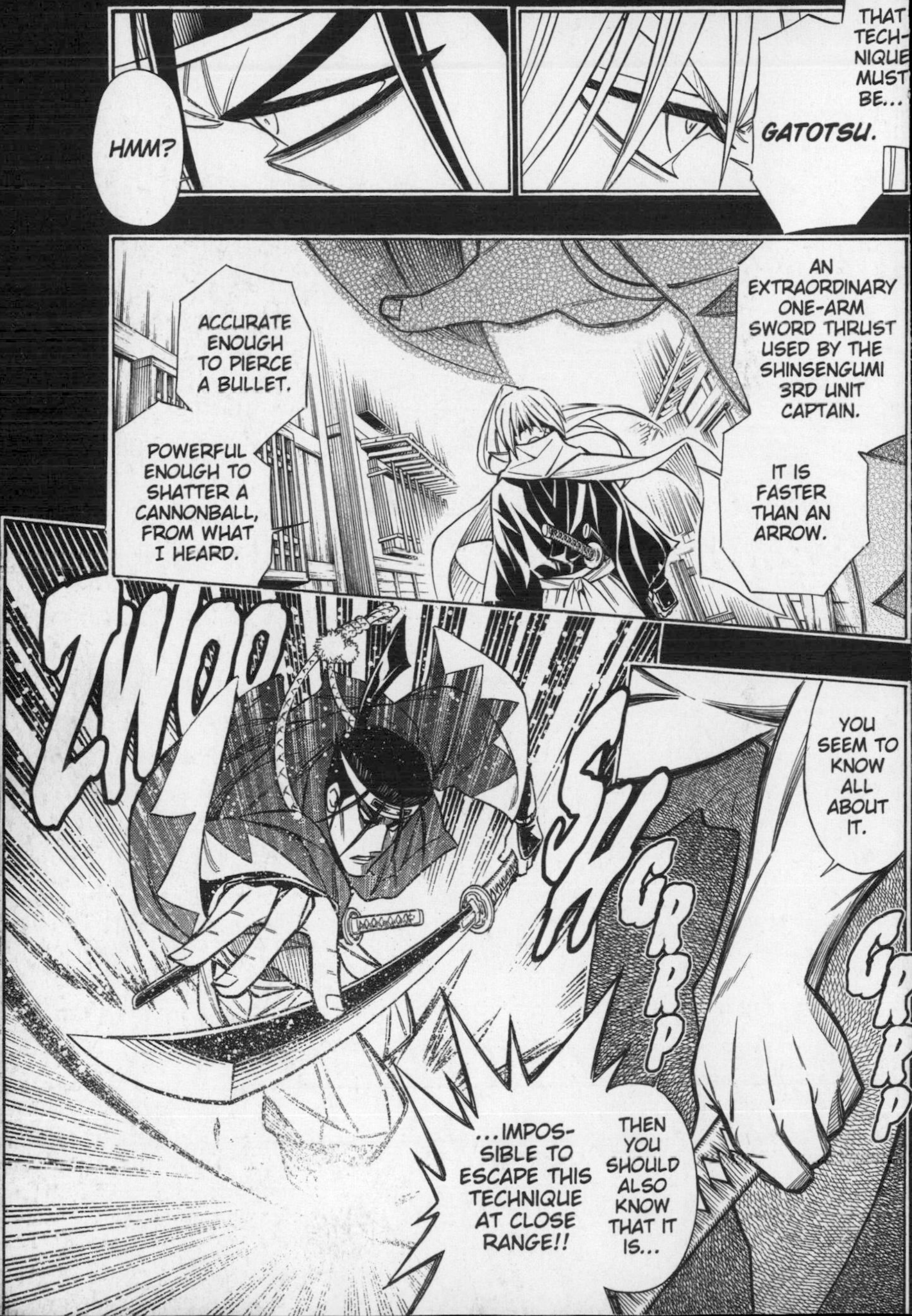
THAT TECH-NIQUE MUST BE...
GATOTSU.
HMM?
AN EXTRAORDINARY ONE-ARM SWORD THRUST USED BY THE SHINSENGUMI 3RD UNIT CAPTAIN.
IT IS FASTER THAN AN ARROW.
ACCURATE ENOUGH TO PIERCE A BULLET.
POWERFUL ENOUGH TO SHATTER A CANNONBALL, FROM WHAT I HEARD.
GRRP
GRRP
YOU SEEM TO KNOW ALL ABOUT IT.
ZWOO
SH
THEN YOU SHOULD ALSO KNOW THAT IT IS...
...IMPOS-SIBLE TO ESCAPE THIS TECHNIQUE AT CLOSE RANGE!!

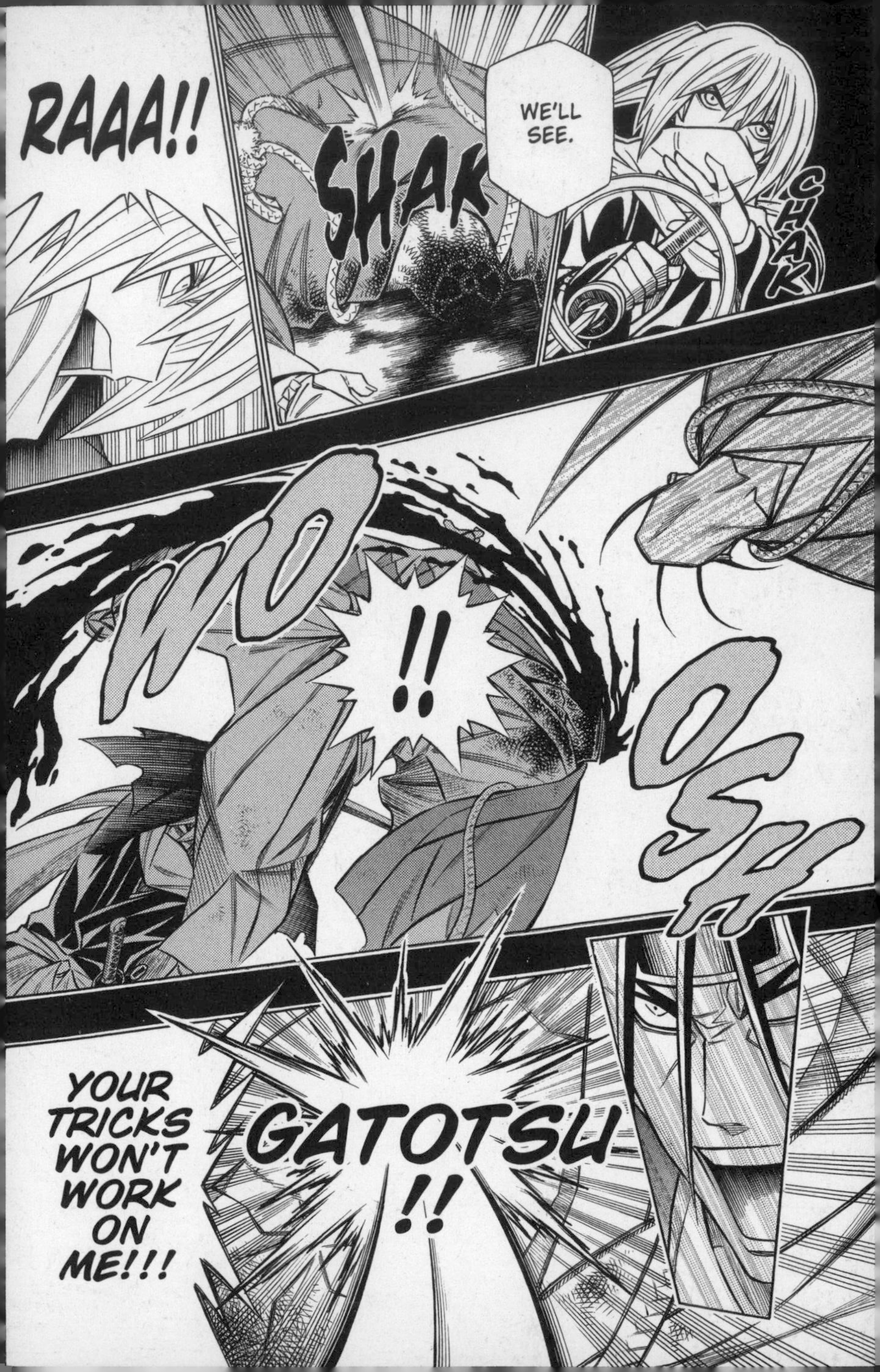
WE'LL SEE.
CHAK
SHAK
RAAA!!
WHO
!!
OSH
GATOTSU!!
YOUR TRICKS WON'T WORK ON ME!!!

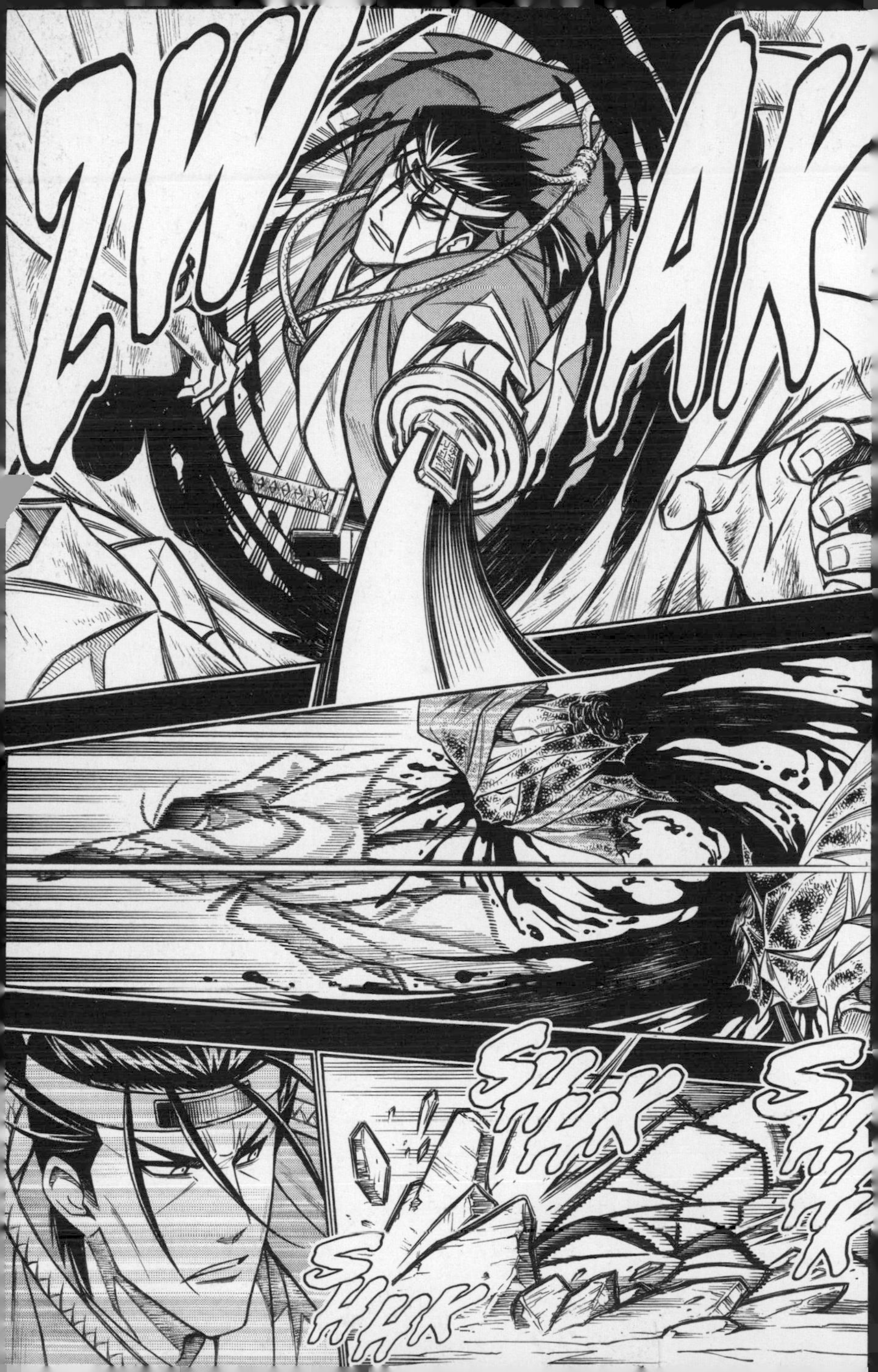
ZWAK
SHHK
SHHK
SHHK

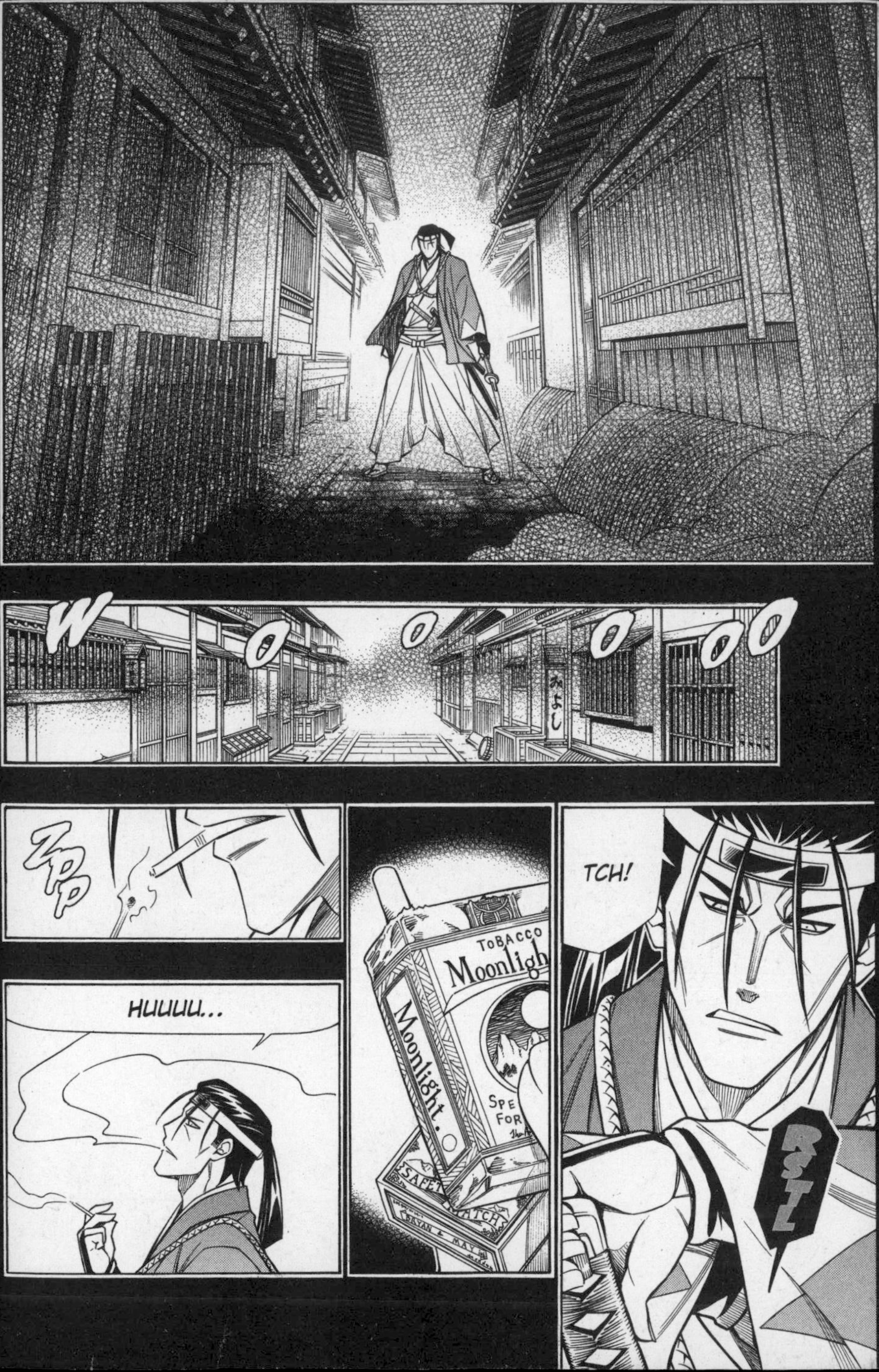
WOOOOO
TCH!
RSTL
TOBACCO
Moonligh
Moonlight.
SPE
FOR
ZPP
HUUUU...

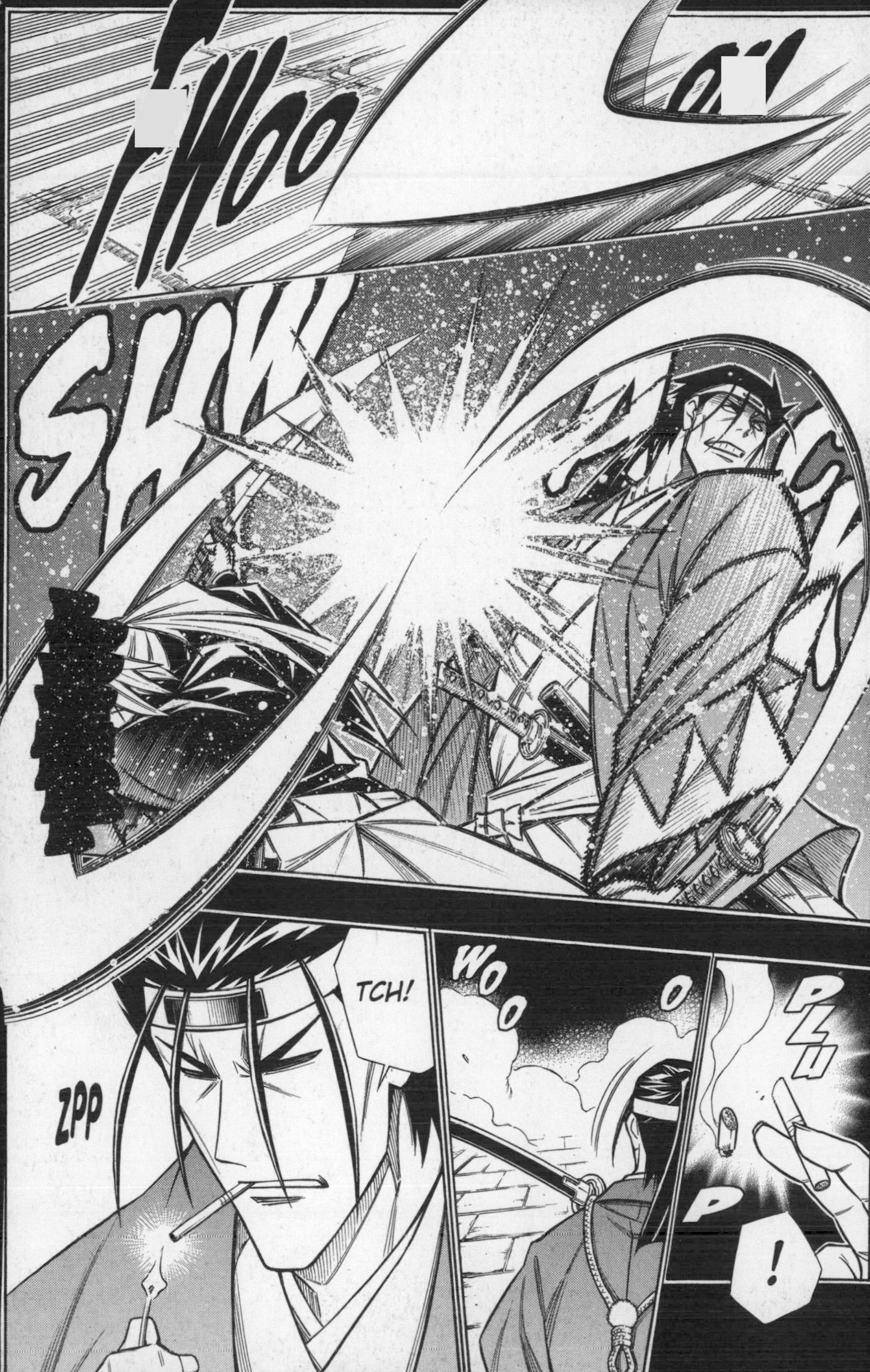

Woo
PLU
P
!
WOO
O
TCH!
ZPP

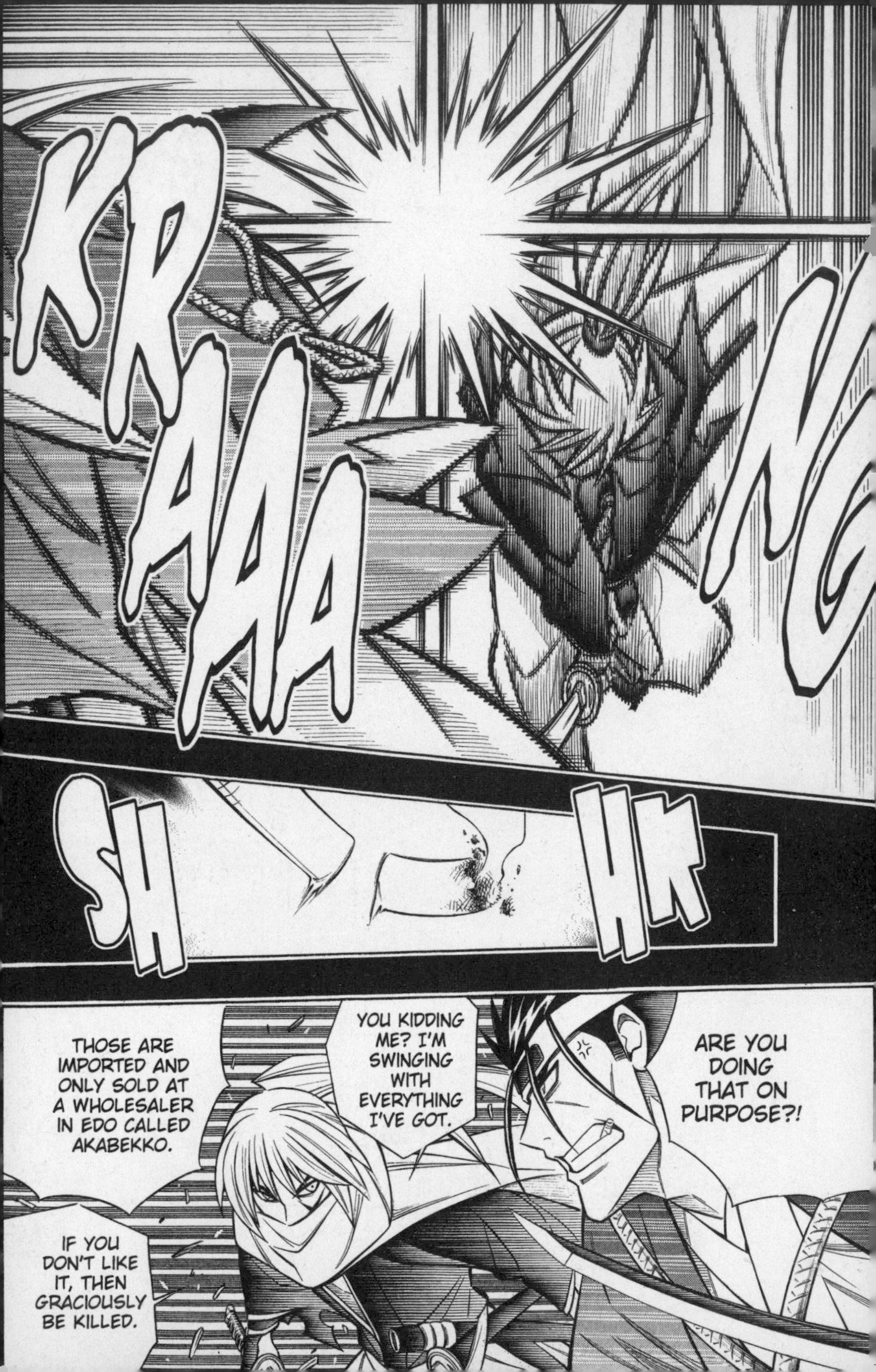
KRAAANG
SHHK
ARE YOU DOING THAT ON PURPOSE?!
YOU KIDDING ME? I'M SWINGING WITH EVERYTHING I'VE GOT.
THOSE ARE IMPORTED AND ONLY SOLD AT A WHOLESALER IN EDO CALLED AKABEKKO.
IF YOU DON'T LIKE IT, THEN GRACIOUSLY BE KILLED.

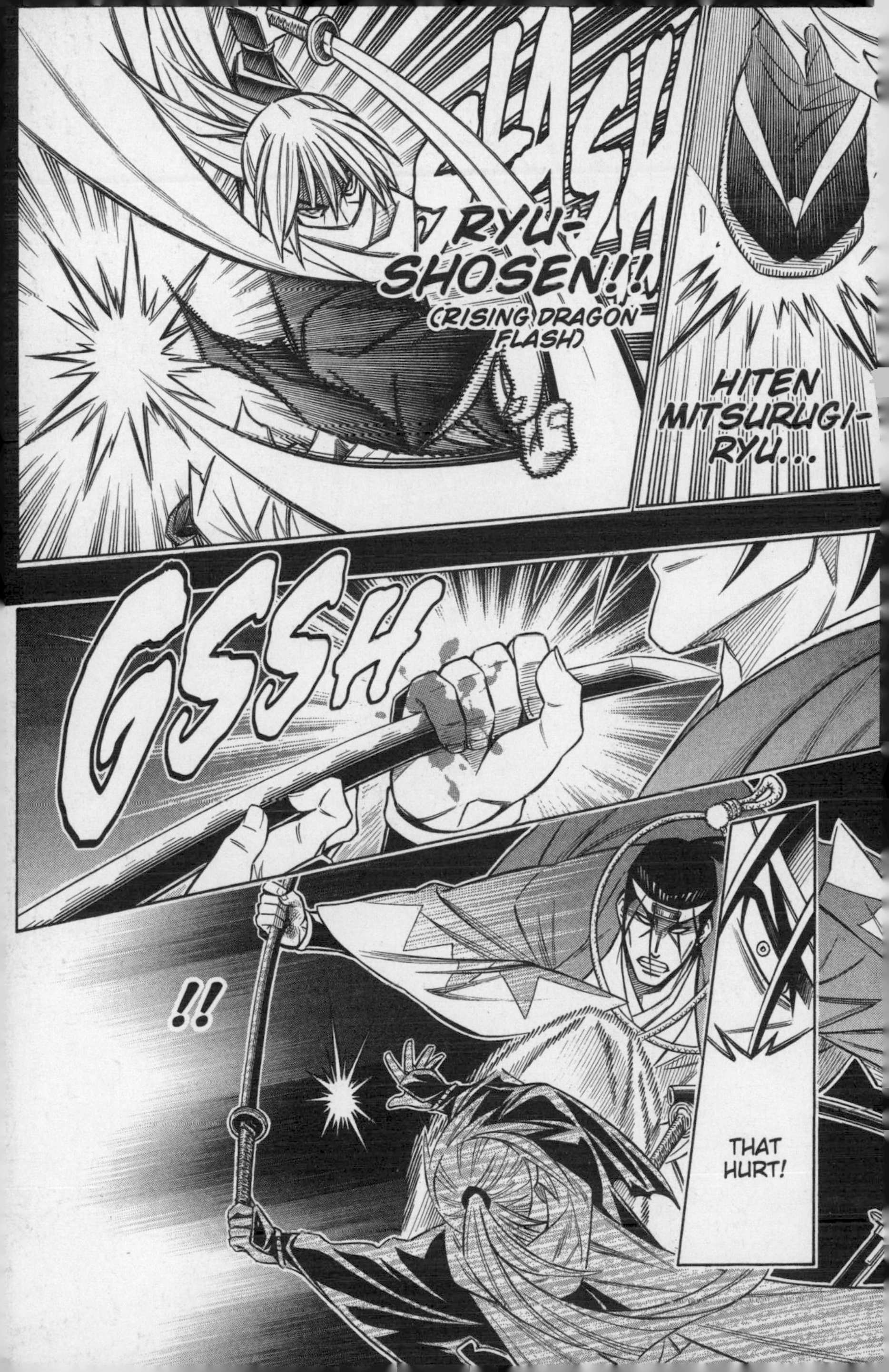

HITEN MITSURUGI-RYU...
RYU-SHOSEN!!
(RISING DRAGON FLASH)
GSSH
THAT HURT!
!!

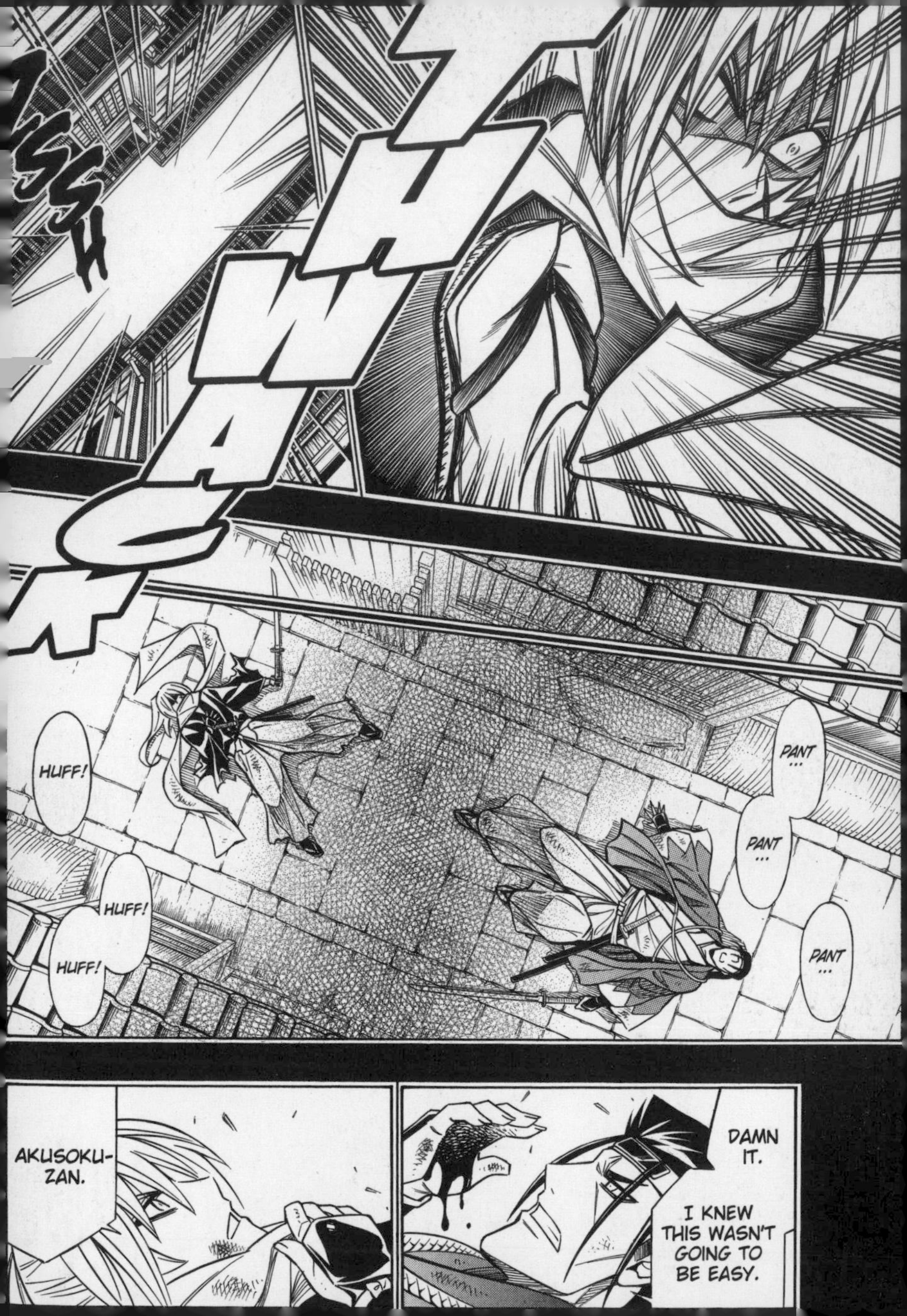
WHACK
SSH
PANT...
PANT...
PANT...
HUFF!
HUFF!
HUFF!
DAMN IT.
I KNEW THIS WASN'T GOING TO BE EASY.
AKUSOKU-ZAN.

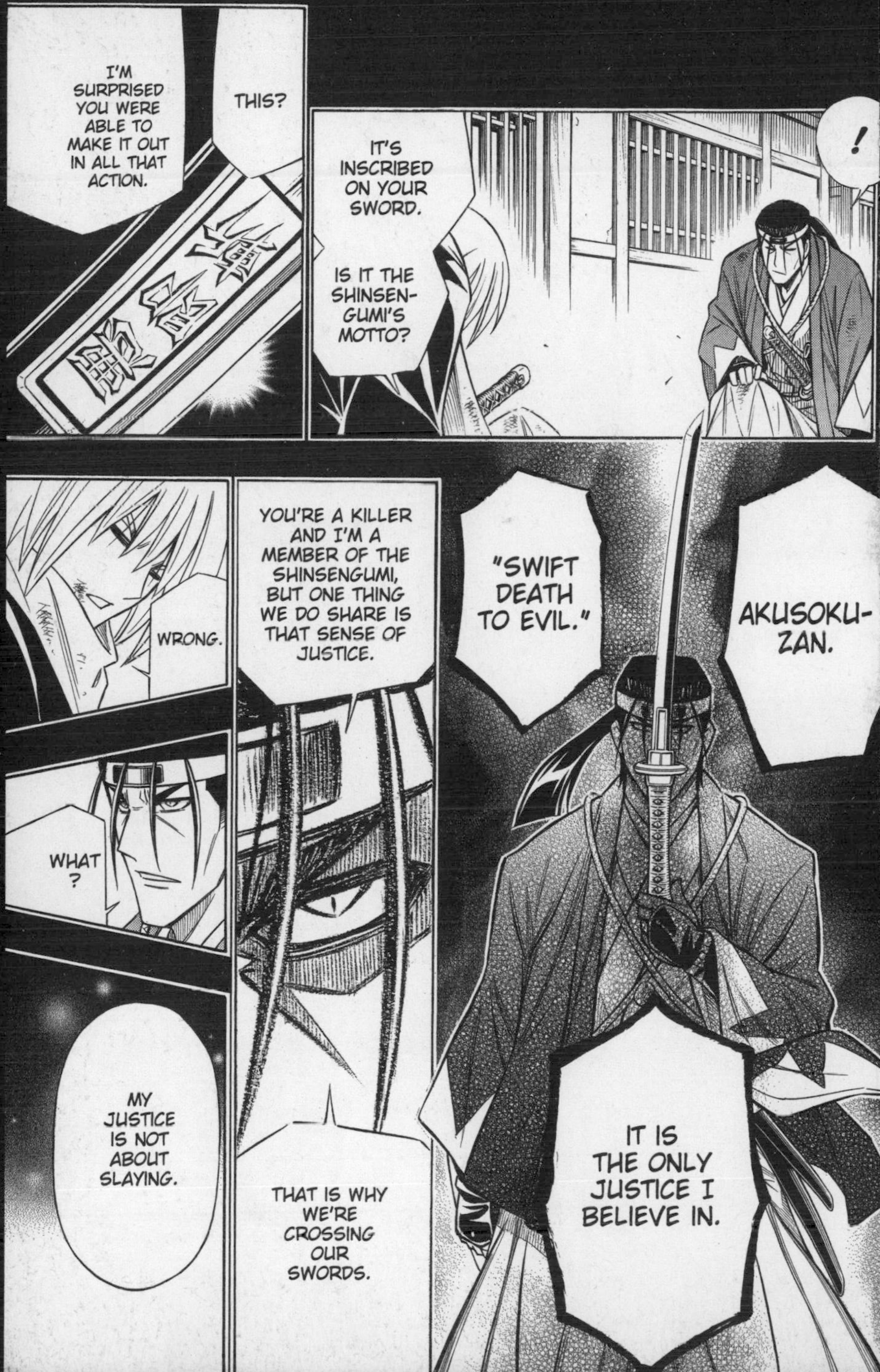
!
IT'S INSCRIBED ON YOUR SWORD.
IS IT THE SHINSENGUMI'S MOTTO?
THIS?
I'M SURPRISED YOU WERE ABLE TO MAKE IT OUT IN ALL THAT ACTION.
AKUSOKU-ZAN.
"SWIFT DEATH TO EVIL."
IT IS THE ONLY JUSTICE I BELIEVE IN.
YOU'RE A KILLER AND I'M A MEMBER OF THE SHINSENGUMI, BUT ONE THING WE DO SHARE IS THAT SENSE OF JUSTICE.
WRONG.
WHAT ?
MY JUSTICE IS NOT ABOUT SLAYING.
THAT IS WHY WE'RE CROSSING OUR SWORDS.

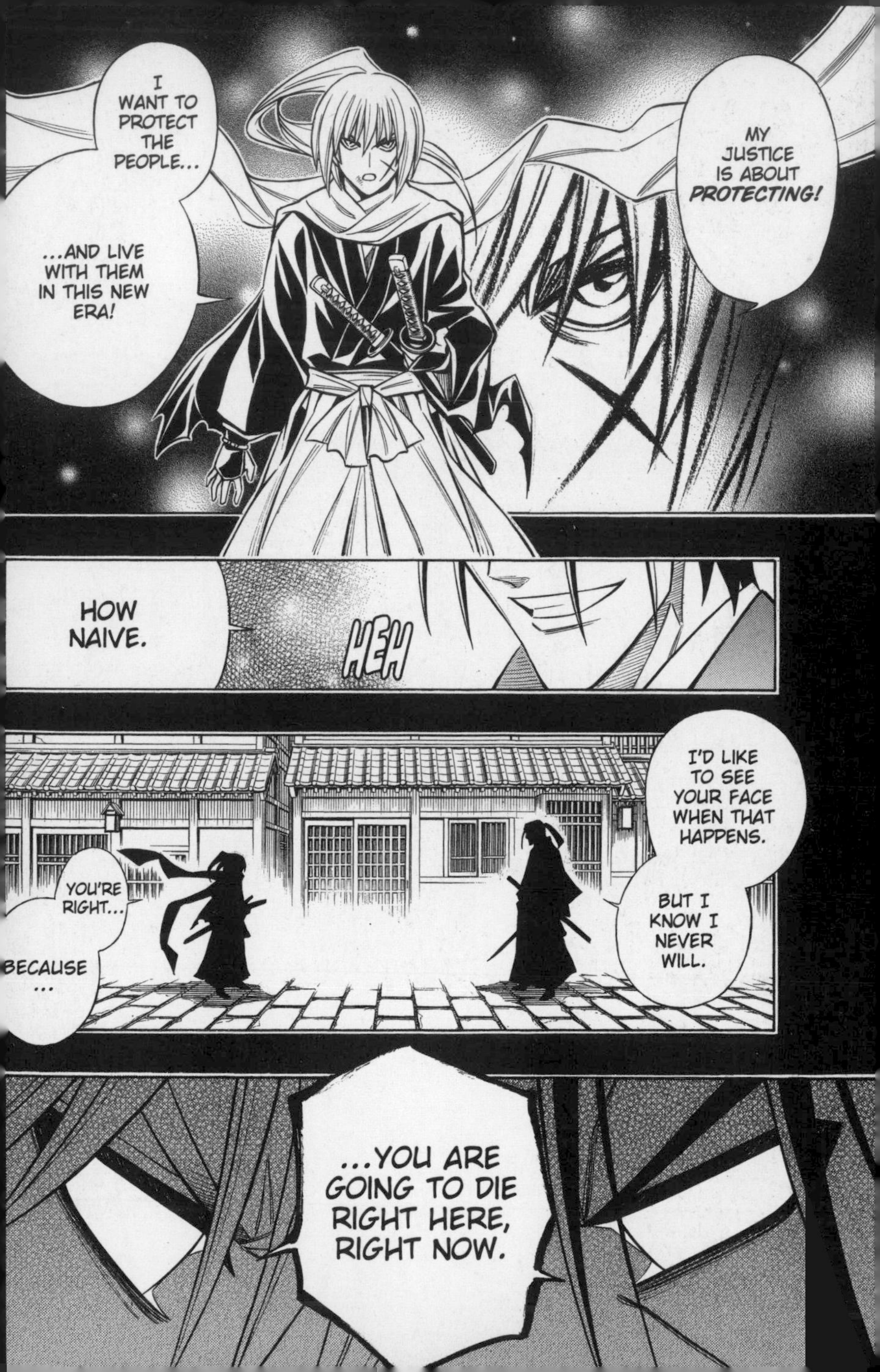
MY JUSTICE IS ABOUT *PROTECTING!*
I WANT TO PROTECT THE PEOPLE...
...AND LIVE WITH THEM IN THIS NEW ERA!
HEH
HOW NAIVE.
I'D LIKE TO SEE YOUR FACE WHEN THAT HAPPENS.
BUT I KNOW I NEVER WILL.
YOU'RE RIGHT...
BECAUSE ...
...YOU ARE GOING TO DIE RIGHT HERE, RIGHT NOW.

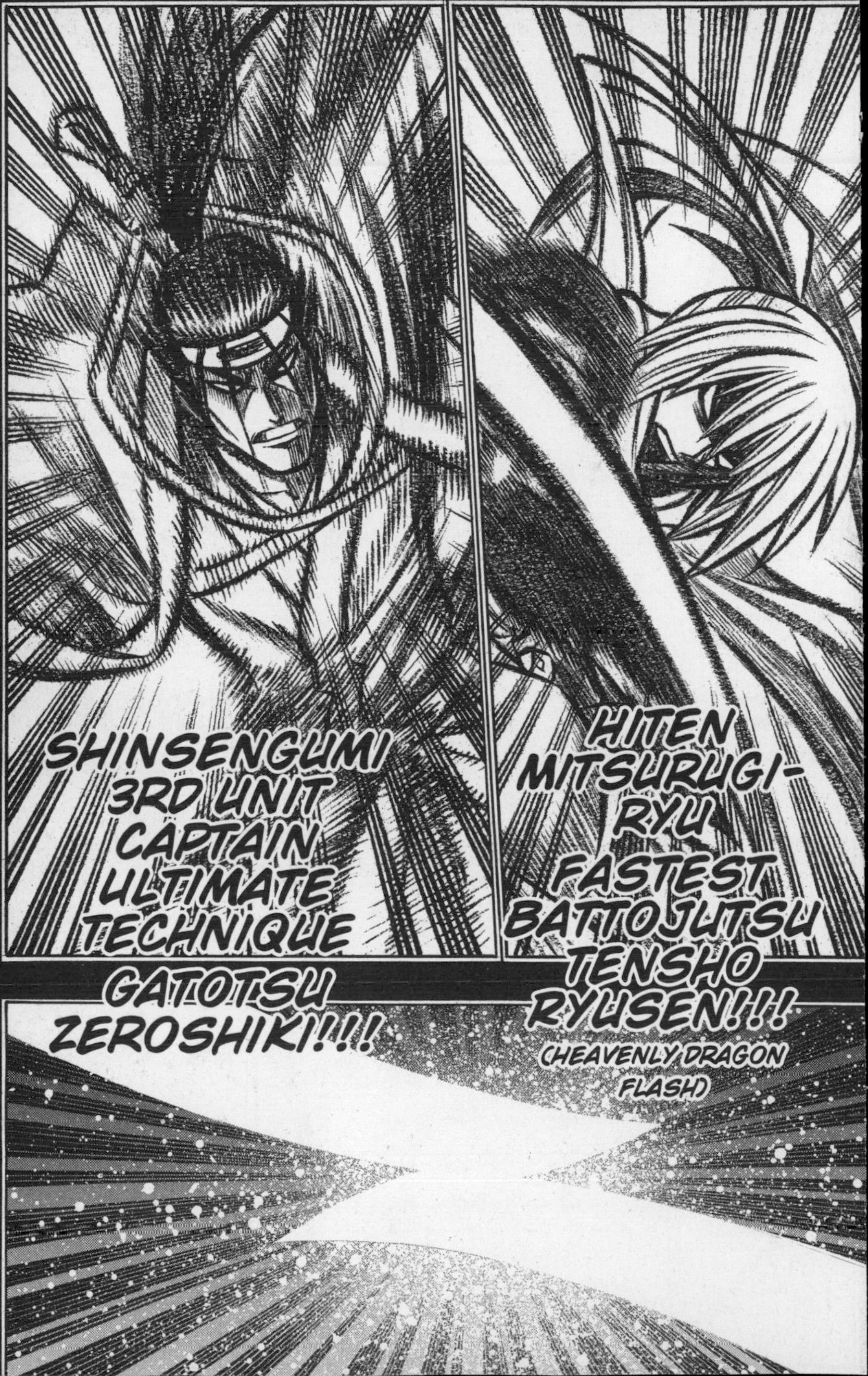
HITEN MITSURUGI-RYU FASTEST BATTOJUTSU TENSHO RYUSEN!!!
(HEAVENLY DRAGON FLASH)
SHINSENGUMI 3RD UNIT CAPTAIN ULTIMATE TECHNIQUE GATOTSU ZEROSHIKI!!!

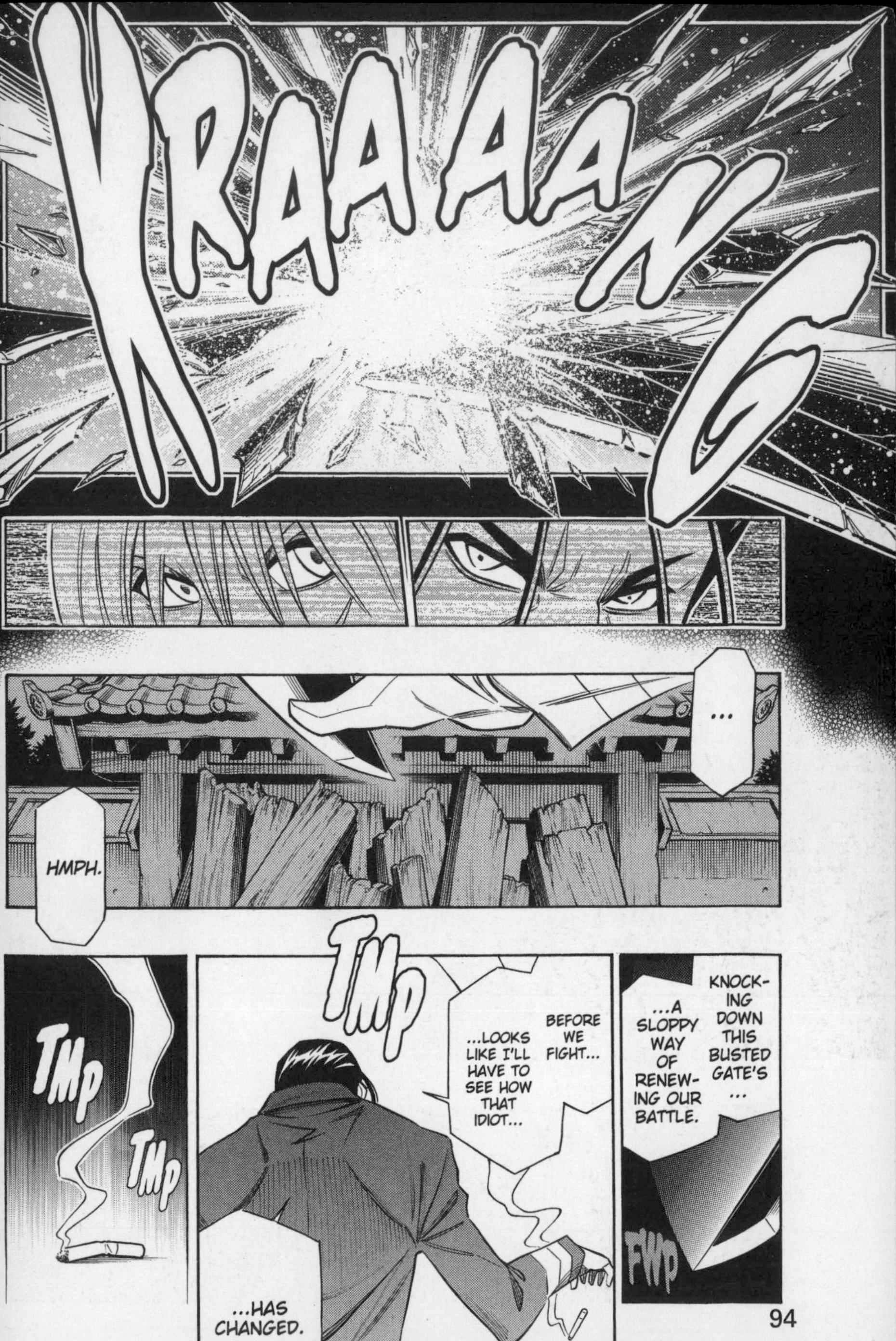
KRAAANG
...
HMPH.
KNOCKING DOWN THIS BUSTED GATE'S...
...A SLOPPY WAY OF RENEWING OUR BATTLE.
FWP
TMP
BEFORE WE FIGHT...
...LOOKS LIKE I'LL HAVE TO SEE HOW THAT IDIOT...
...HAS CHANGED.
TMP
TMP

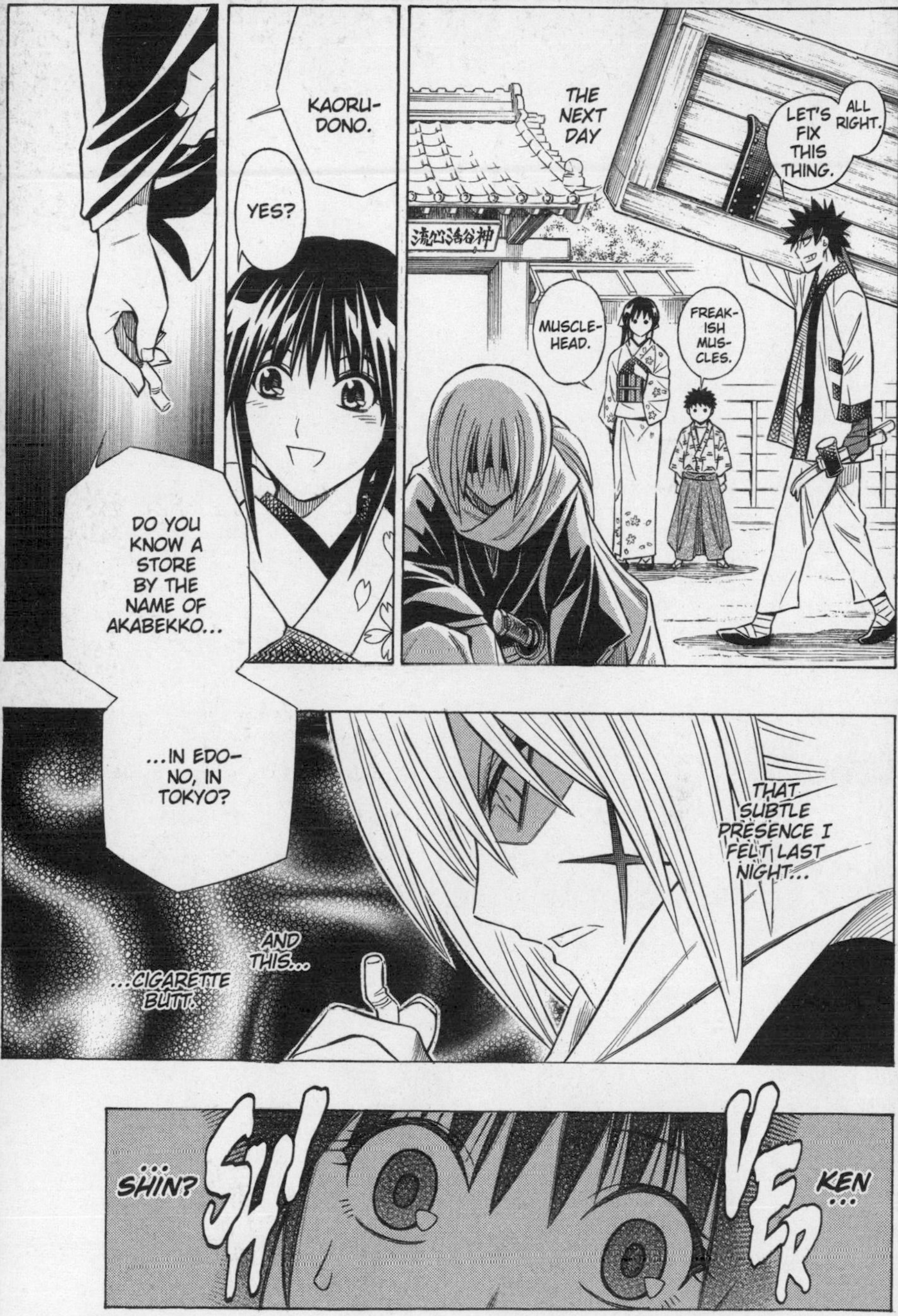
ALL RIGHT.
LET'S FIX THIS THING.
THE NEXT DAY
FREAK-ISH MUS-CLES.
MUSCLE-HEAD.
KAORU-DONO.
YES?
DO YOU KNOW A STORE BY THE NAME OF AKABEKKO...
...IN EDO-NO, IN TOKYO?
THAT SUBTLE PRESENCE I FELT LAST NIGHT...
AND THIS...
...CIGARETTE BUTT.
KEN...
SHIVER
...SHIN?

Rurouni Kenshin
RESTORATION

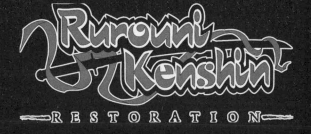

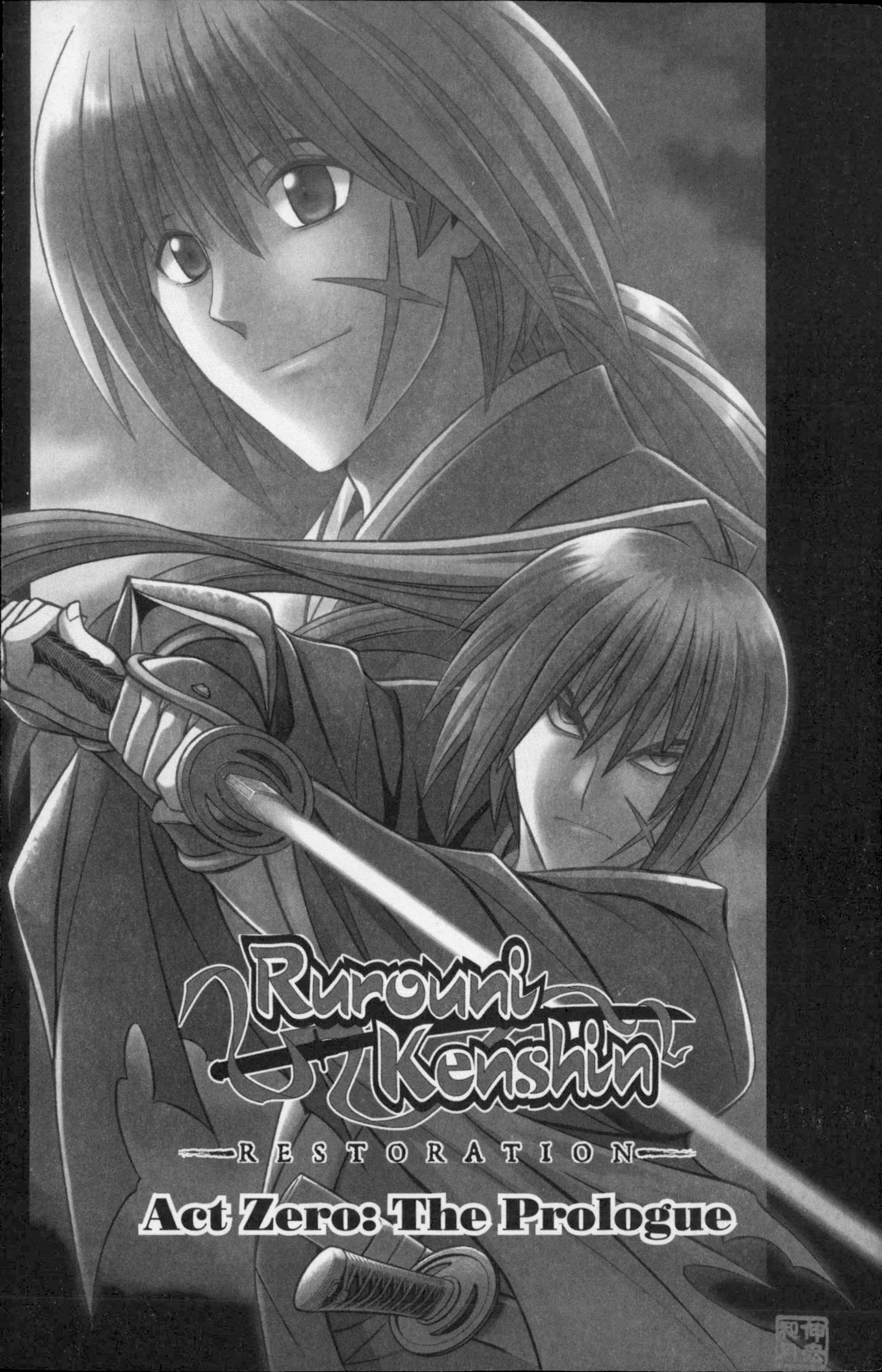
Rurouni Kenshin
RESTORATION
Act Zero: The Prologue

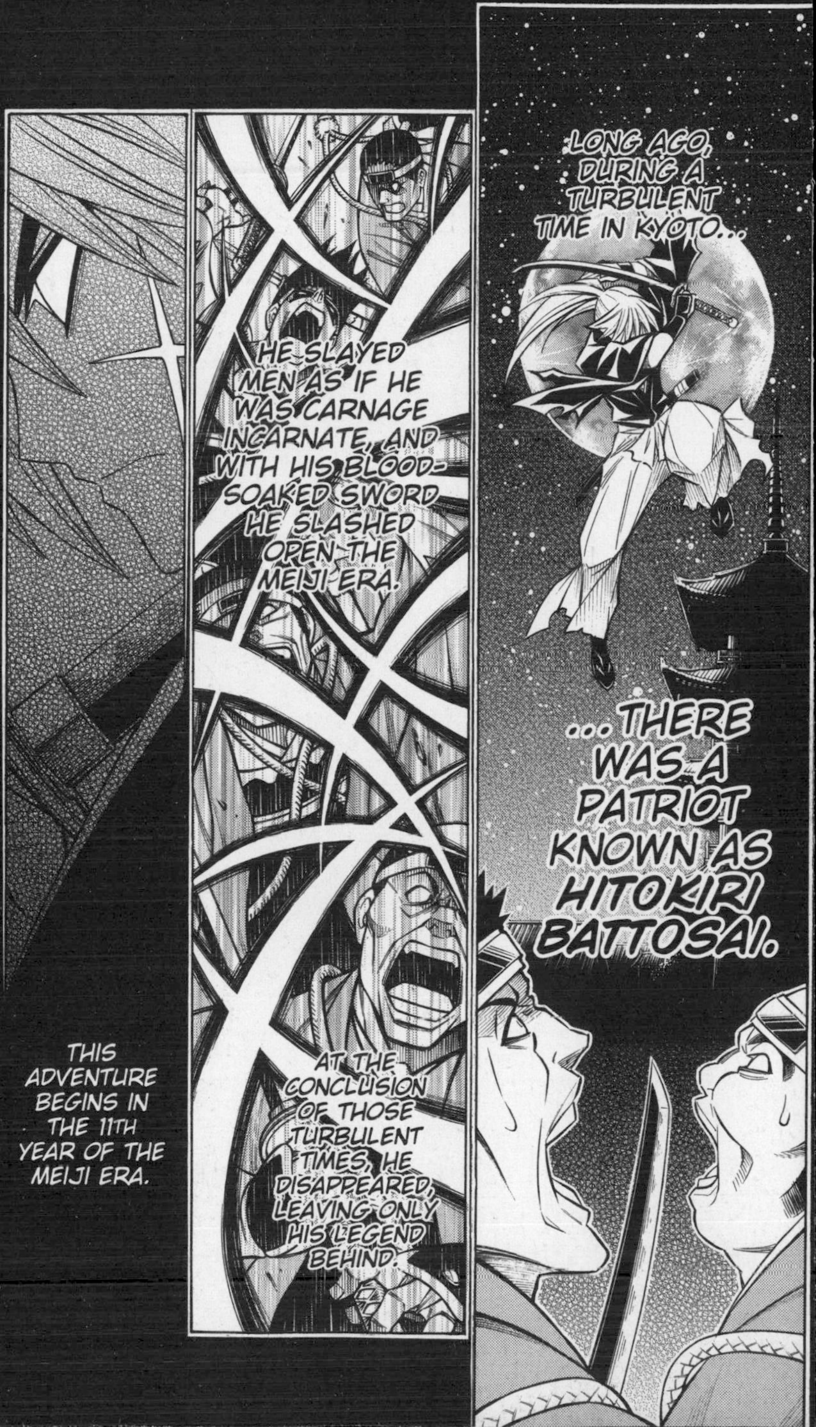
LONG AGO, DURING A TURBULENT TIME IN KYOTO...
...THERE WAS A PATRIOT KNOWN AS HITOKIRI BATTOSAI.
HE SLAYED MEN AS IF HE WAS CARNAGE INCARNATE, AND WITH HIS BLOOD-SOAKED SWORD HE SLASHED OPEN THE MEIJI ERA.
AT THE CONCLUSION OF THOSE TURBULENT TIMES, HE DISAPPEARED, LEAVING ONLY HIS LEGEND BEHIND.
THIS ADVENTURE BEGINS IN THE 11TH YEAR OF THE MEIJI ERA.

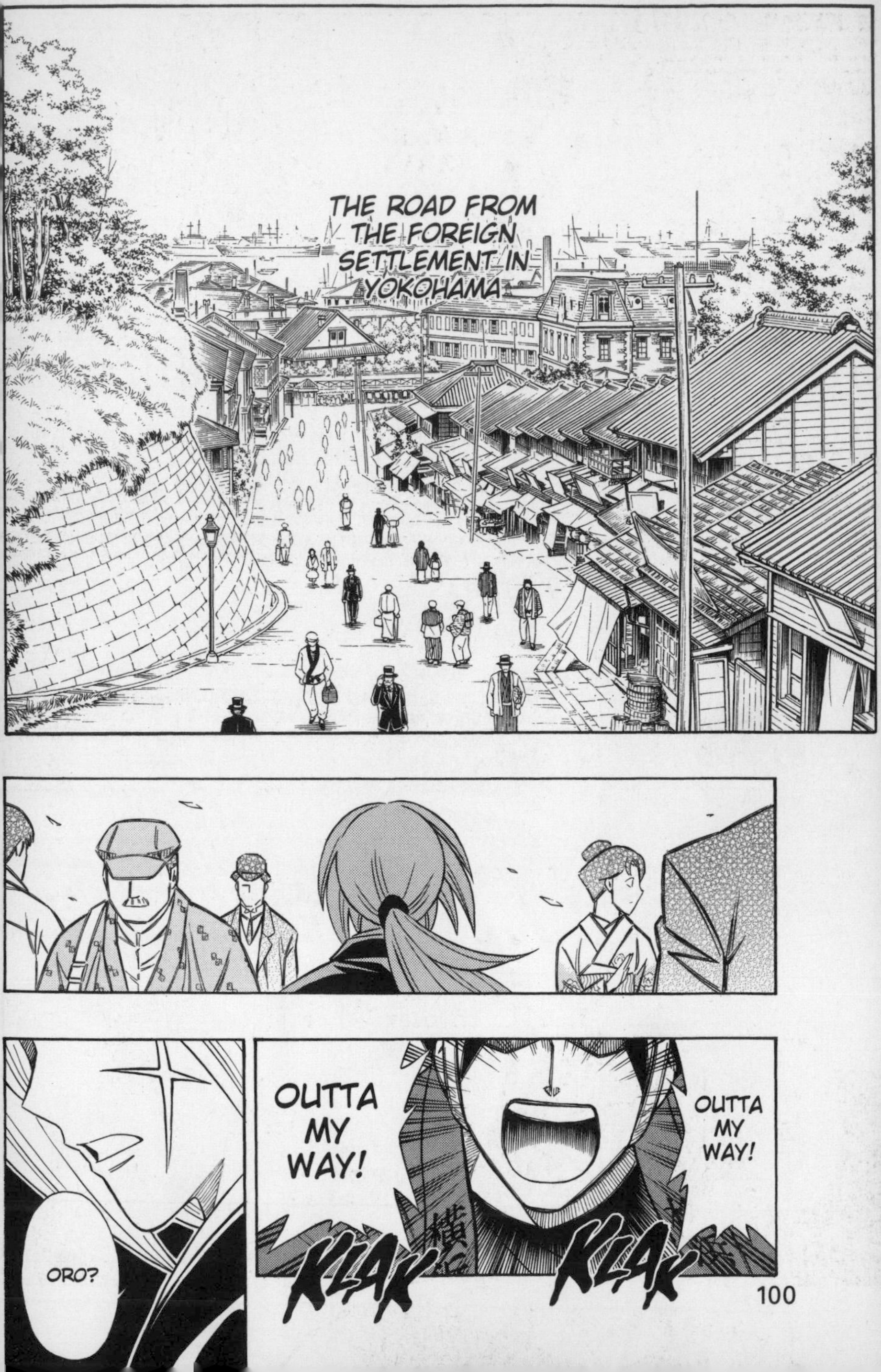
THE ROAD FROM THE FOREIGN SETTLEMENT IN YOKOHAMA
OUTTA MY WAY!
OUTTA MY WAY!
KLAK
KLAK
ORO?

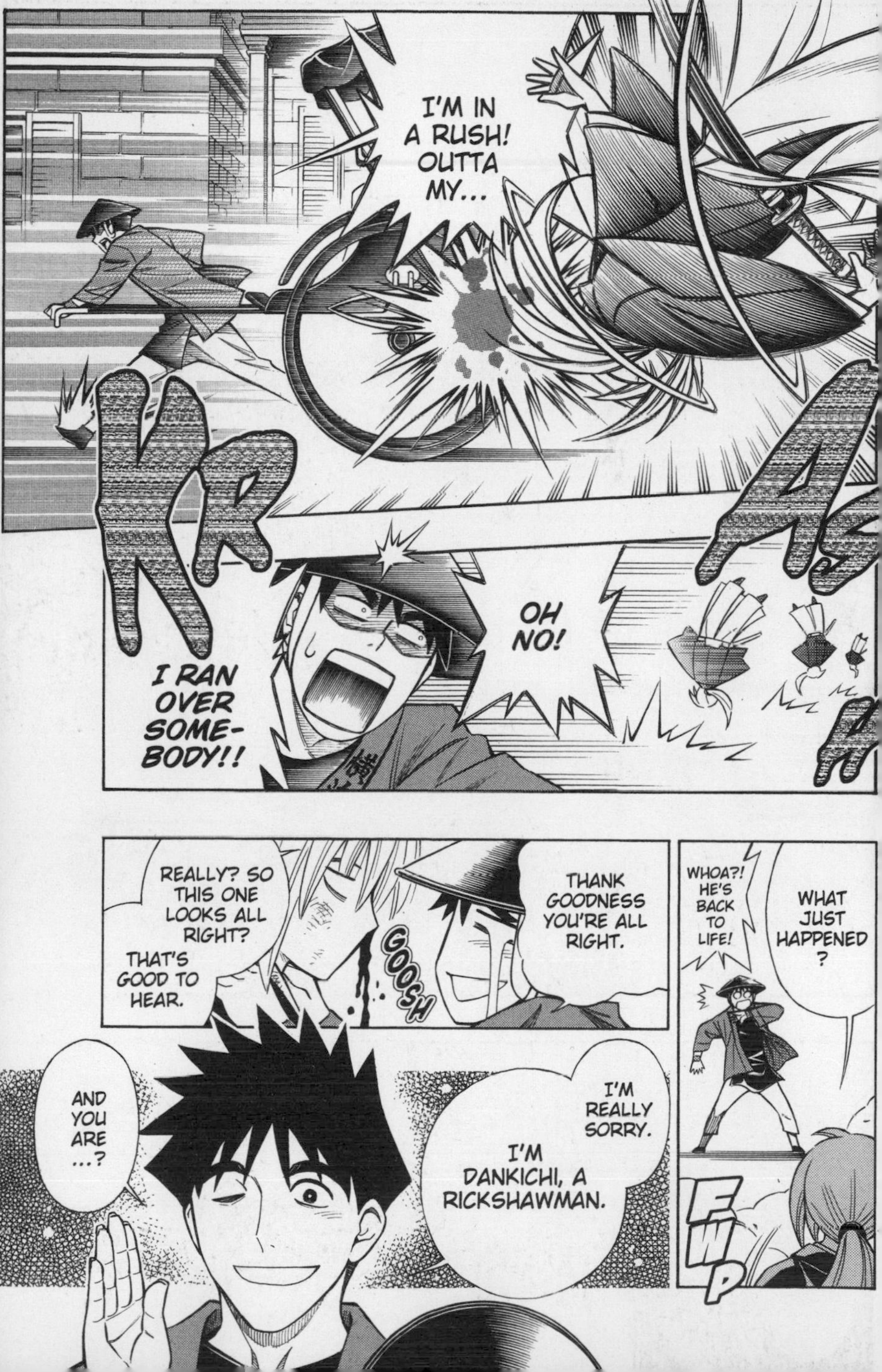
I'M IN A RUSH! OUTTA MY...
KR
AS
OH NO!
I RAN OVER SOMEBODY!!
WHAT JUST HAPPENED?
WHOA?! HE'S BACK TO LIFE!
FWP
THANK GOODNESS YOU'RE ALL RIGHT.
GOOSH
REALLY? SO THIS ONE LOOKS ALL RIGHT?
THAT'S GOOD TO HEAR.
I'M REALLY SORRY.
I'M DANKICHI, A RICKSHAWMAN.
AND YOU ARE ...?

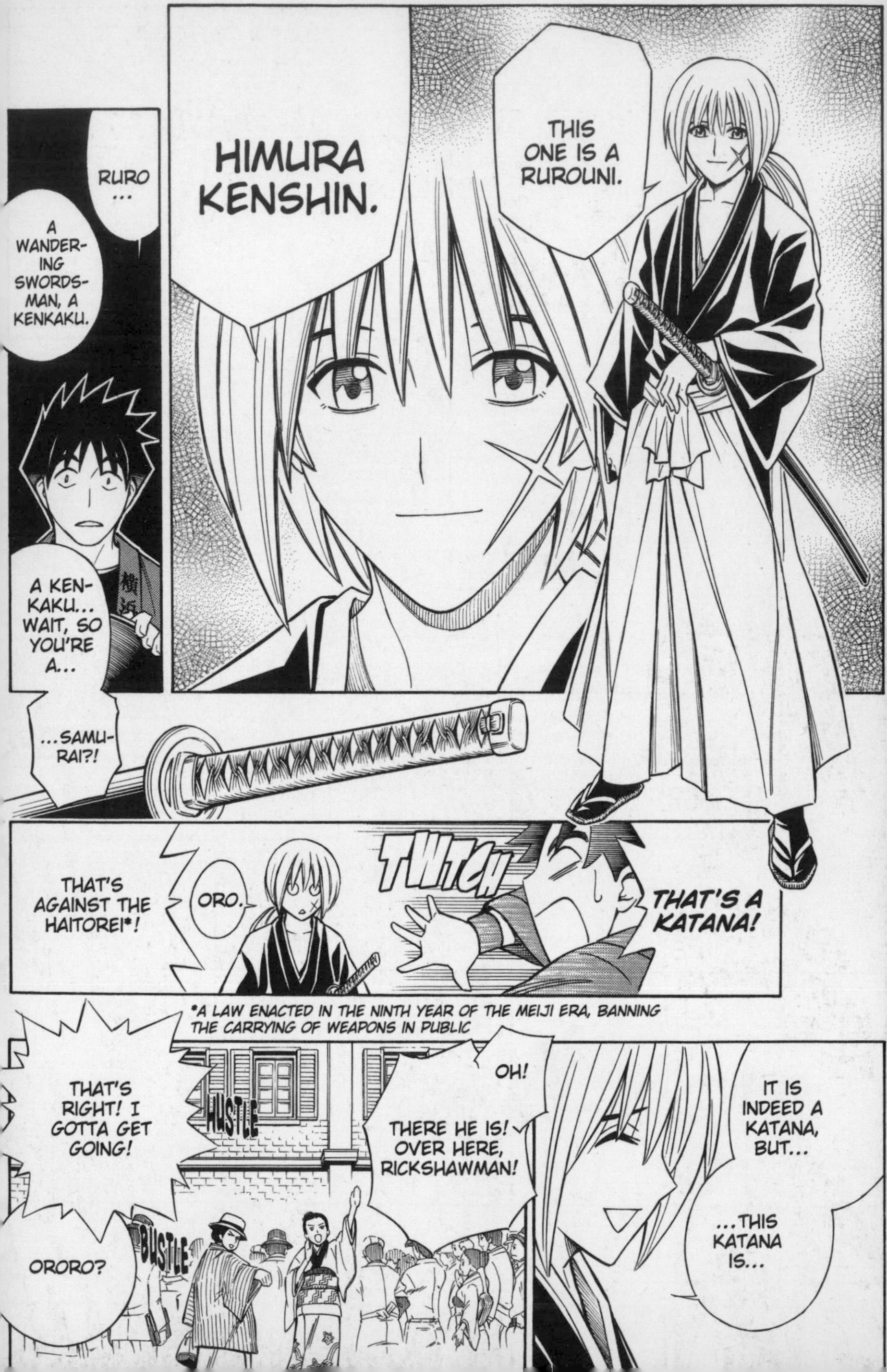
THIS ONE IS A RUROUNI.
HIMURA KENSHIN.
RURO...
A WANDER-ING SWORDS-MAN, A KENKAKU.
A KEN-KAKU... WAIT, SO YOU'RE A...
...SAMU-RAI?!
THAT'S A KATANA!
TWTCH
ORO.
THAT'S AGAINST THE HAITOREI*!
*A LAW ENACTED IN THE NINTH YEAR OF THE MEIJI ERA, BANNING THE CARRYING OF WEAPONS IN PUBLIC
IT IS INDEED A KATANA, BUT...
...THIS KATANA IS...
OH!
THERE HE IS! OVER HERE, RICKSHAWMAN!
THAT'S RIGHT! I GOTTA GET GOING!
HUSTLE
BUSTLE
ORORO?

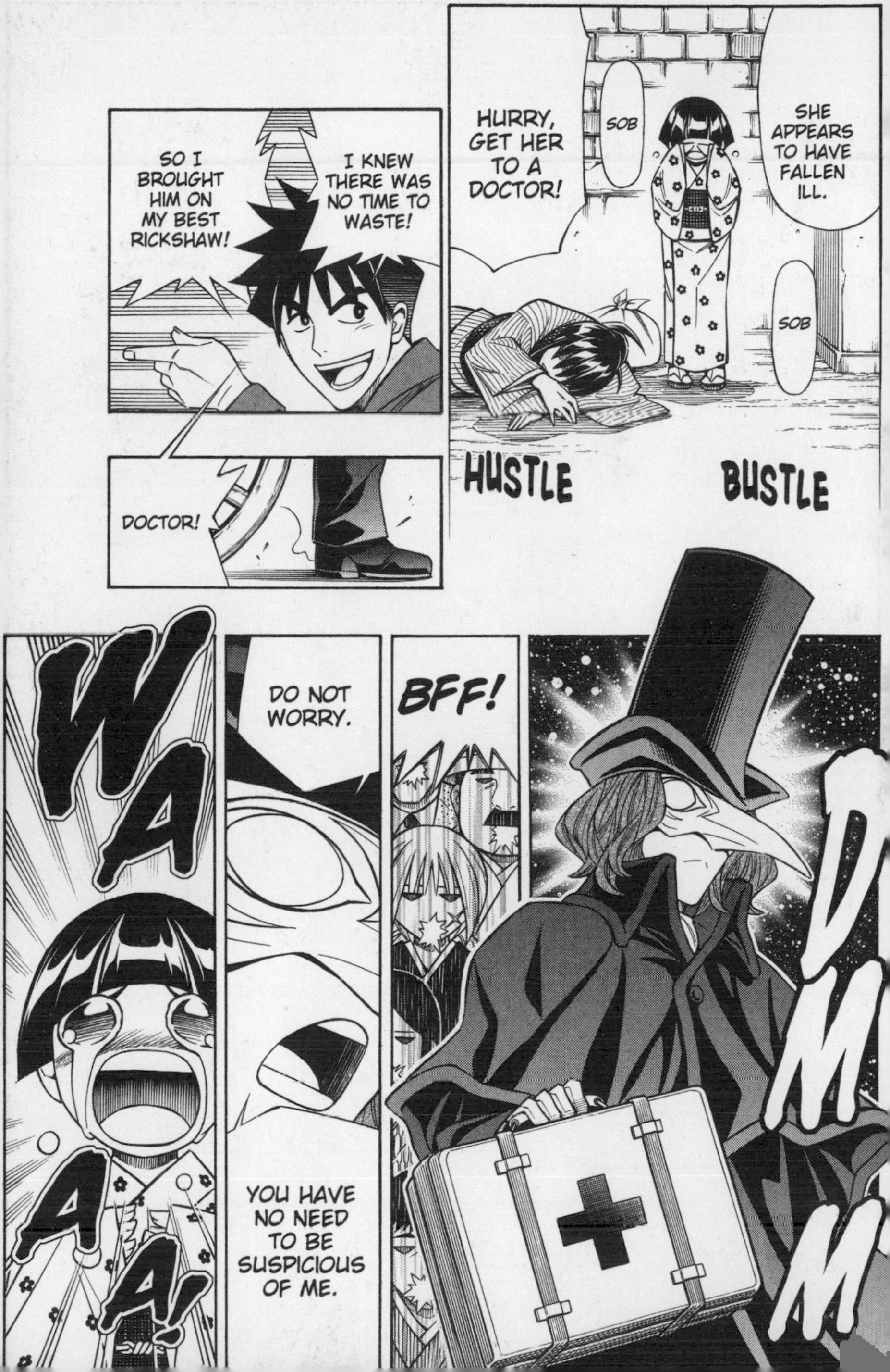
SHE APPEARS TO HAVE FALLEN ILL.
SOB
HURRY, GET HER TO A DOCTOR!
SOB
BUSTLE
HUSTLE
I KNEW THERE WAS NO TIME TO WASTE!
SO I BROUGHT HIM ON MY BEST RICKSHAW!
DOCTOR!
DMM
BFF!
DO NOT WORRY.
YOU HAVE NO NEED TO BE SUSPICIOUS OF ME.
WAAA!

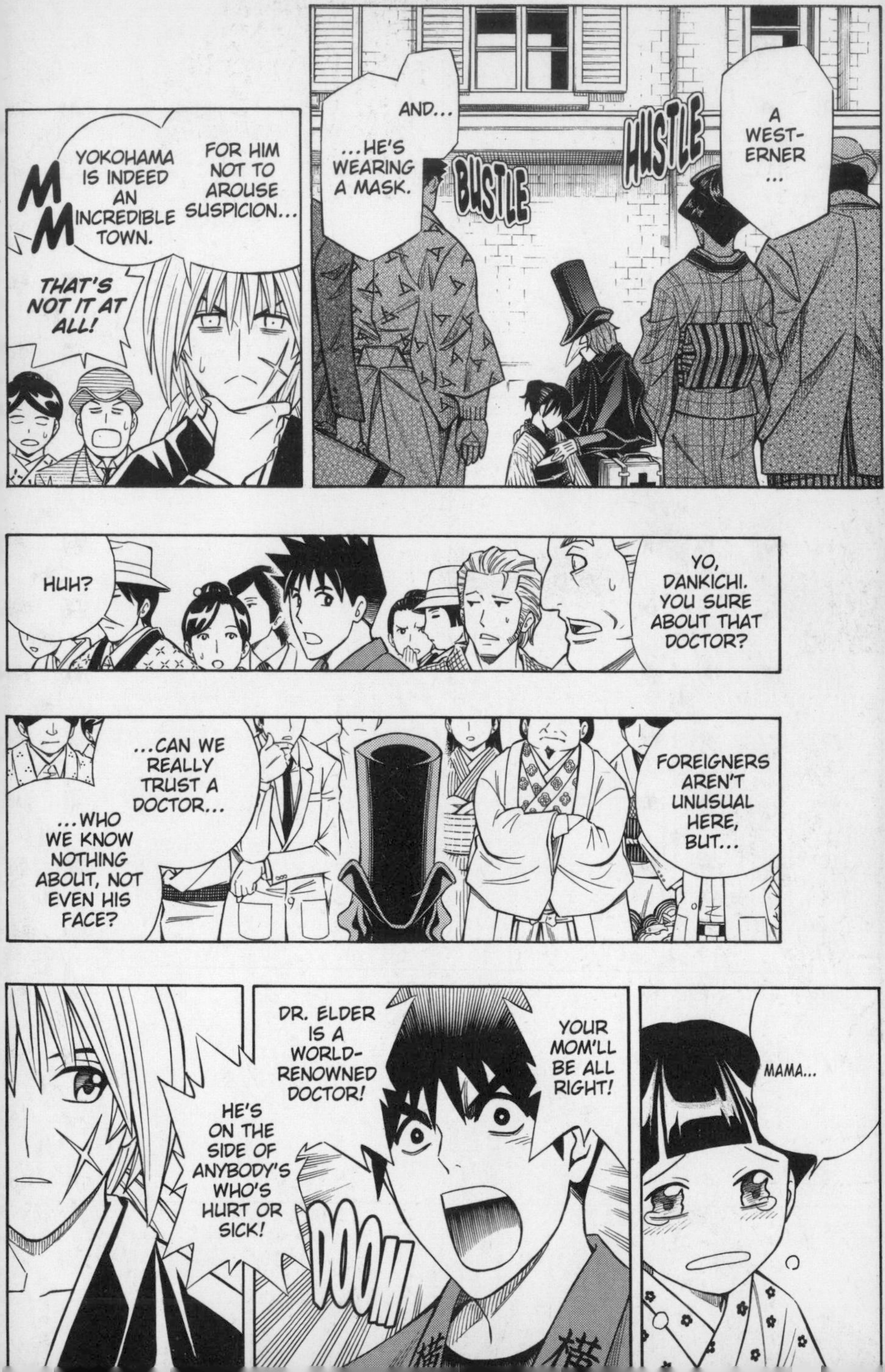
A WEST-ERNER...
HUSTLE
BUSTLE
AND...
...HE'S WEARING A MASK.
FOR HIM NOT TO AROUSE SUSPICION...
YOKOHAMA IS INDEED AN INCREDIBLE TOWN.
MM
THAT'S NOT IT AT ALL!
YO, DANKICHI. YOU SURE ABOUT THAT DOCTOR?
HUH?
FOREIGNERS AREN'T UNUSUAL HERE, BUT...
...CAN WE REALLY TRUST A DOCTOR...
...WHO WE KNOW NOTHING ABOUT, NOT EVEN HIS FACE?
MAMA...
YOUR MOM'LL BE ALL RIGHT!
DR. ELDER IS A WORLD-RENOWNED DOCTOR!
HE'S ON THE SIDE OF ANYBODY'S WHO'S HURT OR SICK!
DOOM

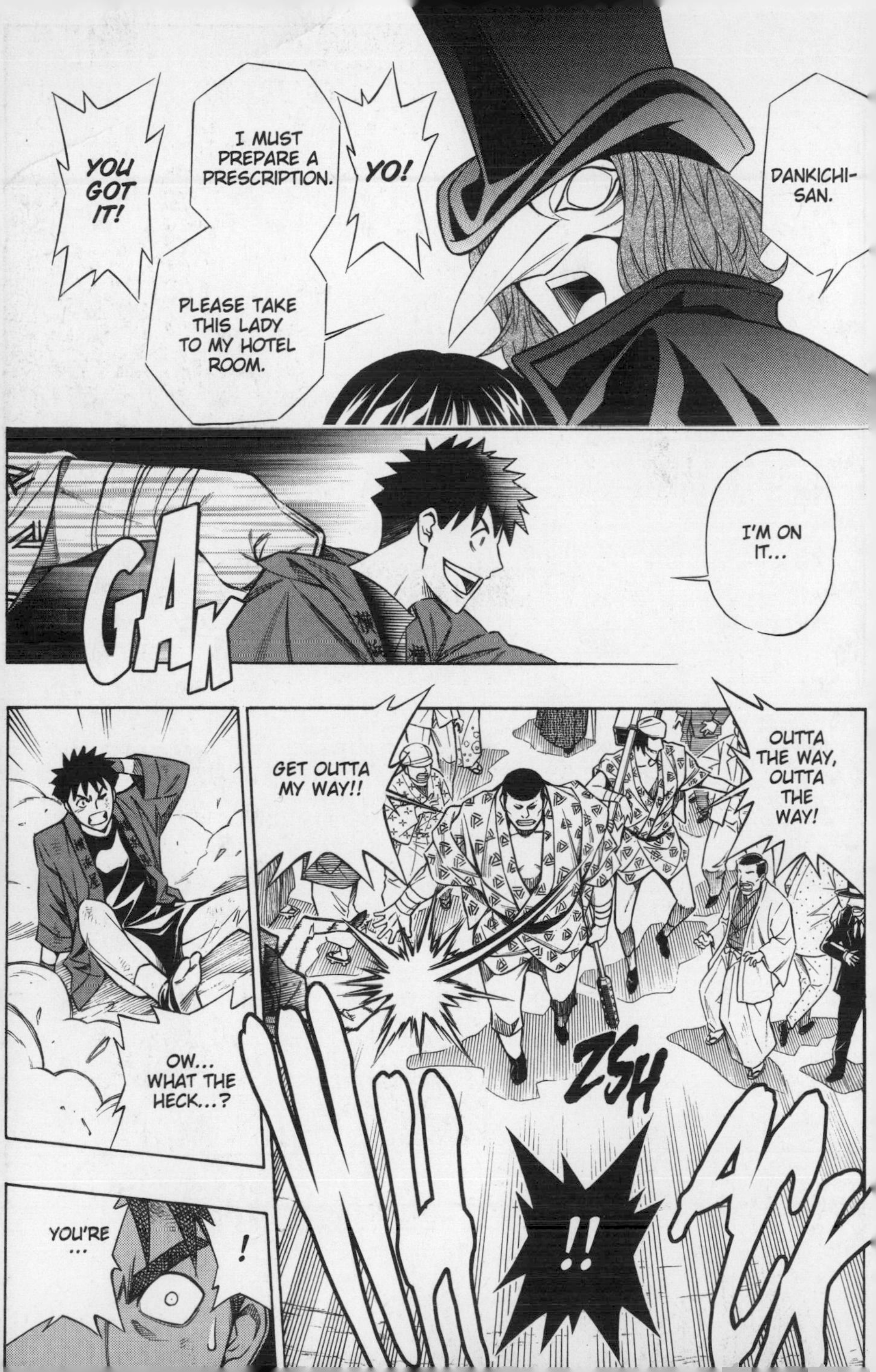
DANKICHI-SAN.
YO!
I MUST PREPARE A PRESCRIPTION.
PLEASE TAKE THIS LADY TO MY HOTEL ROOM.
YOU GOT IT!
I'M ON IT...
GAK
OUTTA THE WAY, OUTTA THE WAY!
GET OUTTA MY WAY!!
ZSH
!!
WHACK
OW... WHAT THE HECK...?
YOU'RE ...
!

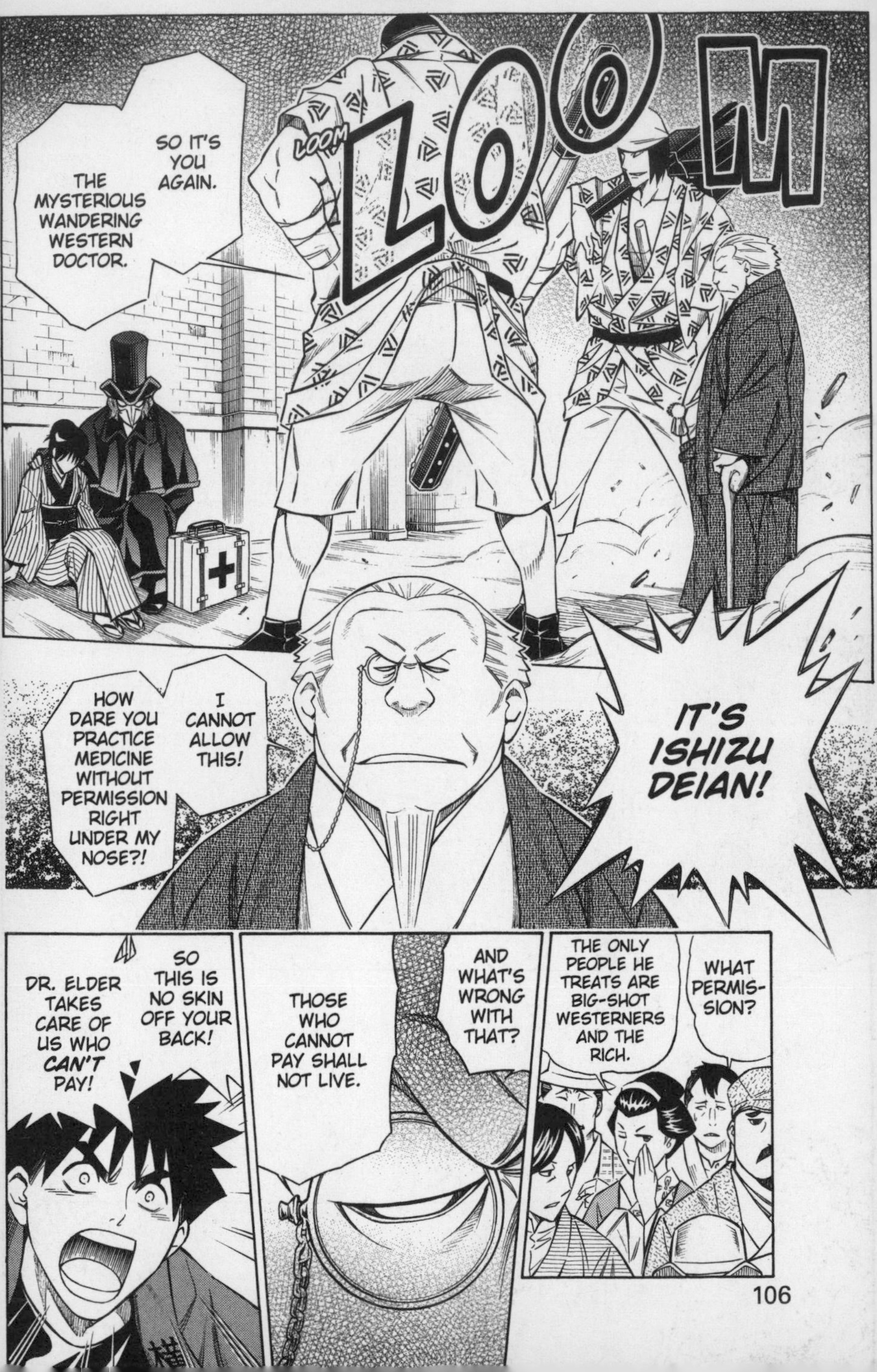
ZOOOM
LOOM
SO IT'S YOU AGAIN.
THE MYSTERIOUS WANDERING WESTERN DOCTOR.
IT'S ISHIZU DEIAN!
I CANNOT ALLOW THIS!
HOW DARE YOU PRACTICE MEDICINE WITHOUT PERMISSION RIGHT UNDER MY NOSE?!
WHAT PERMIS-SION?
THE ONLY PEOPLE HE TREATS ARE BIG-SHOT WESTERNERS AND THE RICH.
AND WHAT'S WRONG WITH THAT?
THOSE WHO CANNOT PAY SHALL NOT LIVE.
SO THIS IS NO SKIN OFF YOUR BACK!
DR. ELDER TAKES CARE OF US WHO *CAN'T* PAY!

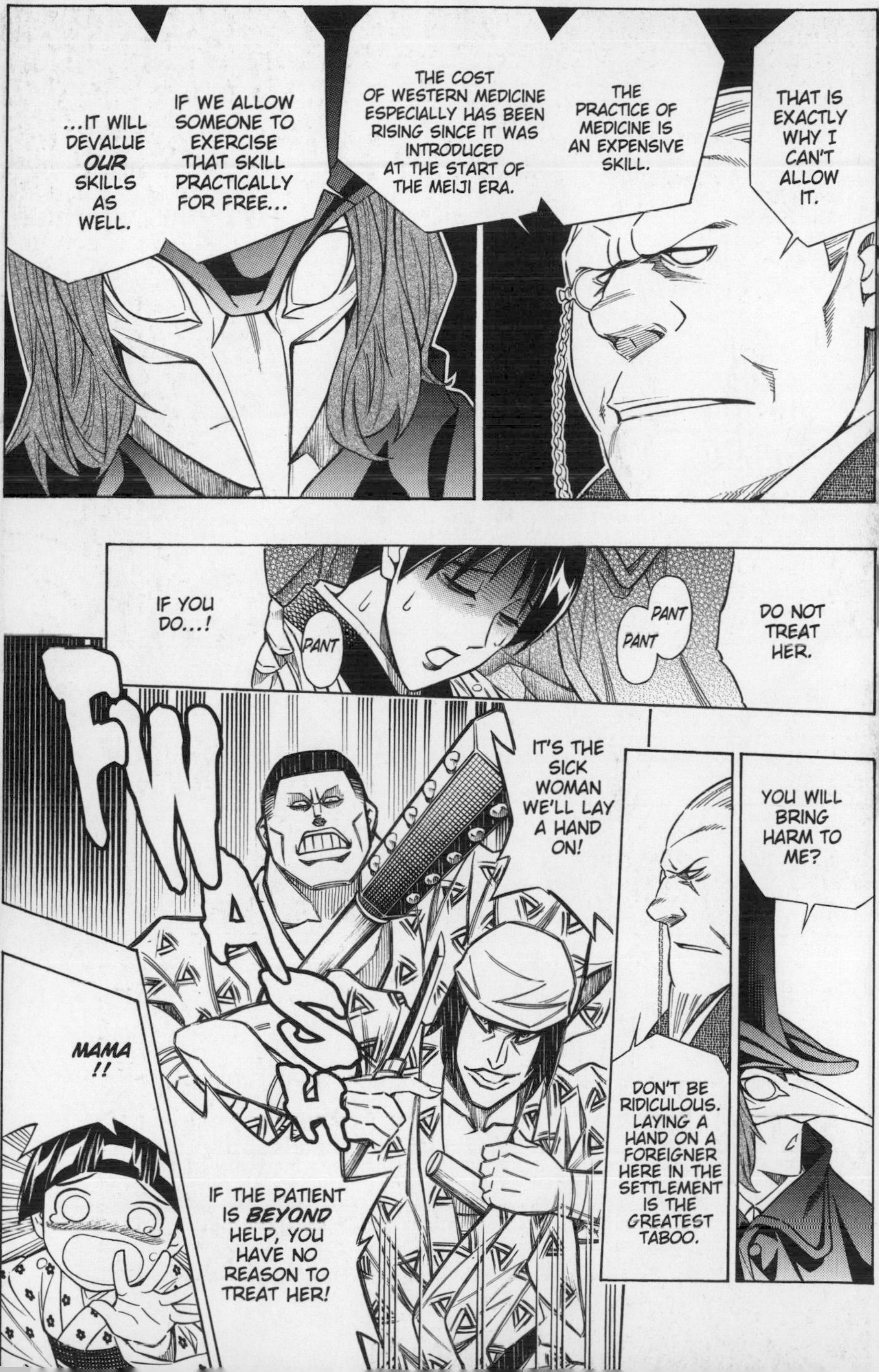
THAT IS EXACTLY WHY I CAN'T ALLOW IT.
THE PRACTICE OF MEDICINE IS AN EXPENSIVE SKILL.
THE COST OF WESTERN MEDICINE ESPECIALLY HAS BEEN RISING SINCE IT WAS INTRODUCED AT THE START OF THE MEIJI ERA.
IF WE ALLOW SOMEONE TO EXERCISE THAT SKILL PRACTICALLY FOR FREE...
...IT WILL DEVALUE OUR SKILLS AS WELL.
DO NOT TREAT HER.
PANT PANT
PANT
IF YOU DO...!
YOU WILL BRING HARM TO ME?
DON'T BE RIDICULOUS. LAYING A HAND ON A FOREIGNER HERE IN THE SETTLEMENT IS THE GREATEST TABOO.
IT'S THE SICK WOMAN WE'LL LAY A HAND ON!
FWASH
IF THE PATIENT IS BEYOND HELP, YOU HAVE NO REASON TO TREAT HER!
MAMA!!

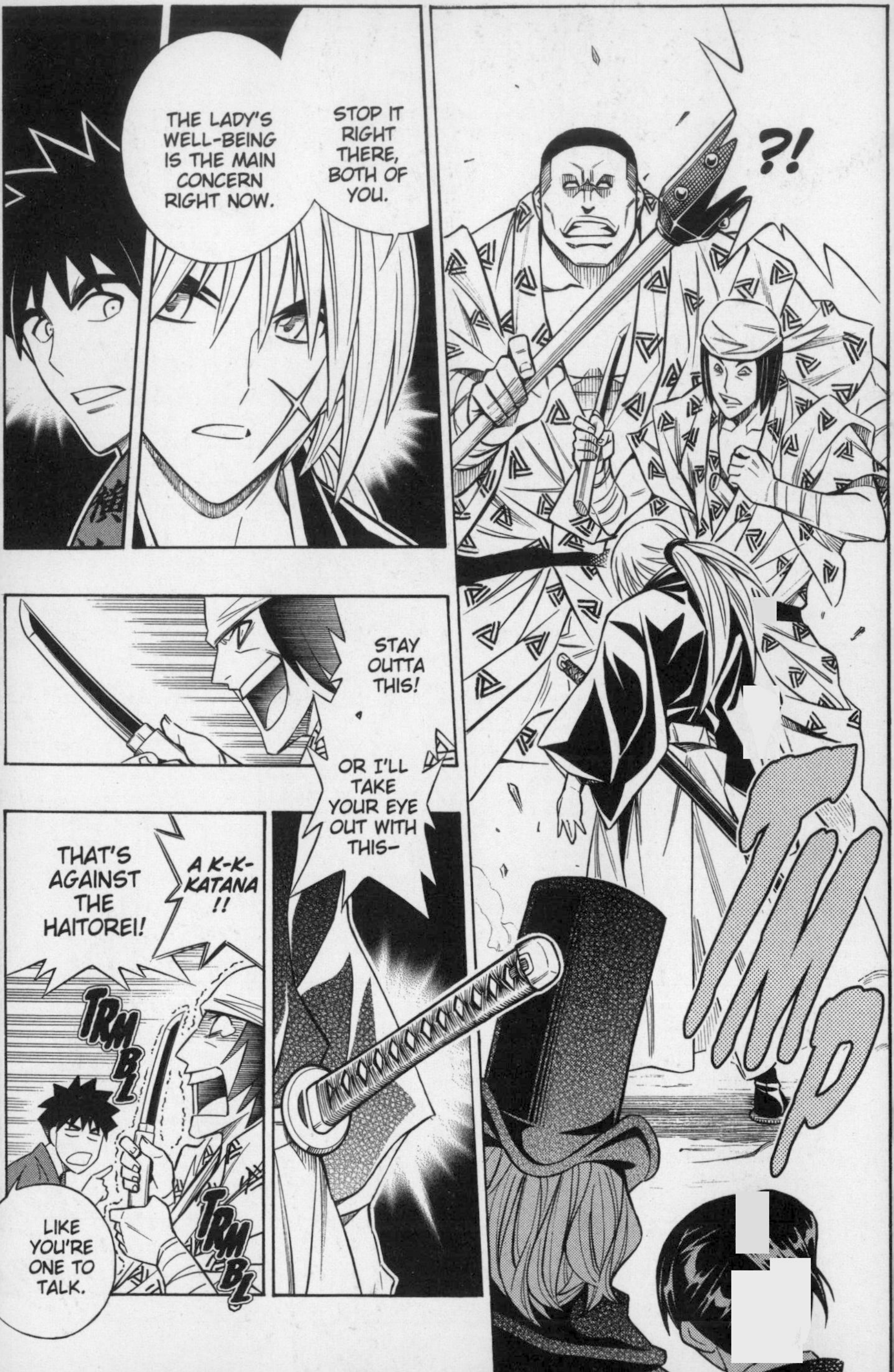
?!
STOP IT RIGHT THERE, BOTH OF YOU.
THE LADY'S WELL-BEING IS THE MAIN CONCERN RIGHT NOW.
STAY OUTTA THIS!
OR I'LL TAKE YOUR EYE OUT WITH THIS-
A K-K-KATANA !!
THAT'S AGAINST THE HAITOREI!
TRMBL
TRMBL
LIKE YOU'RE ONE TO TALK.

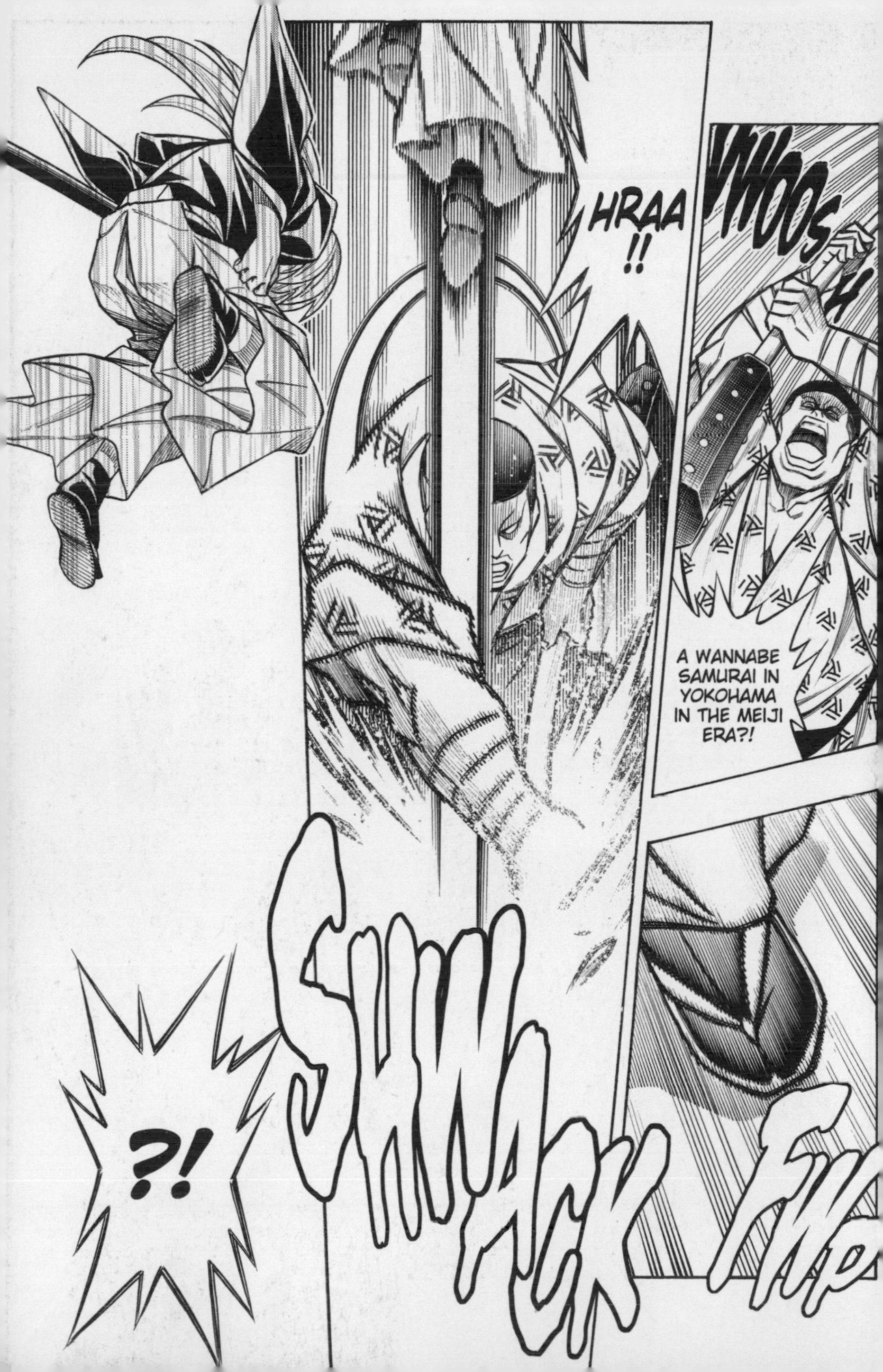
A WANNABE SAMURAI IN YOKOHAMA IN THE MEIJI ERA?!
HRAA !!
SHWACK
?!

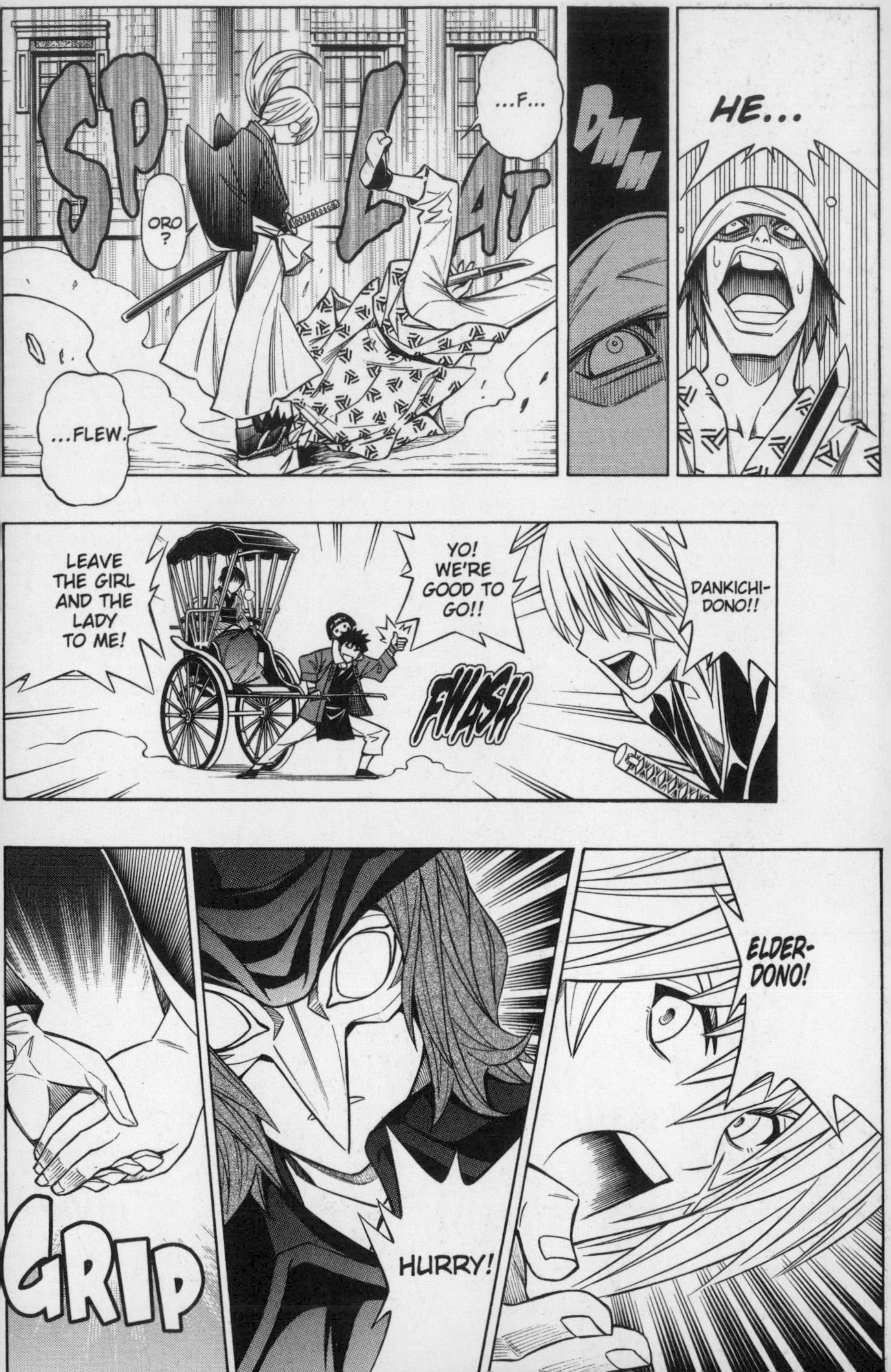
HE...
...F...
SPLAT
ORO ?
...FLEW.
DANKICHI-DONO!!
FWASH
YO! WE'RE GOOD TO GO!!
LEAVE THE GIRL AND THE LADY TO ME!
ELDER-DONO!
HURRY!
GRIP

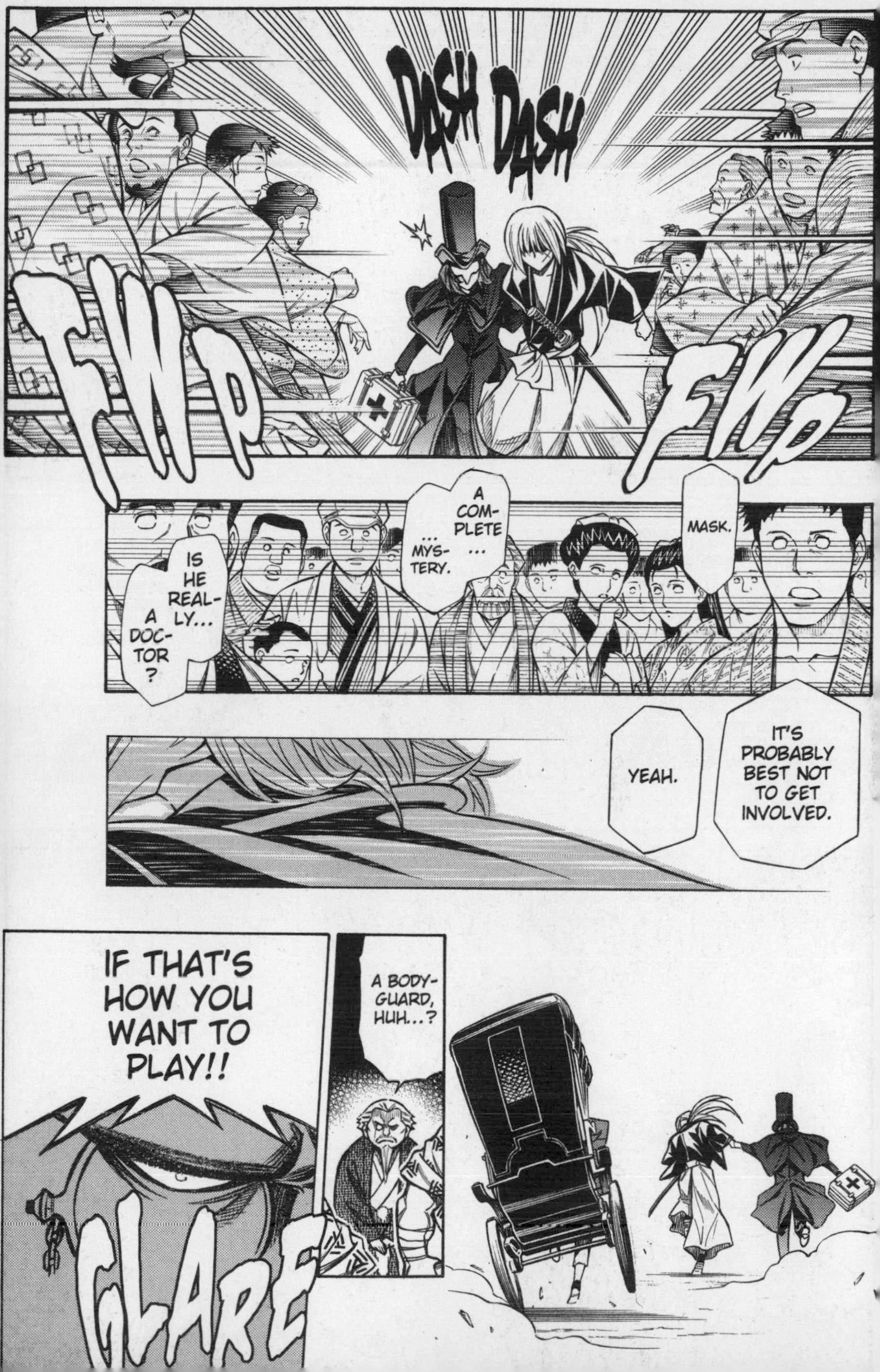
DASH DASH
FWP
FWP
MASK.
A COMPLETE... ...MYSTERY.
IS HE REALLY... A DOCTOR?
IT'S PROBABLY BEST NOT TO GET INVOLVED.
YEAH.
A BODYGUARD, HUH...?
IF THAT'S HOW YOU WANT TO PLAY!!
GLARE

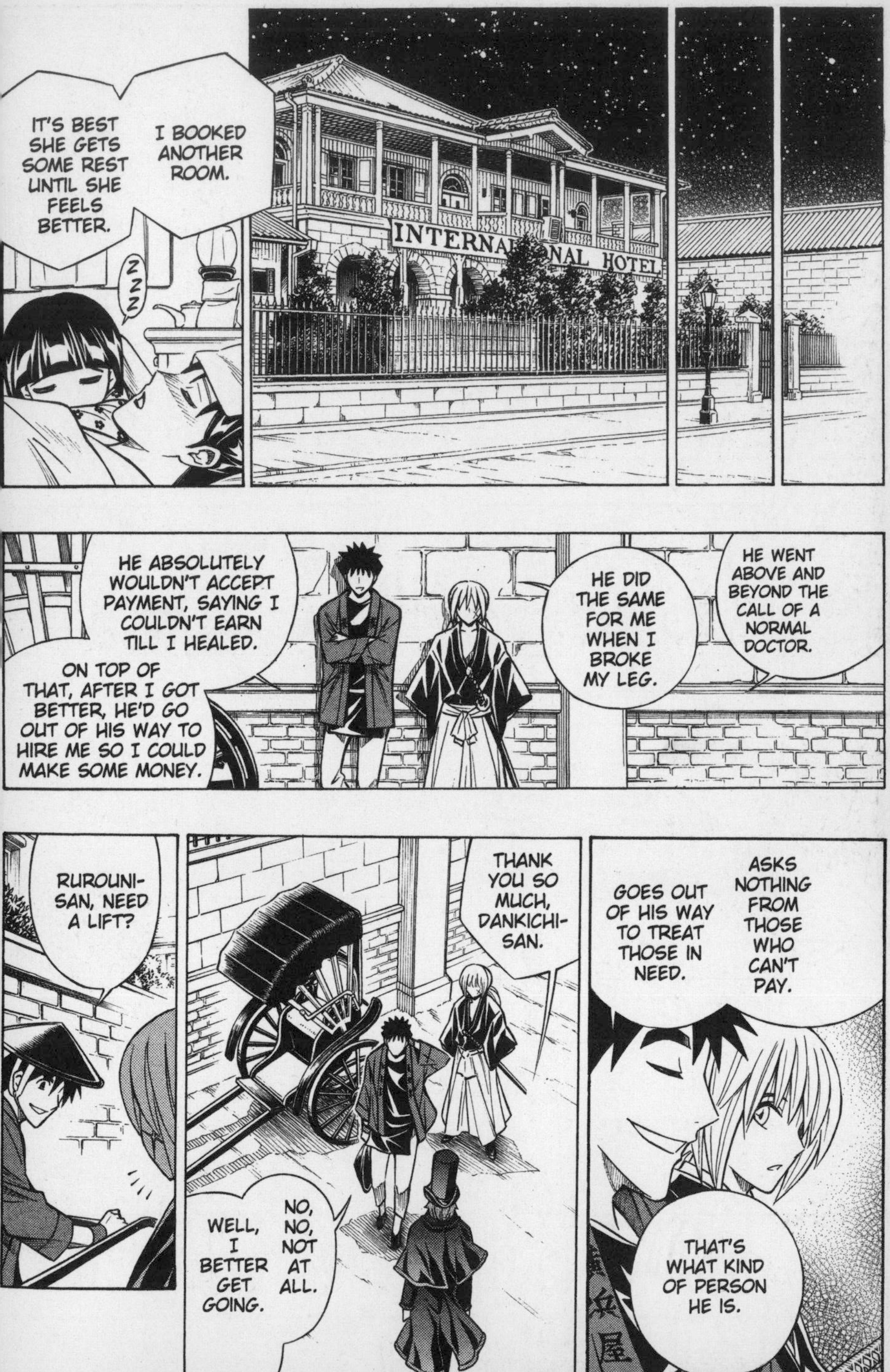

I BOOKED ANOTHER ROOM.
IT'S BEST SHE GETS SOME REST UNTIL SHE FEELS BETTER.
ZZZ
HE WENT ABOVE AND BEYOND THE CALL OF A NORMAL DOCTOR.
HE DID THE SAME FOR ME WHEN I BROKE MY LEG.
HE ABSOLUTELY WOULDN'T ACCEPT PAYMENT, SAYING I COULDN'T EARN TILL I HEALED.
ON TOP OF THAT, AFTER I GOT BETTER, HE'D GO OUT OF HIS WAY TO HIRE ME SO I COULD MAKE SOME MONEY.
ASKS NOTHING FROM THOSE WHO CAN'T PAY.
GOES OUT OF HIS WAY TO TREAT THOSE IN NEED.
THAT'S WHAT KIND OF PERSON HE IS.
THANK YOU SO MUCH, DANKICHI-SAN.
NO, NO, NOT AT ALL.
WELL, I BETTER GET GOING.
RUROUNI-SAN, NEED A LIFT?

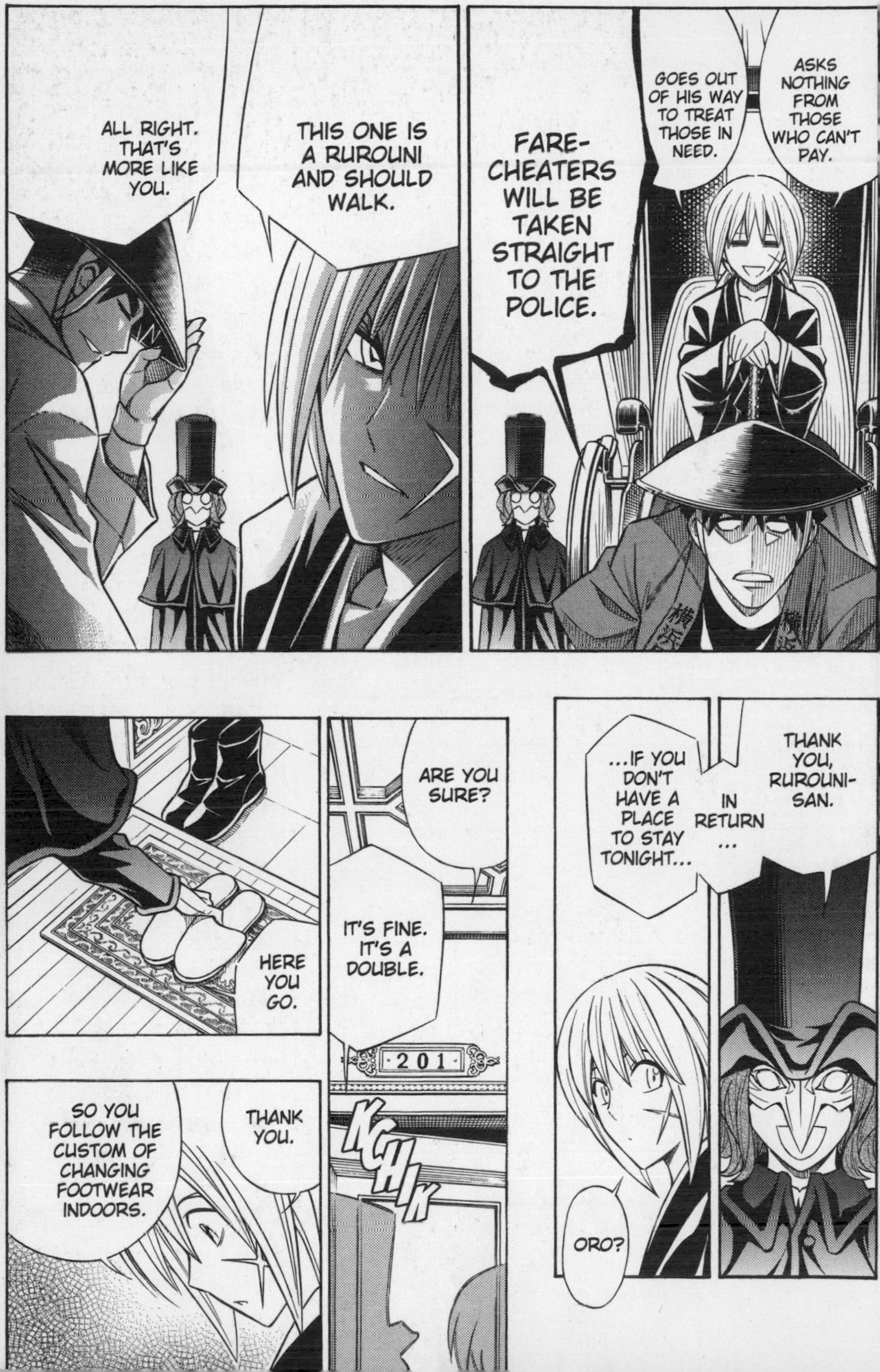
ASKS NOTHING FROM THOSE WHO CAN'T PAY.
GOES OUT OF HIS WAY TO TREAT THOSE IN NEED.
FARE-CHEATERS WILL BE TAKEN STRAIGHT TO THE POLICE.
THIS ONE IS A RUROUNI AND SHOULD WALK.
ALL RIGHT. THAT'S MORE LIKE YOU.
THANK YOU, RUROUNI-SAN.
IN RETURN...
...IF YOU DON'T HAVE A PLACE TO STAY TONIGHT...
ORO?
ARE YOU SURE?
IT'S FINE. IT'S A DOUBLE.
201
KCHIK
HERE YOU GO.
THANK YOU.
SO YOU FOLLOW THE CUSTOM OF CHANGING FOOTWEAR INDOORS.

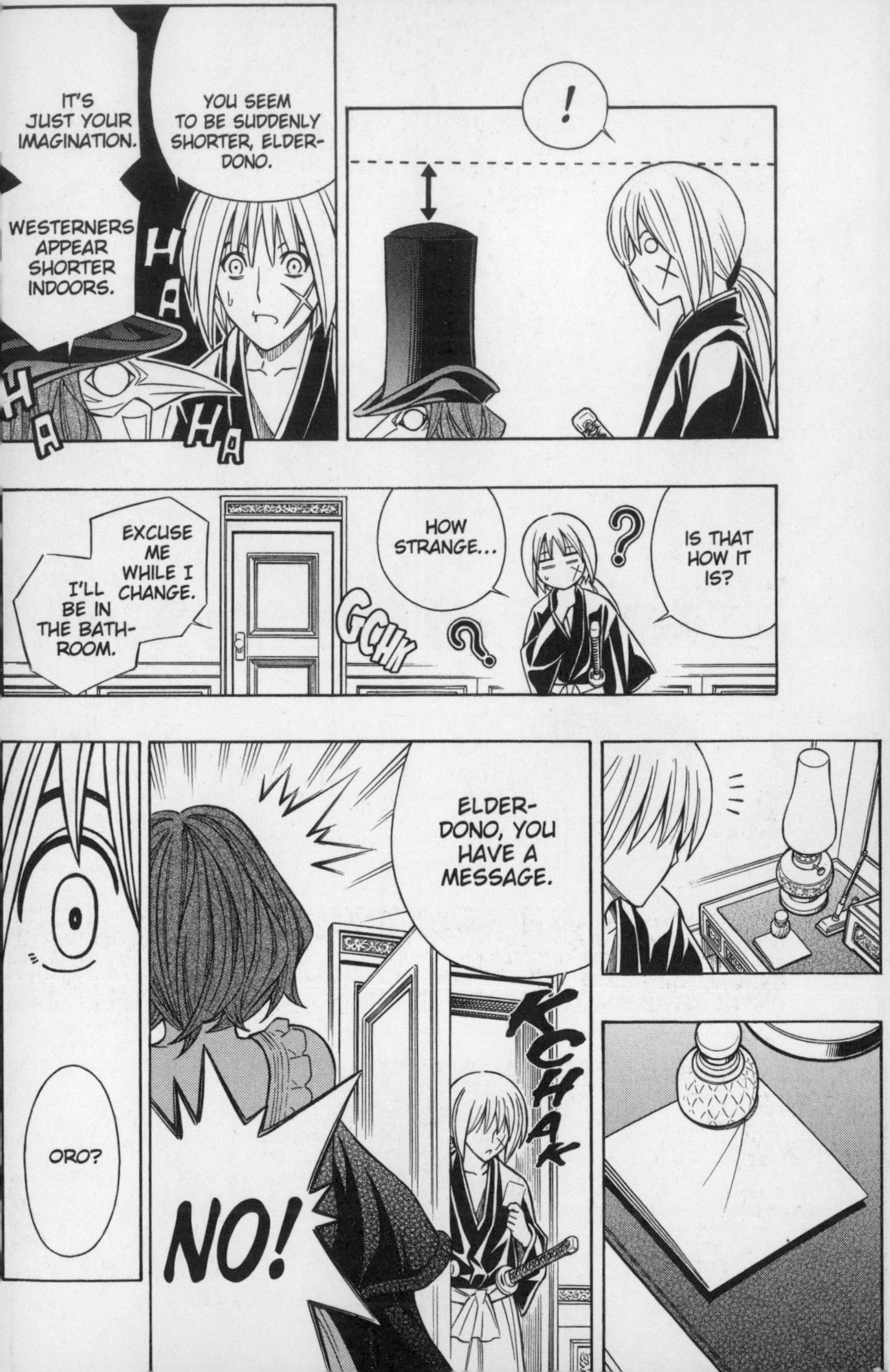
!
YOU SEEM TO BE SUDDENLY SHORTER, ELDER-DONO.
IT'S JUST YOUR IMAGINATION.
WESTERNERS APPEAR SHORTER INDOORS.
HA HA HA HA
IS THAT HOW IT IS?
HOW STRANGE...
GCHK
EXCUSE ME WHILE I CHANGE.
I'LL BE IN THE BATHROOM.
ELDER-DONO, YOU HAVE A MESSAGE.
KCHAK
NO!
ORO?

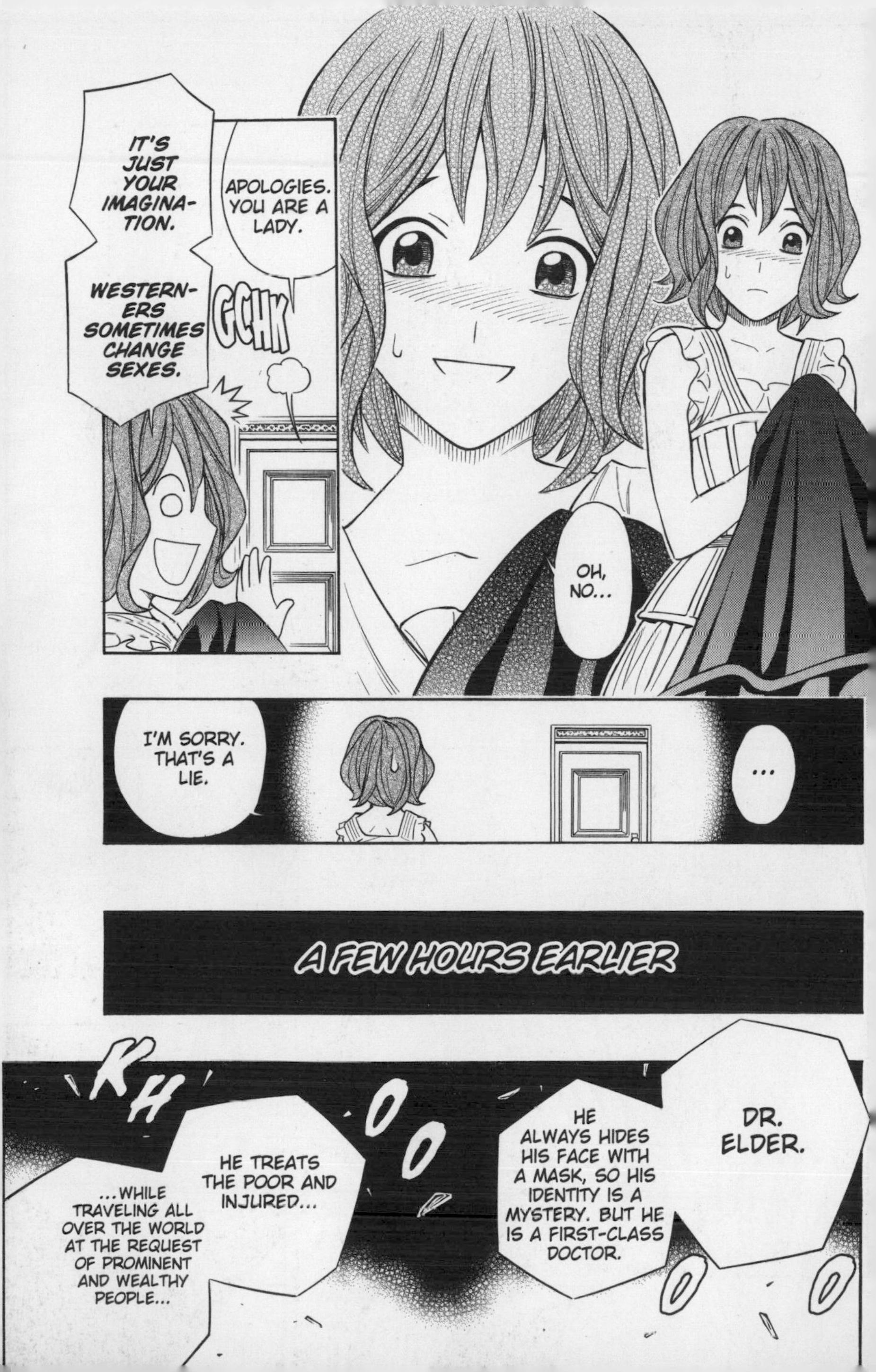
OH, NO...
IT'S JUST YOUR IMAGINATION.
WESTERNERS SOMETIMES CHANGE SEXES.
GCHK
APOLOGIES. YOU ARE A LADY.
...
I'M SORRY. THAT'S A LIE.
A FEW HOURS EARLIER
DR. ELDER.
HE ALWAYS HIDES HIS FACE WITH A MASK, SO HIS IDENTITY IS A MYSTERY. BUT HE IS A FIRST-CLASS DOCTOR.
KHOO
HE TREATS THE POOR AND INJURED...
...WHILE TRAVELING ALL OVER THE WORLD AT THE REQUEST OF PROMINENT AND WEALTHY PEOPLE...

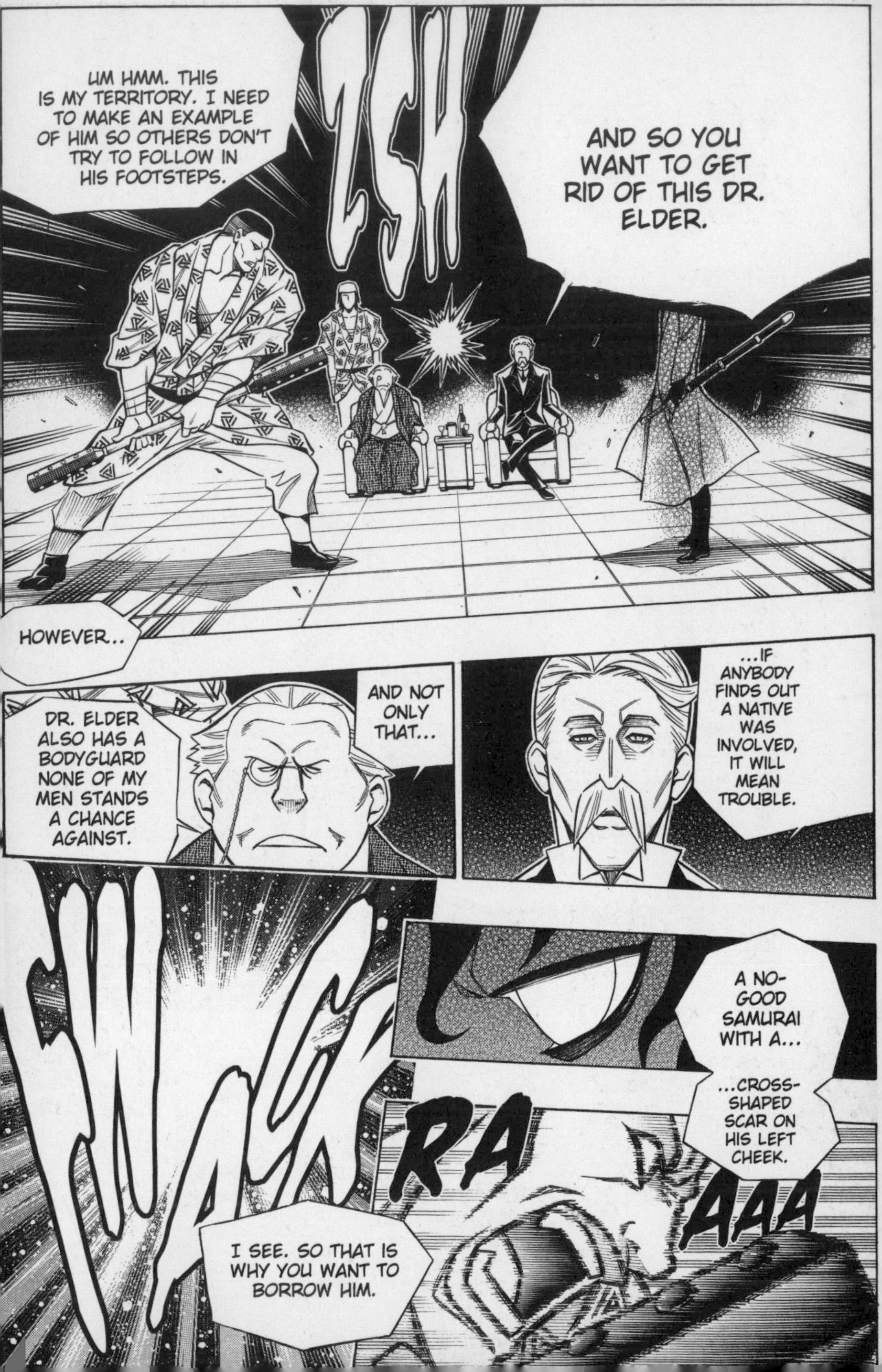
AND SO YOU WANT TO GET RID OF THIS DR. ELDER.
UM HMM. THIS IS MY TERRITORY. I NEED TO MAKE AN EXAMPLE OF HIM SO OTHERS DON'T TRY TO FOLLOW IN HIS FOOTSTEPS.
HOWEVER...
...IF ANYBODY FINDS OUT A NATIVE WAS INVOLVED, IT WILL MEAN TROUBLE.
AND NOT ONLY THAT...
DR. ELDER ALSO HAS A BODYGUARD NONE OF MY MEN STANDS A CHANCE AGAINST.
A NO-GOOD SAMURAI WITH A...
...CROSS-SHAPED SCAR ON HIS LEFT CHEEK.
RA
AAA
I SEE. SO THAT IS WHY YOU WANT TO BORROW HIM.

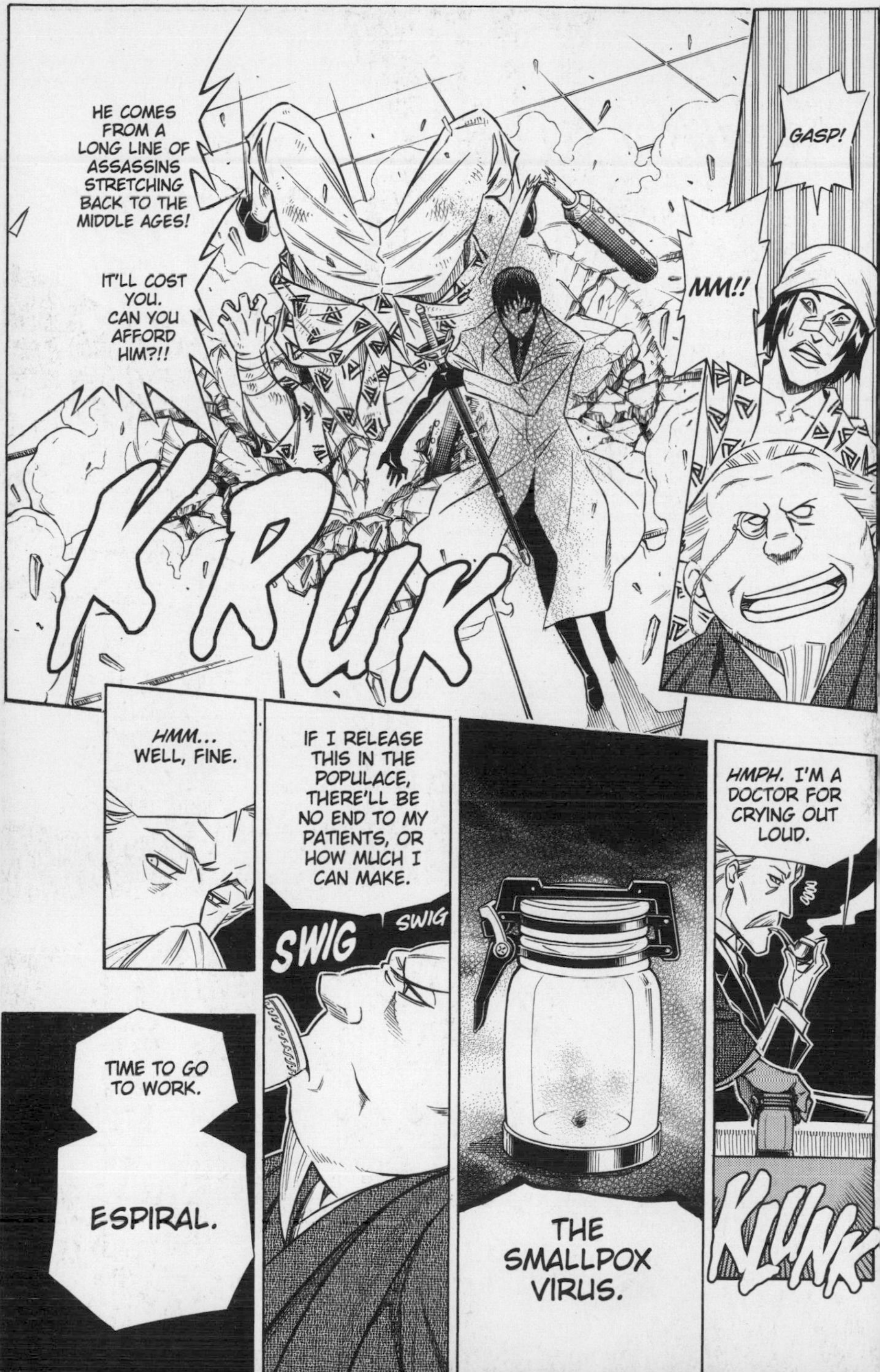
GASP!
MM!!
HE COMES FROM A LONG LINE OF ASSASSINS STRETCHING BACK TO THE MIDDLE AGES!
IT'LL COST YOU. CAN YOU AFFORD HIM?!!
KRUK
HMPH. I'M A DOCTOR FOR CRYING OUT LOUD.
KLUNK
THE SMALLPOX VIRUS.
IF I RELEASE THIS IN THE POPULACE, THERE'LL BE NO END TO MY PATIENTS, OR HOW MUCH I CAN MAKE.
SWIG
SWIG
HMM... WELL, FINE.
TIME TO GO TO WORK.
ESPIRAL.

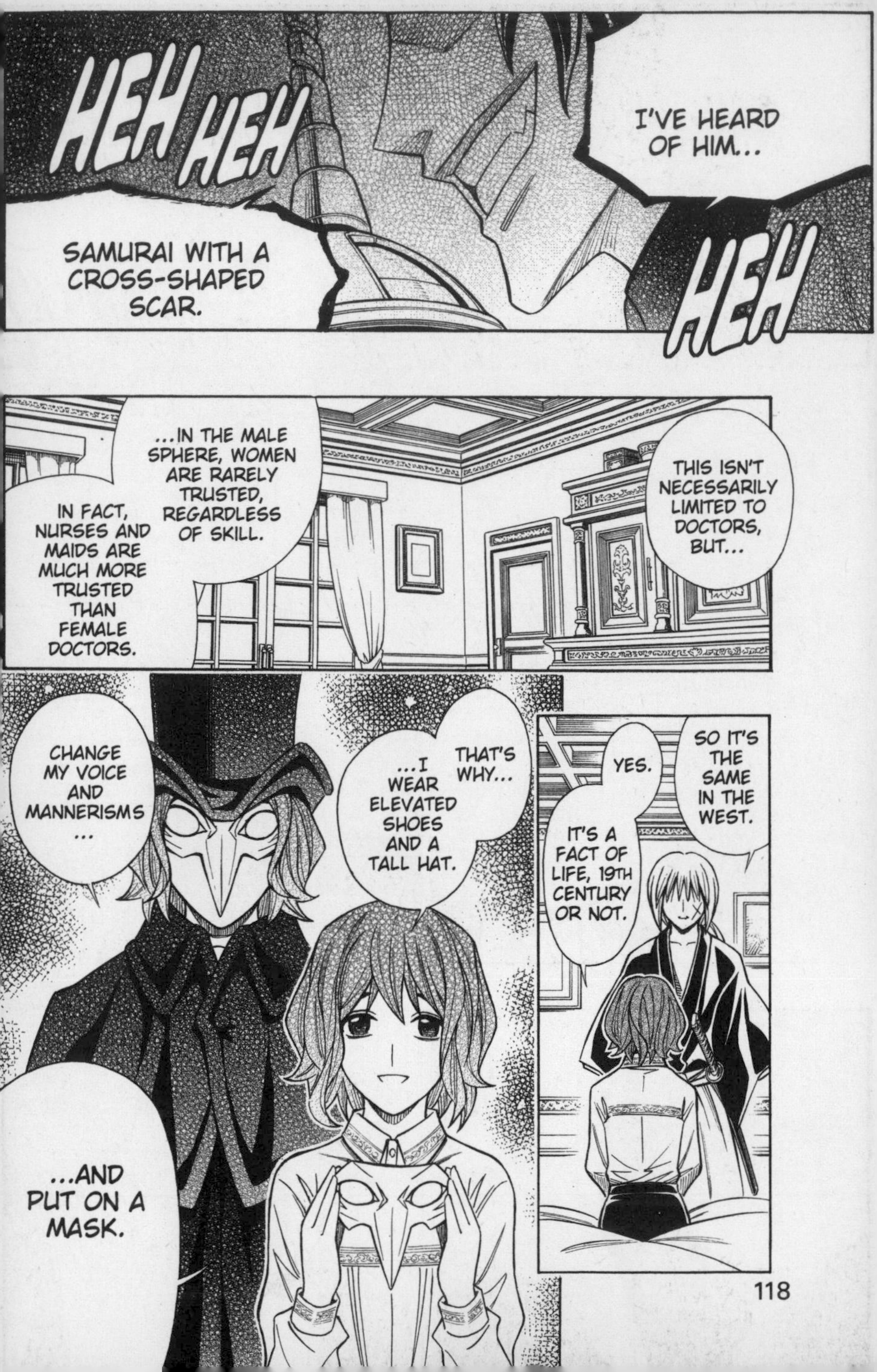
I'VE HEARD OF HIM...
HEH HEH
HEH
SAMURAI WITH A CROSS-SHAPED SCAR.
THIS ISN'T NECESSARILY LIMITED TO DOCTORS, BUT...
...IN THE MALE SPHERE, WOMEN ARE RARELY TRUSTED, REGARDLESS OF SKILL.
IN FACT, NURSES AND MAIDS ARE MUCH MORE TRUSTED THAN FEMALE DOCTORS.
SO IT'S THE SAME IN THE WEST.
YES.
IT'S A FACT OF LIFE, 19TH CENTURY OR NOT.
THAT'S WHY...
...I WEAR ELEVATED SHOES AND A TALL HAT.
CHANGE MY VOICE AND MANNERISMS...
...AND PUT ON A MASK.

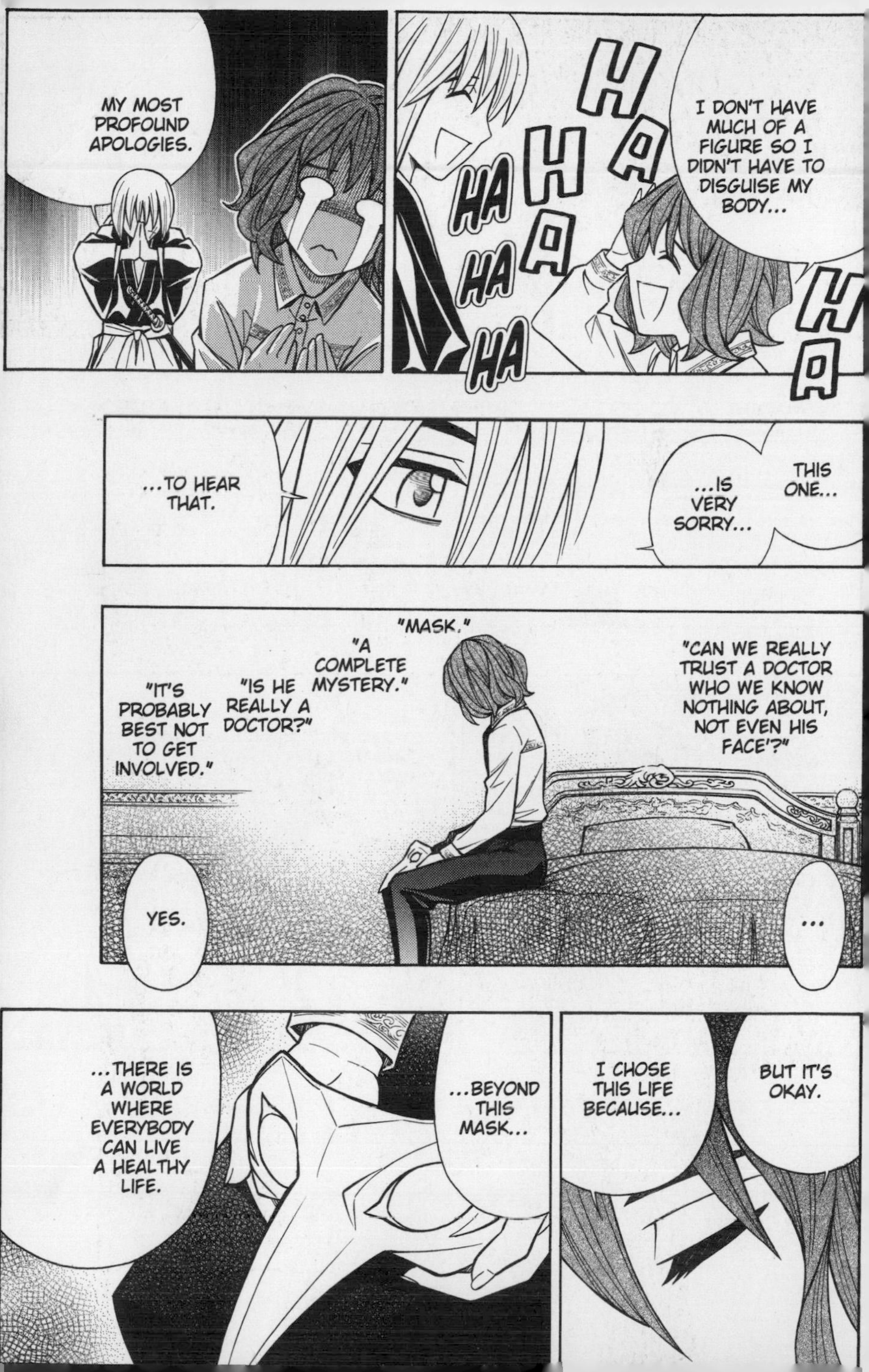
I DON'T HAVE MUCH OF A FIGURE SO I DIDN'T HAVE TO DISGUISE MY BODY...
HA
HAHA
HAHA
HA HA HA HA
MY MOST PROFOUND APOLOGIES.
THIS ONE...
...IS VERY SORRY...
...TO HEAR THAT.
"CAN WE REALLY TRUST A DOCTOR WHO WE KNOW NOTHING ABOUT, NOT EVEN HIS FACE'?"
"MASK."
"A COMPLETE MYSTERY."
"IS HE REALLY A DOCTOR?"
"IT'S PROBABLY BEST NOT TO GET INVOLVED."
...
YES.
BUT IT'S OKAY.
I CHOSE THIS LIFE BECAUSE...
...BEYOND THIS MASK...
...THERE IS A WORLD WHERE EVERYBODY CAN LIVE A HEALTHY LIFE.

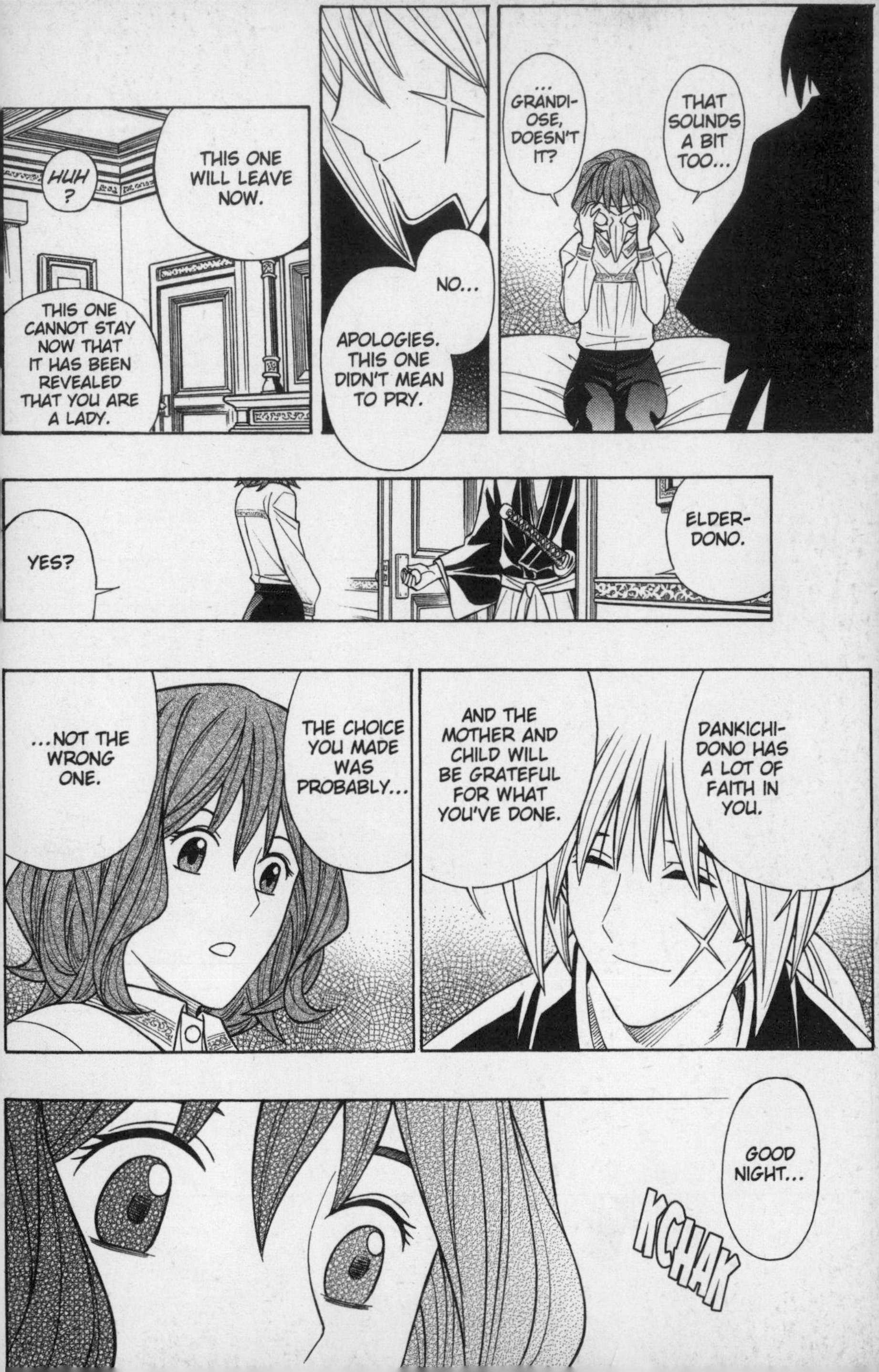
THAT SOUNDS A BIT TOO...
...GRANDIOSE, DOESN'T IT?
NO...
APOLOGIES. THIS ONE DIDN'T MEAN TO PRY.
THIS ONE WILL LEAVE NOW.
HUH?
THIS ONE CANNOT STAY NOW THAT IT HAS BEEN REVEALED THAT YOU ARE A LADY.
ELDER-DONO.
YES?
DANKICHI-DONO HAS A LOT OF FAITH IN YOU.
AND THE MOTHER AND CHILD WILL BE GRATEFUL FOR WHAT YOU'VE DONE.
THE CHOICE YOU MADE WAS PROBABLY...
...NOT THE WRONG ONE.
GOOD NIGHT...
KCHAK

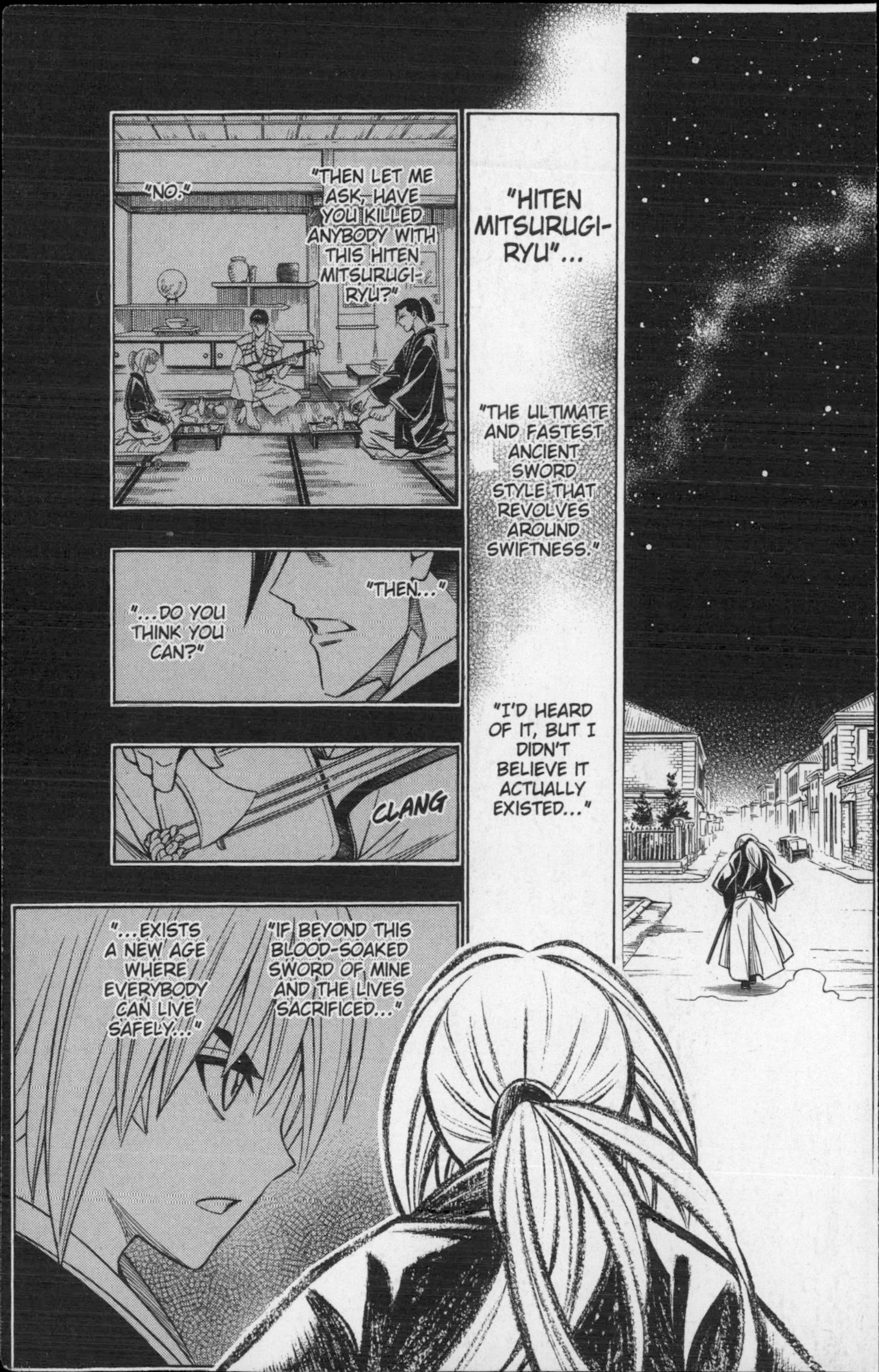
"HITEN MITSURUGI-RYU"...
"THE ULTIMATE AND FASTEST ANCIENT SWORD STYLE THAT REVOLVES AROUND SWIFTNESS."
"I'D HEARD OF IT, BUT I DIDN'T BELIEVE IT ACTUALLY EXISTED..."
"THEN LET ME ASK, HAVE YOU KILLED ANYBODY WITH THIS HITEN MITSURUGI-RYU?"
"NO."
"THEN..."
"...DO YOU THINK YOU CAN?"
CLANG
"IF BEYOND THIS BLOOD-SOAKED SWORD OF MINE AND THE LIVES SACRIFICED..."
"...EXISTS A NEW AGE WHERE EVERYBODY CAN LIVE SAFELY..."

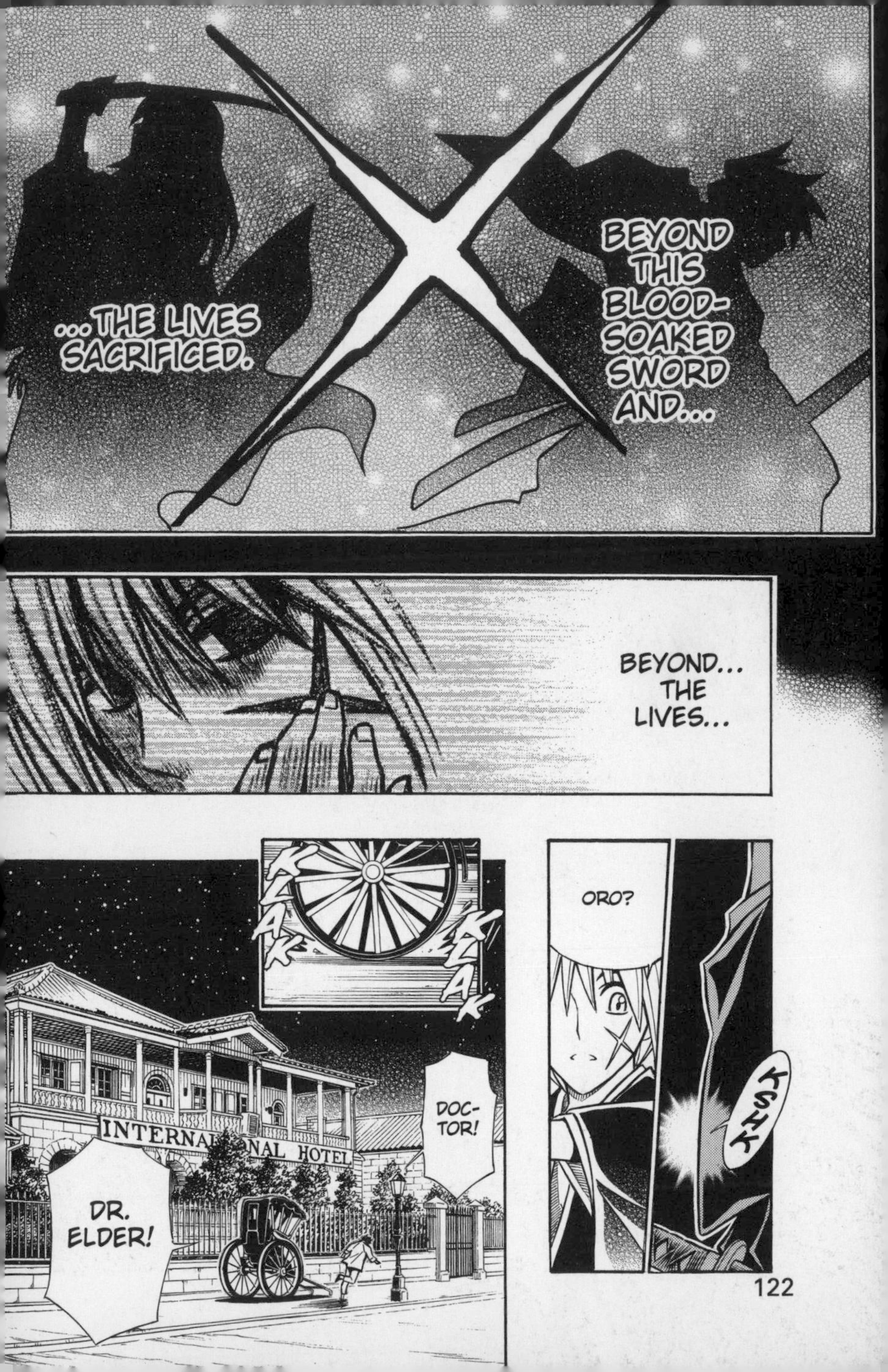

BEYOND THIS BLOOD-SOAKED SWORD AND...
...THE LIVES SACRIFICED.
BEYOND... THE LIVES...
ORO?
KSHK
KLAK
KLAK
DOC-TOR!
DR. ELDER!
INTERNATIONAL HOTEL

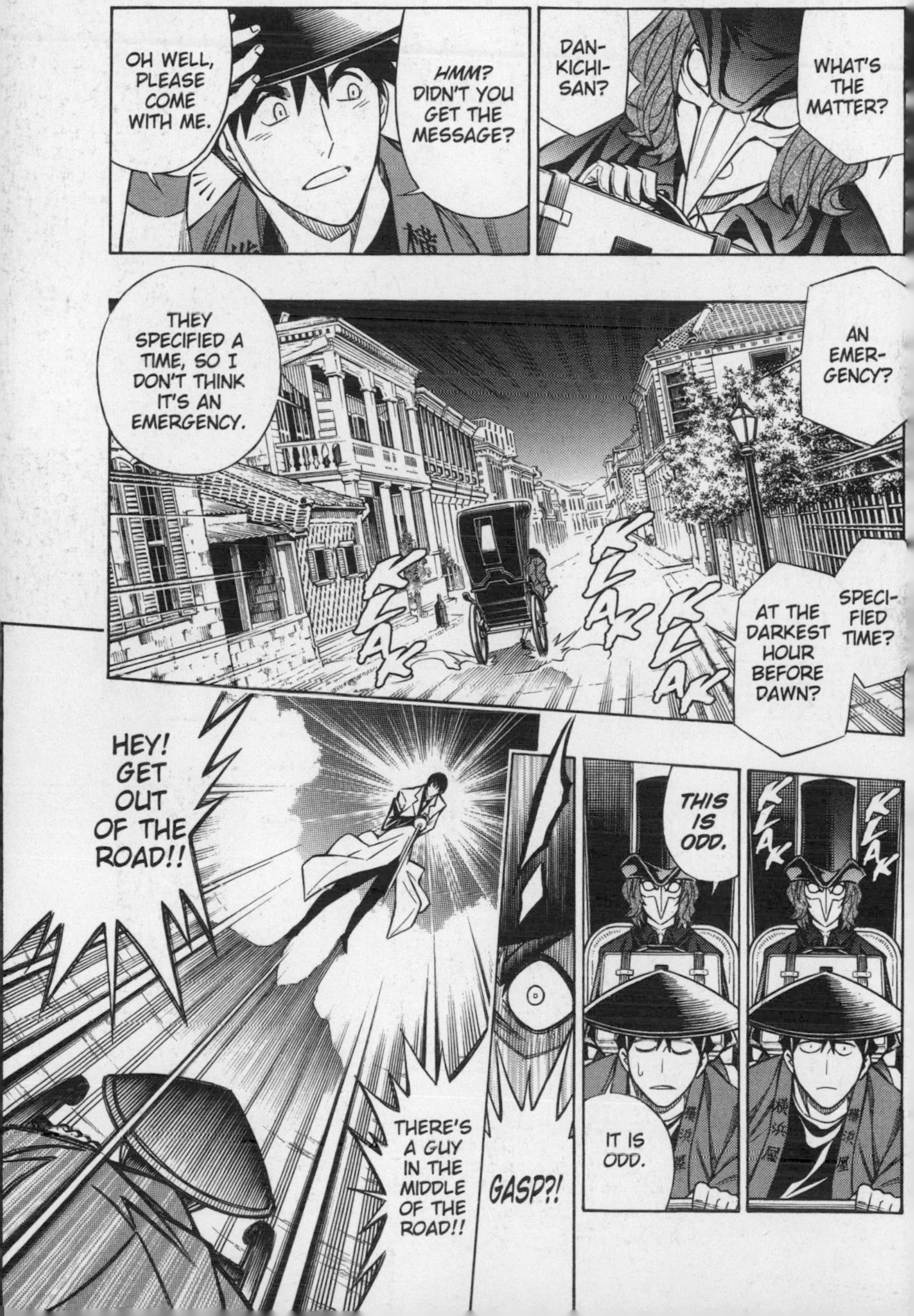
WHAT'S THE MATTER?
DAN-KICHI-SAN?
HMM? DIDN'T YOU GET THE MESSAGE?
OH WELL, PLEASE COME WITH ME.
AN EMERGENCY?
THEY SPECIFIED A TIME, SO I DON'T THINK IT'S AN EMERGENCY.
KLAK
KLAK
KLAK
SPECIFIED TIME?
AT THE DARKEST HOUR BEFORE DAWN?
KLAK
KLAK
THIS IS ODD.
IT IS ODD.
GASP?!
THERE'S A GUY IN THE MIDDLE OF THE ROAD!!
HEY! GET OUT OF THE ROAD!!

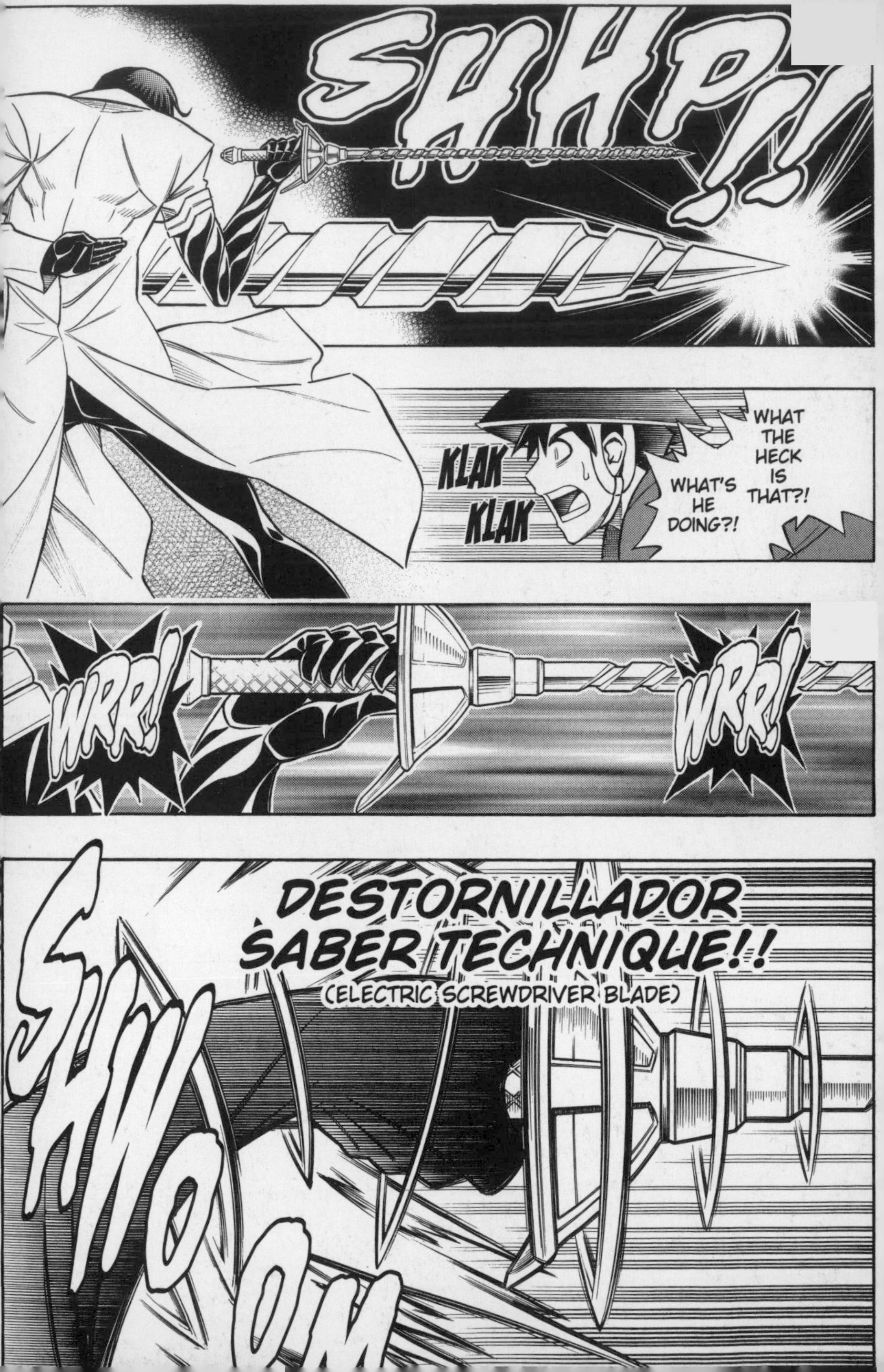
SHHP!!
WHAT THE HECK IS THAT?!
WHAT'S HE DOING?!
KLAK KLAK
WRR!
WRR!
DESTORNILLADOR SABER TECHNIQUE!!
(ELECTRIC SCREWDRIVER BLADE)
SHHOOM

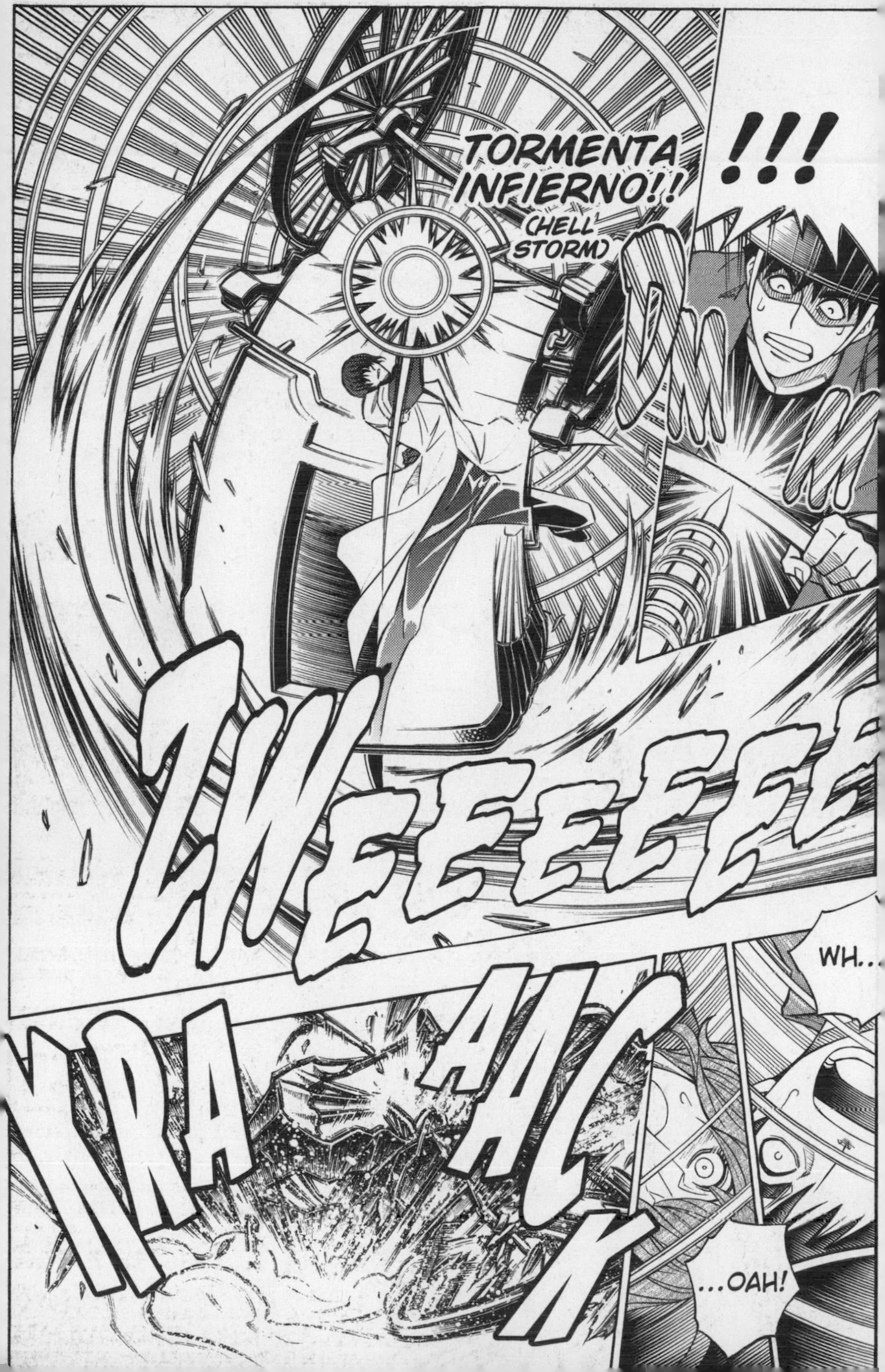
!!!
TORMENTA INFIERNO!!
(HELL STORM)
WH...
...OAH!

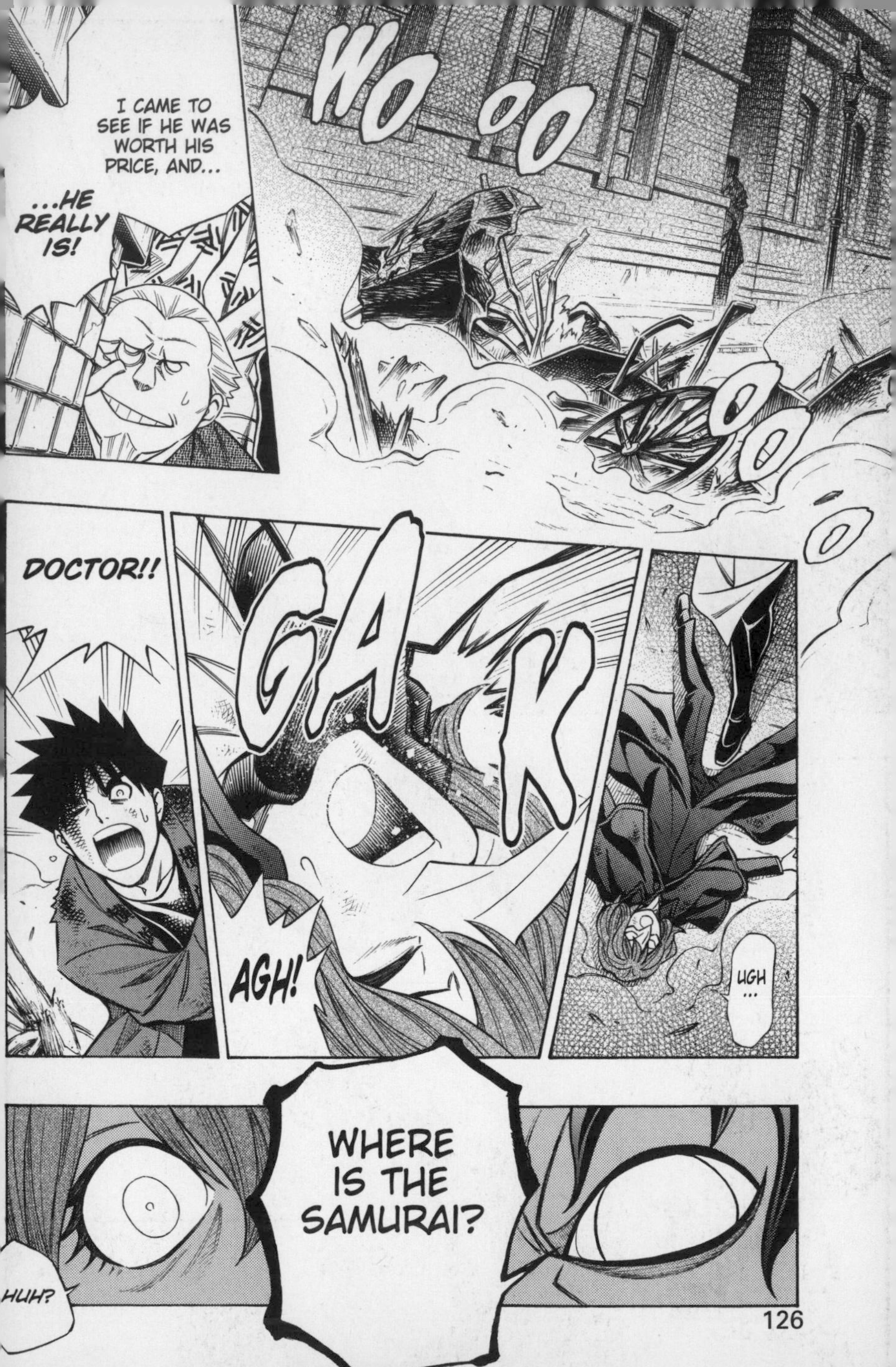
WOOOOOOO
I CAME TO SEE IF HE WAS WORTH HIS PRICE, AND...
...HE REALLY IS!
UGH ...
GAK
AGH!
DOCTOR!!
WHERE IS THE SAMURAI?
HUH?

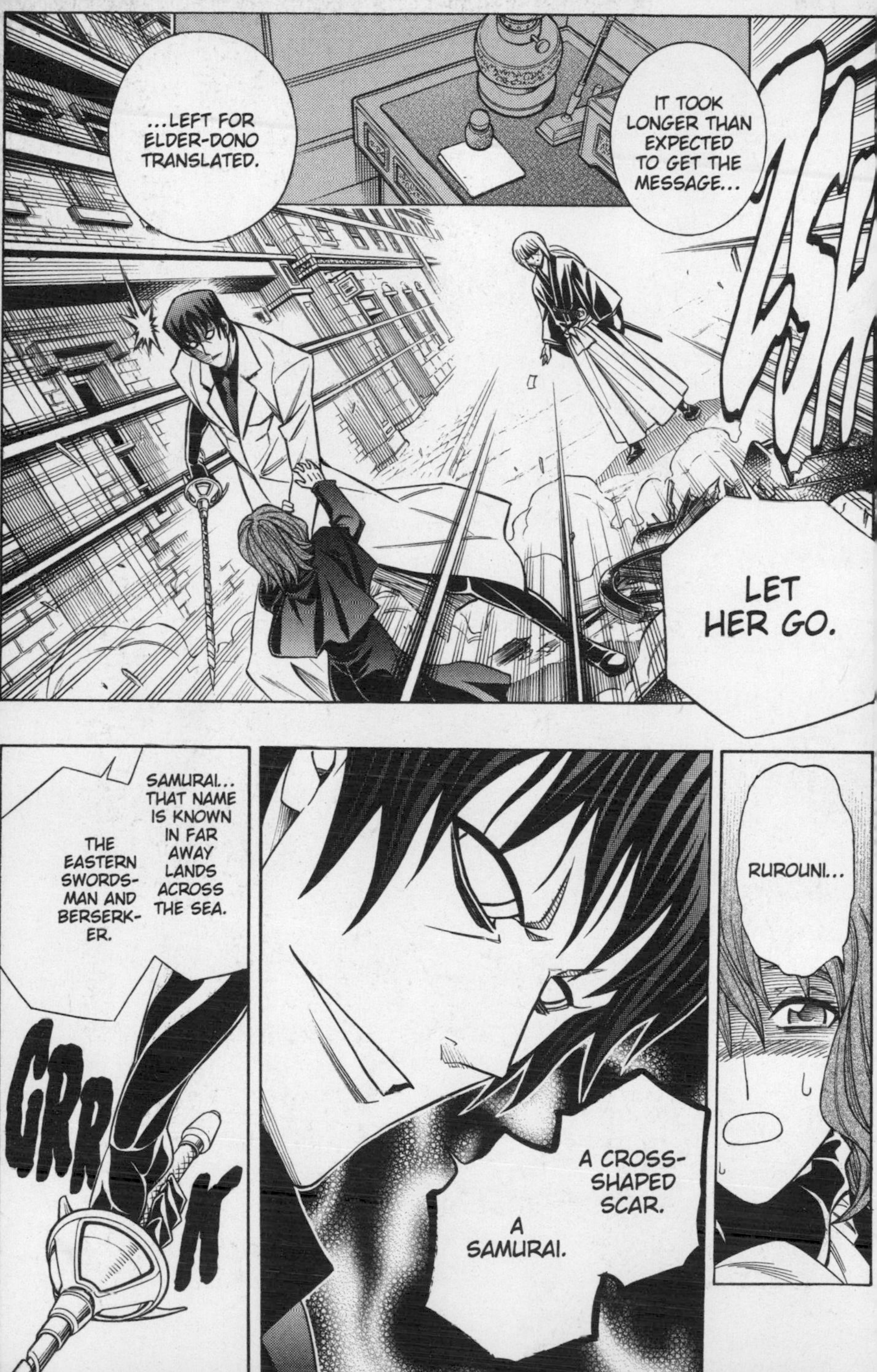
IT TOOK LONGER THAN EXPECTED TO GET THE MESSAGE...
...LEFT FOR ELDER-DONO TRANSLATED.
LET HER GO.
RUROUNI...
A CROSS-SHAPED SCAR.
A SAMURAI.
SAMURAI... THAT NAME IS KNOWN IN FAR AWAY LANDS ACROSS THE SEA.
THE EASTERN SWORDSMAN AND BERSERKER.

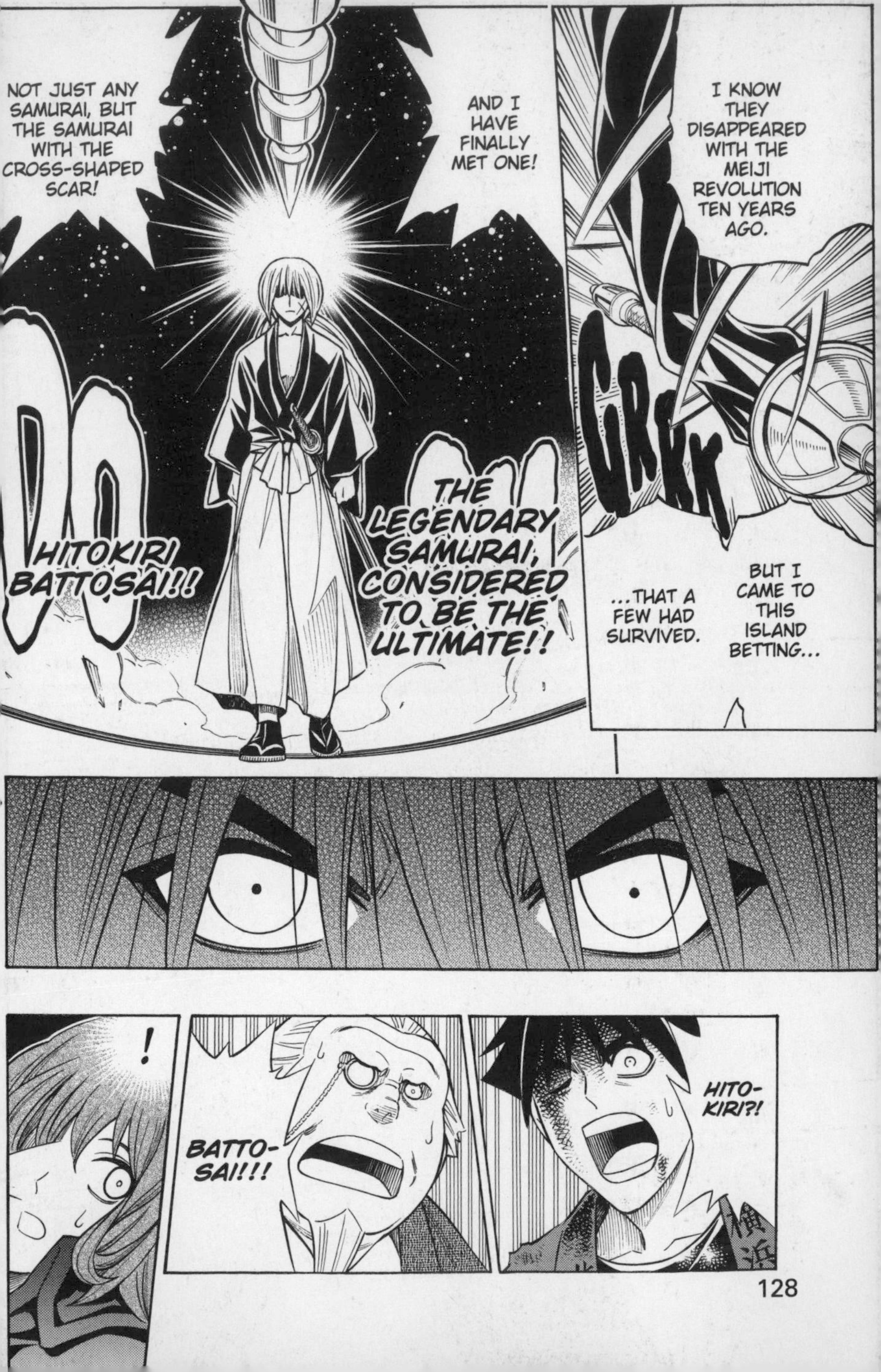
I KNOW THEY DISAPPEARED WITH THE MEIJI REVOLUTION TEN YEARS AGO.
GRKK
BUT I CAME TO THIS ISLAND BETTING...
...THAT A FEW HAD SURVIVED.
AND I HAVE FINALLY MET ONE!
NOT JUST ANY SAMURAI, BUT THE SAMURAI WITH THE CROSS-SHAPED SCAR!
THE LEGENDARY SAMURAI, CONSIDERED TO BE THE ULTIMATE!!
HITOKIRI BATTOSAI!!
DO
HITO-KIRI?!
BATTO-SAI!!!
!

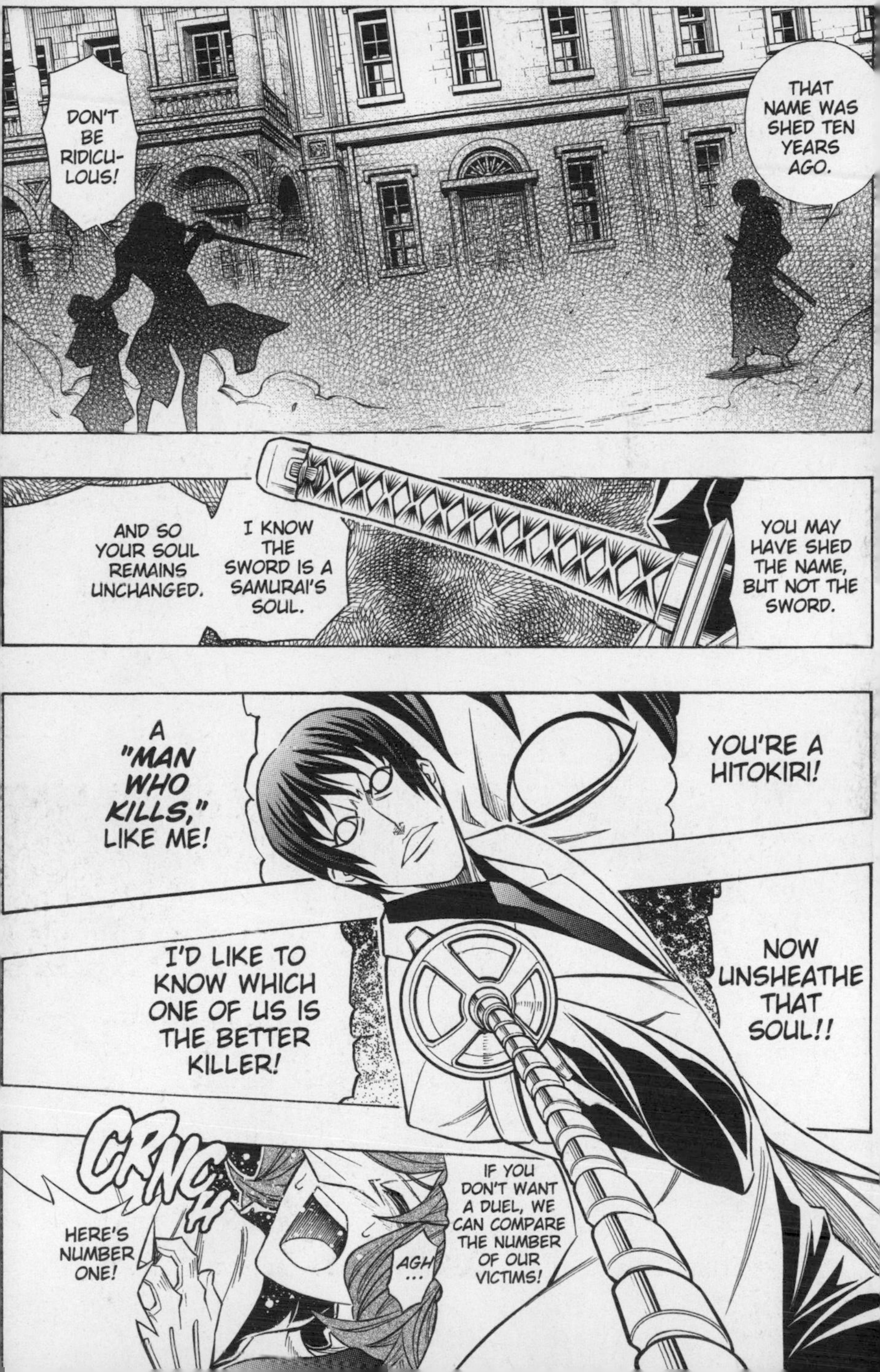
THAT NAME WAS SHED TEN YEARS AGO.
DON'T BE RIDICU-LOUS!
YOU MAY HAVE SHED THE NAME, BUT NOT THE SWORD.
I KNOW THE SWORD IS A SAMURAI'S SOUL.
AND SO YOUR SOUL REMAINS UNCHANGED.
YOU'RE A HITOKIRI!
A *"MAN WHO KILLS,"* LIKE ME!
NOW UNSHEATHE THAT SOUL!!
I'D LIKE TO KNOW WHICH ONE OF US IS THE BETTER KILLER!
IF YOU DON'T WANT A DUEL, WE CAN COMPARE THE NUMBER OF OUR VICTIMS!
AGH...
CRNCH
HERE'S NUMBER ONE!

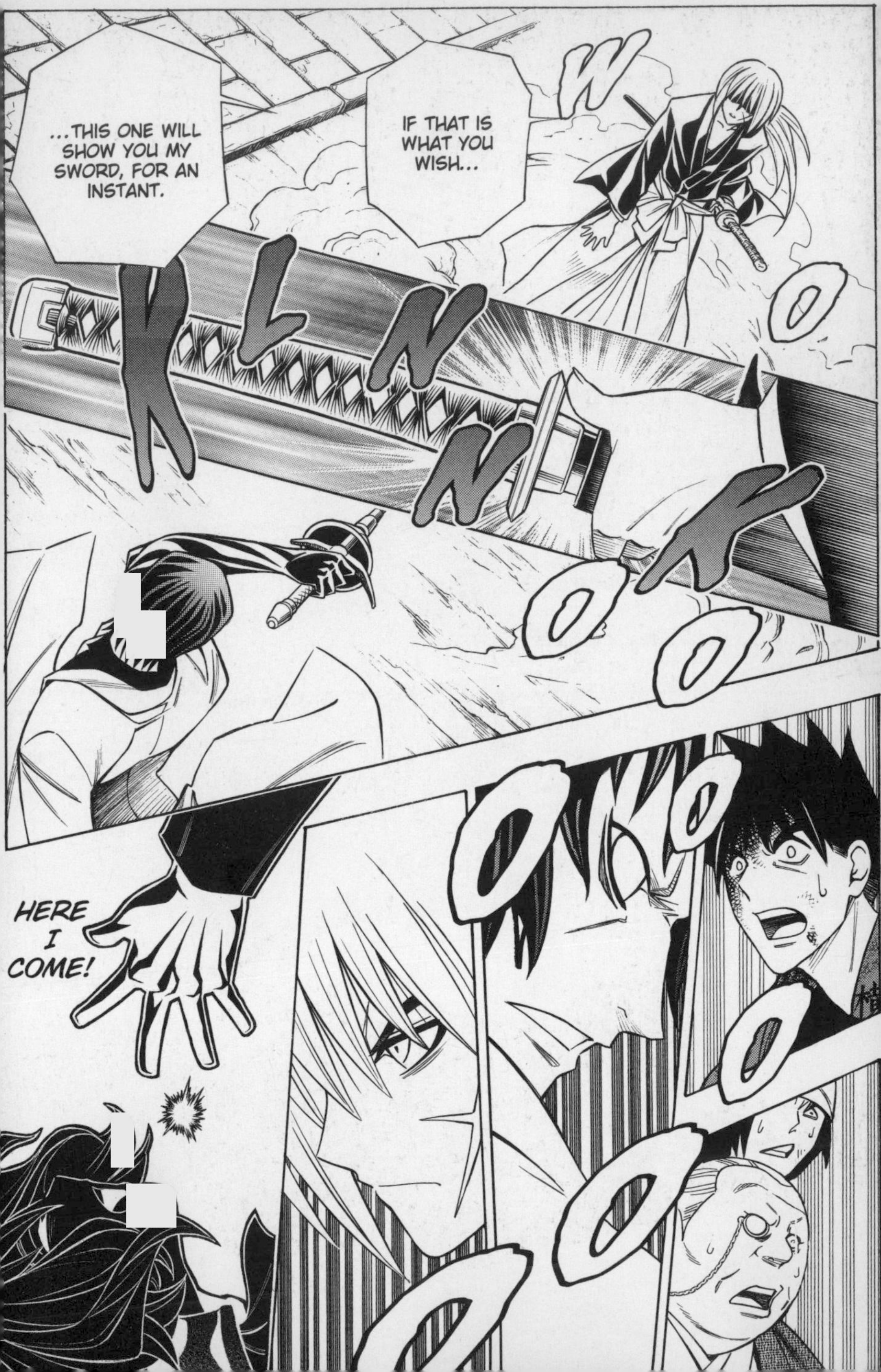
IF THAT IS WHAT YOU WISH...
...THIS ONE WILL SHOW YOU MY SWORD, FOR AN INSTANT.
KLNNK
HERE I COME!

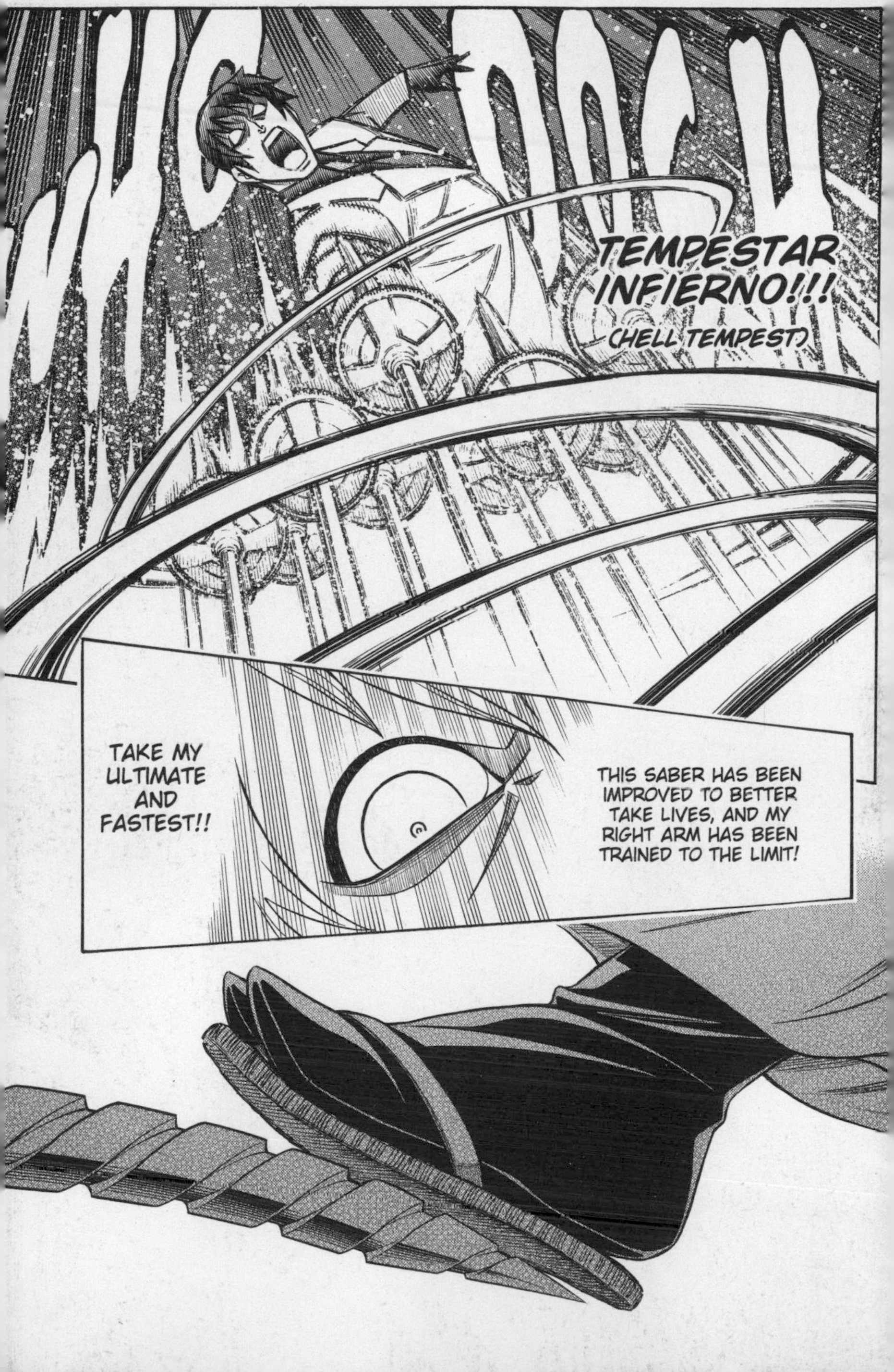
TEMPESTAR INFIERNO!!!
(HELL TEMPEST)
THIS SABER HAS BEEN IMPROVED TO BETTER TAKE LIVES, AND MY RIGHT ARM HAS BEEN TRAINED TO THE LIMIT!
TAKE MY ULTIMATE AND FASTEST!!

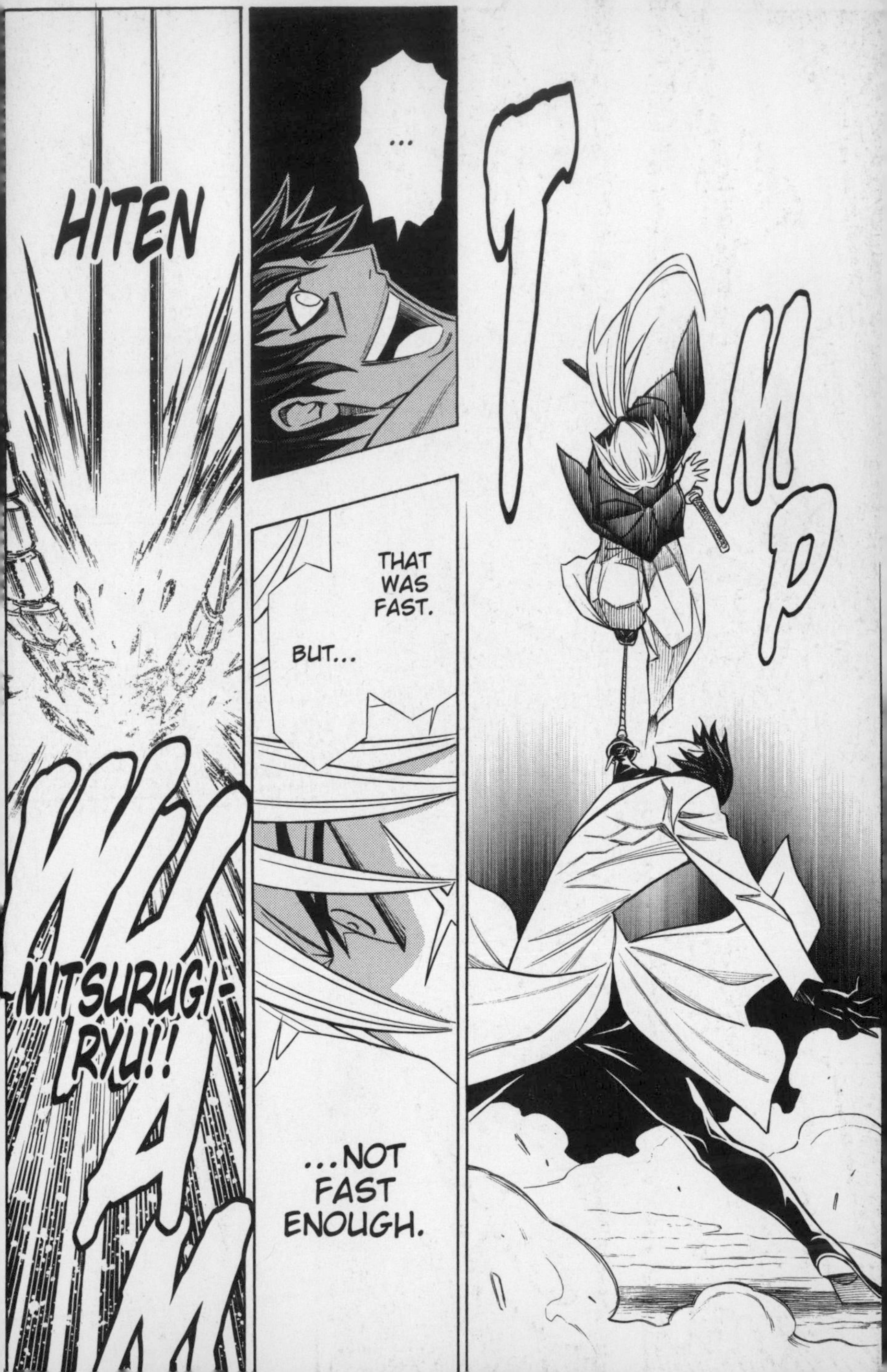
J M P
...
THAT WAS FAST.
BUT...
...NOT FAST ENOUGH.
HITEN
MITSURUGI-RYU!!
WHA

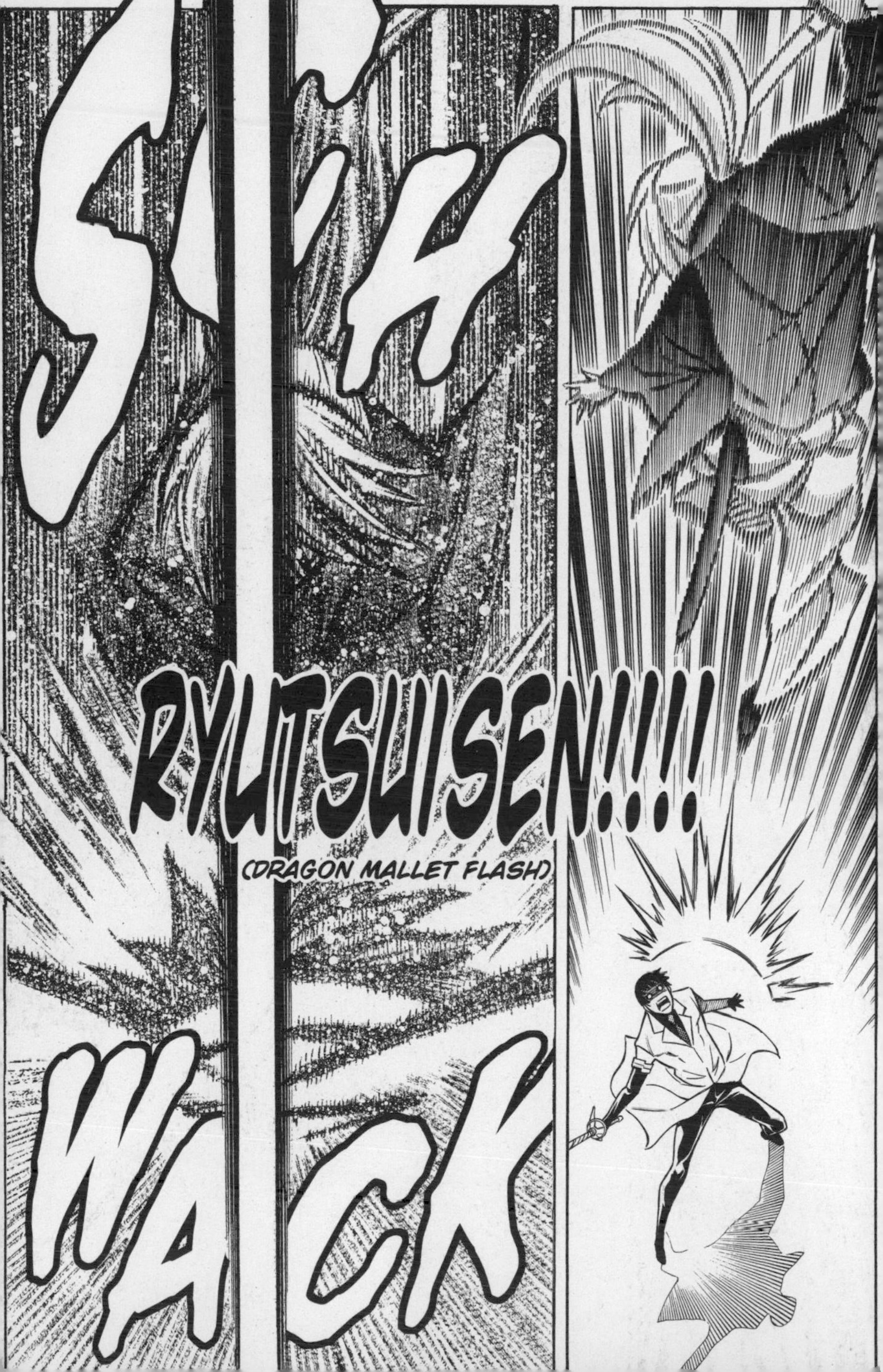
SHH
RYUTSUISEN!!!!
(DRAGON MALLET FLASH)
WACK

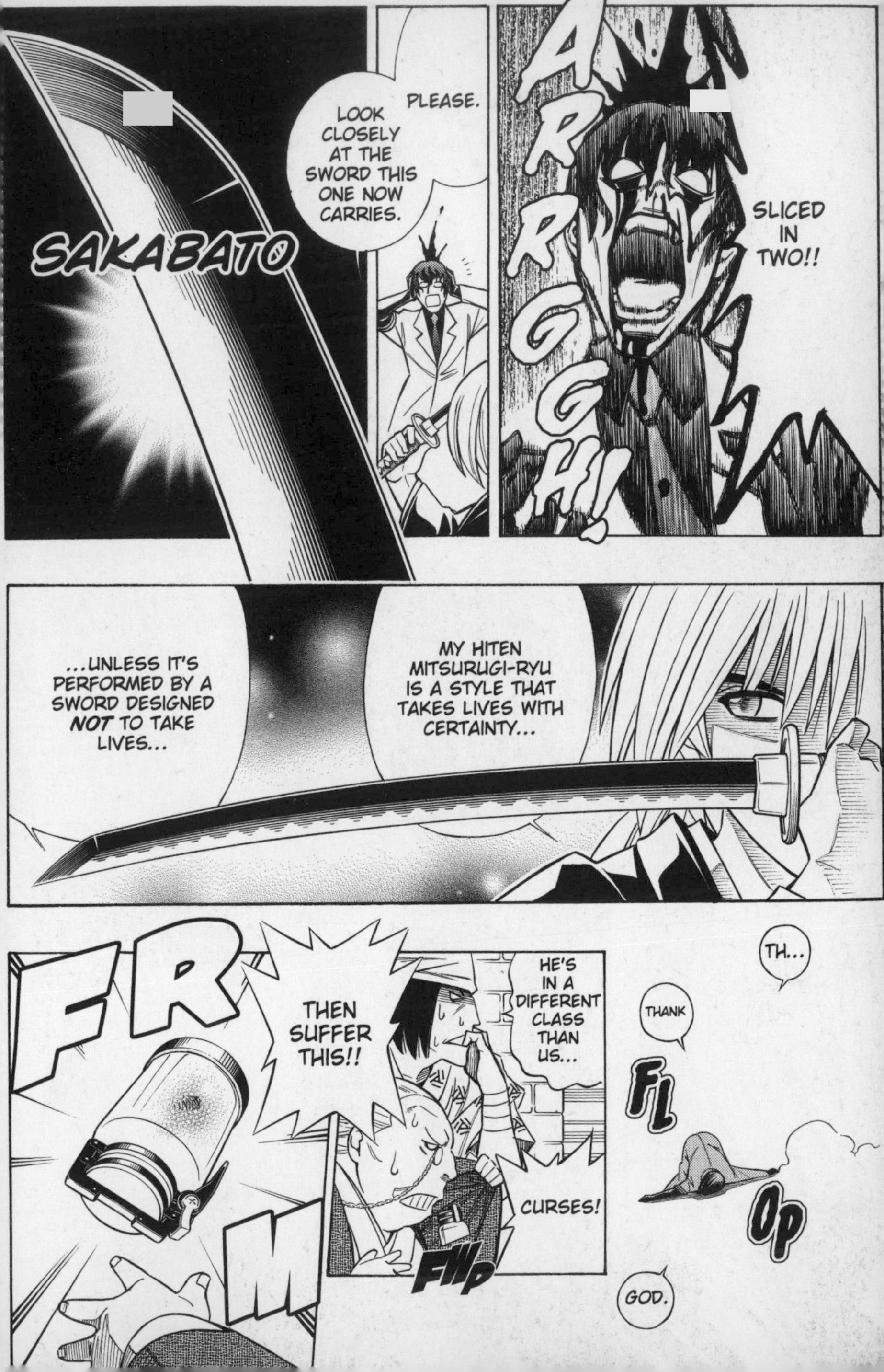
ARRGGGH!!
SLICED IN TWO!!
PLEASE.
LOOK CLOSELY AT THE SWORD THIS ONE NOW CARRIES.
SAKABATO
MY HITEN MITSURUGI-RYU IS A STYLE THAT TAKES LIVES WITH CERTAINTY...
...UNLESS IT'S PERFORMED BY A SWORD DESIGNED NOT TO TAKE LIVES...
TH...
THANK
FLOP
GOD.
HE'S IN A DIFFERENT CLASS THAN US...
CURSES!
FWP
THEN SUFFER THIS!!
FRM

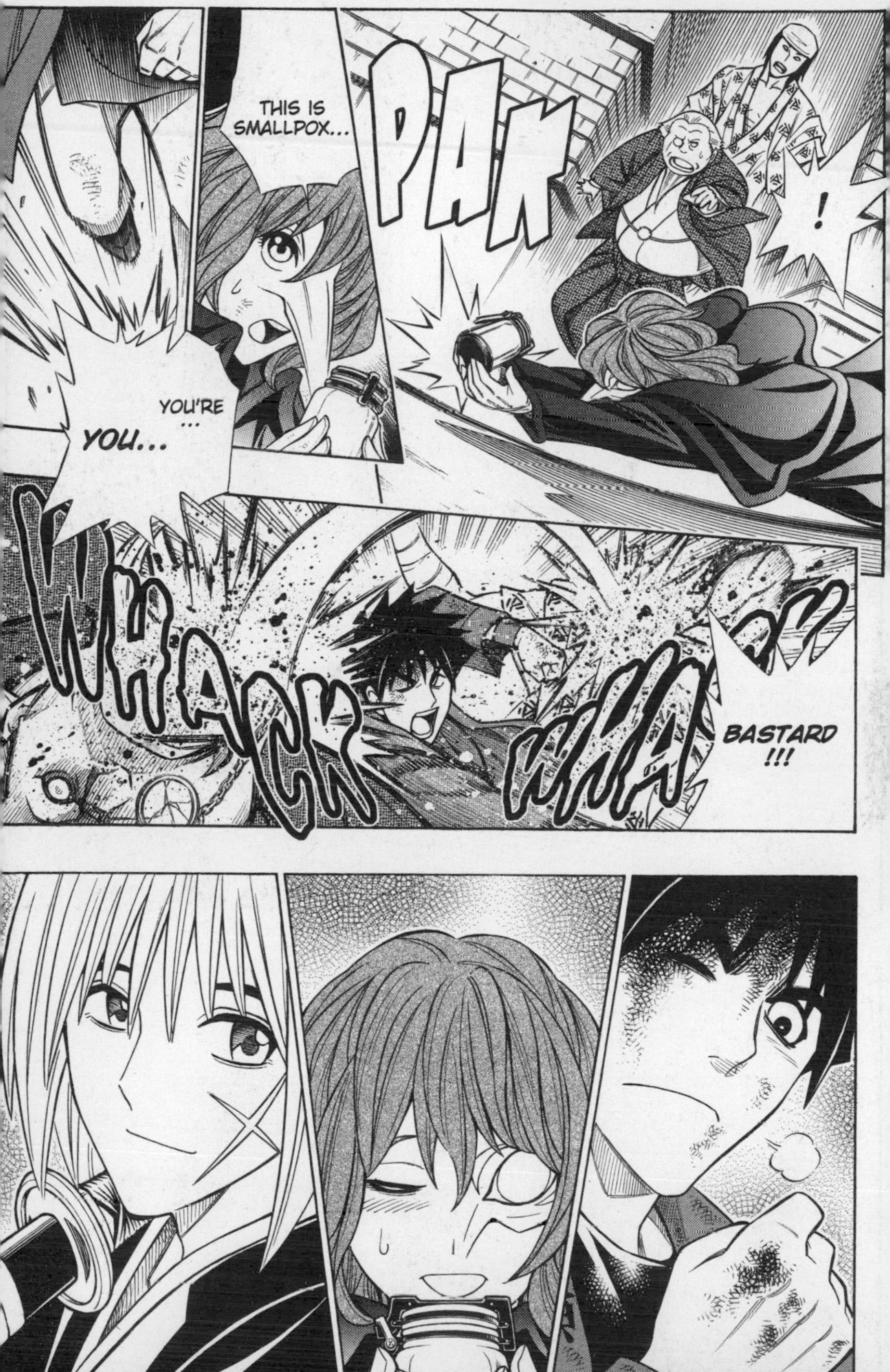
PAK
!
THIS IS SMALLPOX...
YOU'RE ...
YOU...
BASTARD !!!
WHAM
WHACK

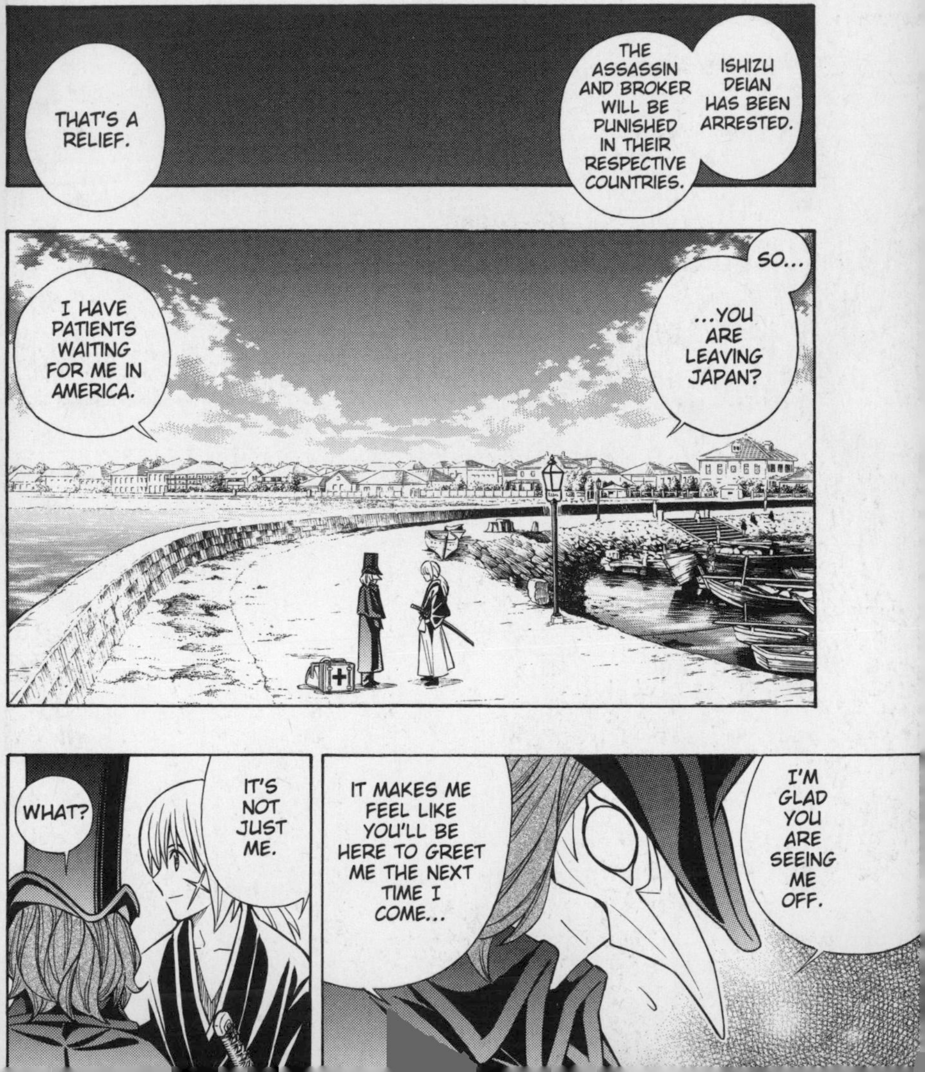
ISHIZU DEIAN HAS BEEN ARRESTED.
THE ASSASSIN AND BROKER WILL BE PUNISHED IN THEIR RESPECTIVE COUNTRIES.
THAT'S A RELIEF.
SO...
...YOU ARE LEAVING JAPAN?
I HAVE PATIENTS WAITING FOR ME IN AMERICA.
I'M GLAD YOU ARE SEEING ME OFF.
IT MAKES ME FEEL LIKE YOU'LL BE HERE TO GREET ME THE NEXT TIME I COME...
IT'S NOT JUST ME.
WHAT?

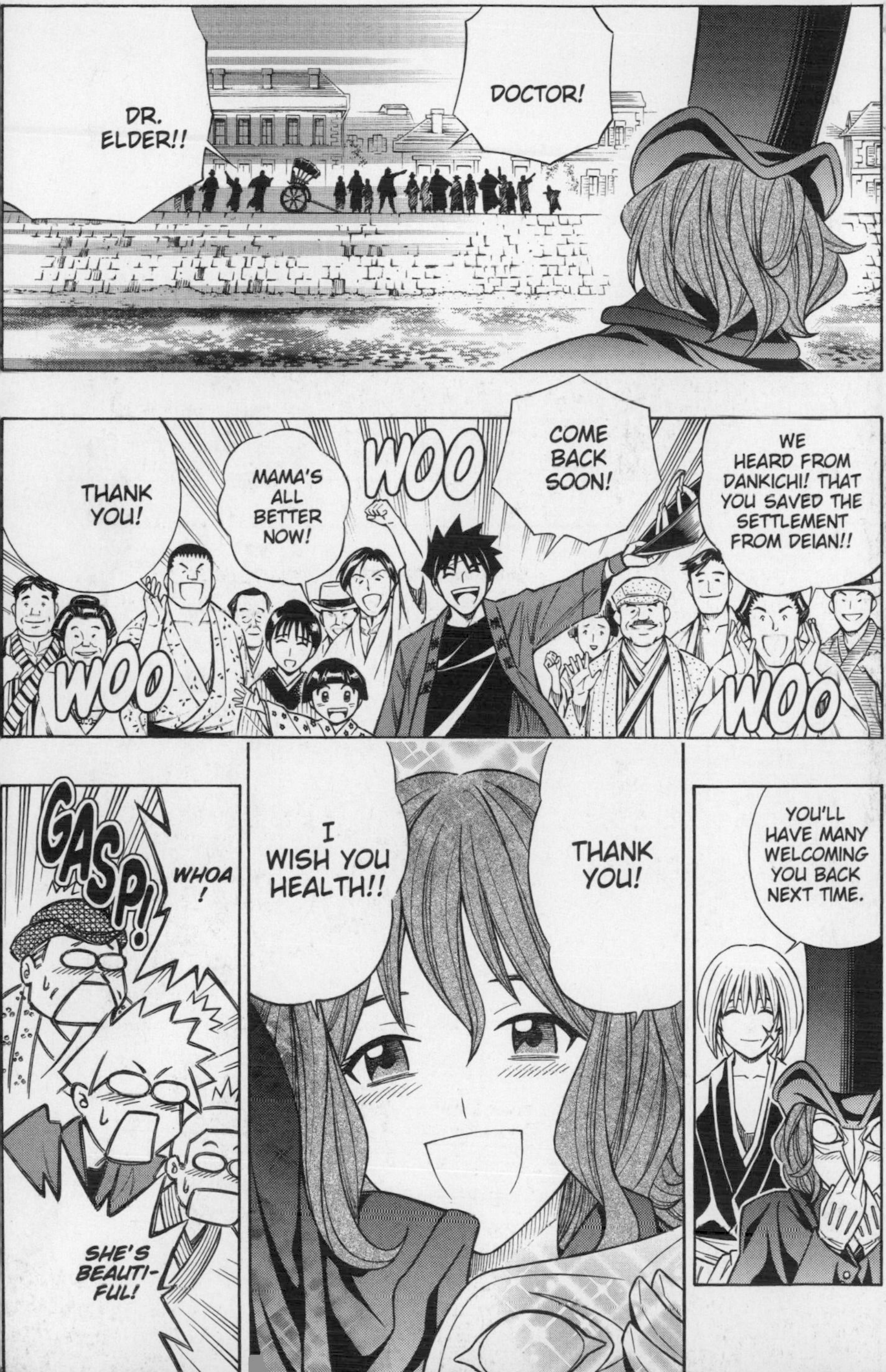
DOCTOR!
DR. ELDER!!
WE HEARD FROM DANKICHI! THAT YOU SAVED THE SETTLEMENT FROM DEIAN!!
WOO
COME BACK SOON!
WOO
MAMA'S ALL BETTER NOW!
THANK YOU!
WOO
YOU'LL HAVE MANY WELCOMING YOU BACK NEXT TIME.
THANK YOU!
I WISH YOU HEALTH!!
GASP!
WHOA!
SHE'S BEAUTI-FUL!

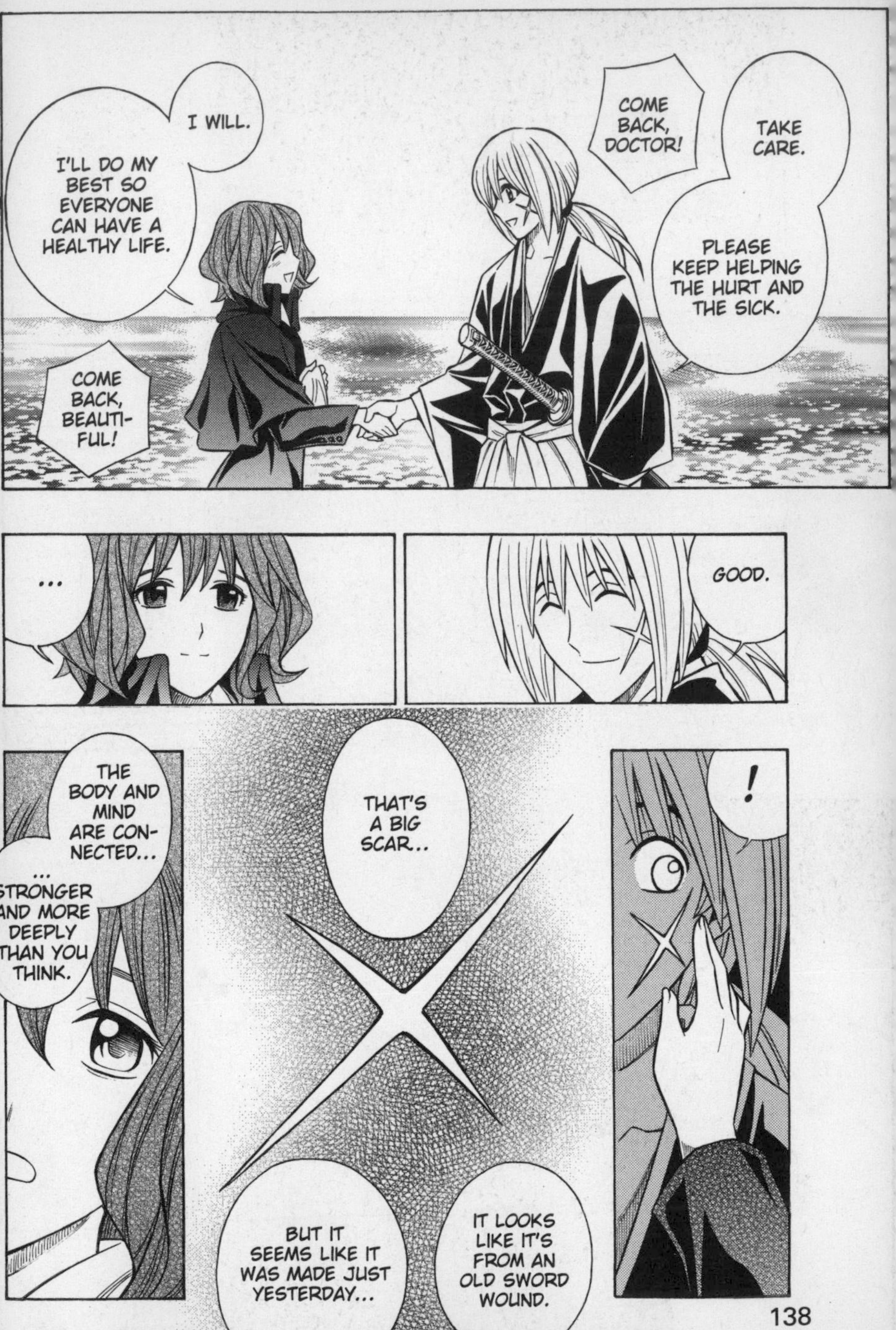
TAKE CARE.
PLEASE KEEP HELPING THE HURT AND THE SICK.
COME BACK, DOCTOR!
I WILL.
I'LL DO MY BEST SO EVERYONE CAN HAVE A HEALTHY LIFE.
COME BACK, BEAUTIFUL!
GOOD.
...
!
THAT'S A BIG SCAR...
IT LOOKS LIKE IT'S FROM AN OLD SWORD WOUND.
BUT IT SEEMS LIKE IT WAS MADE JUST YESTERDAY...
THE BODY AND MIND ARE CONNECTED...
...STRONGER AND MORE DEEPLY THAN YOU THINK.

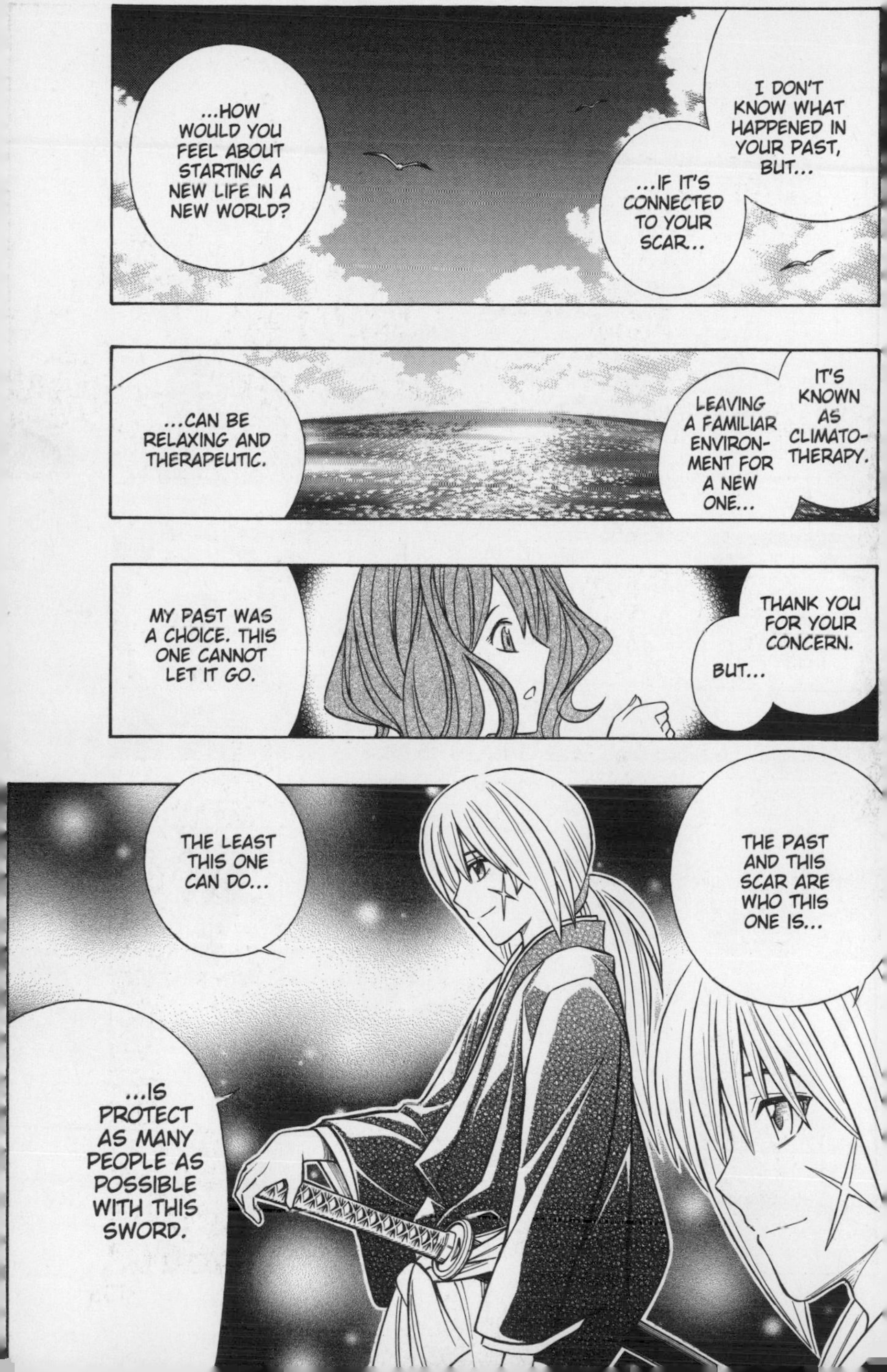
I DON'T KNOW WHAT HAPPENED IN YOUR PAST, BUT...
...IF IT'S CONNECTED TO YOUR SCAR...
...HOW WOULD YOU FEEL ABOUT STARTING A NEW LIFE IN A NEW WORLD?
IT'S KNOWN AS CLIMATO-THERAPY.
LEAVING A FAMILIAR ENVIRON-MENT FOR A NEW ONE...
...CAN BE RELAXING AND THERAPEUTIC.
THANK YOU FOR YOUR CONCERN.
BUT...
MY PAST WAS A CHOICE. THIS ONE CANNOT LET IT GO.
THE PAST AND THIS SCAR ARE WHO THIS ONE IS...
THE LEAST THIS ONE CAN DO...
...IS PROTECT AS MANY PEOPLE AS POSSIBLE WITH THIS SWORD.

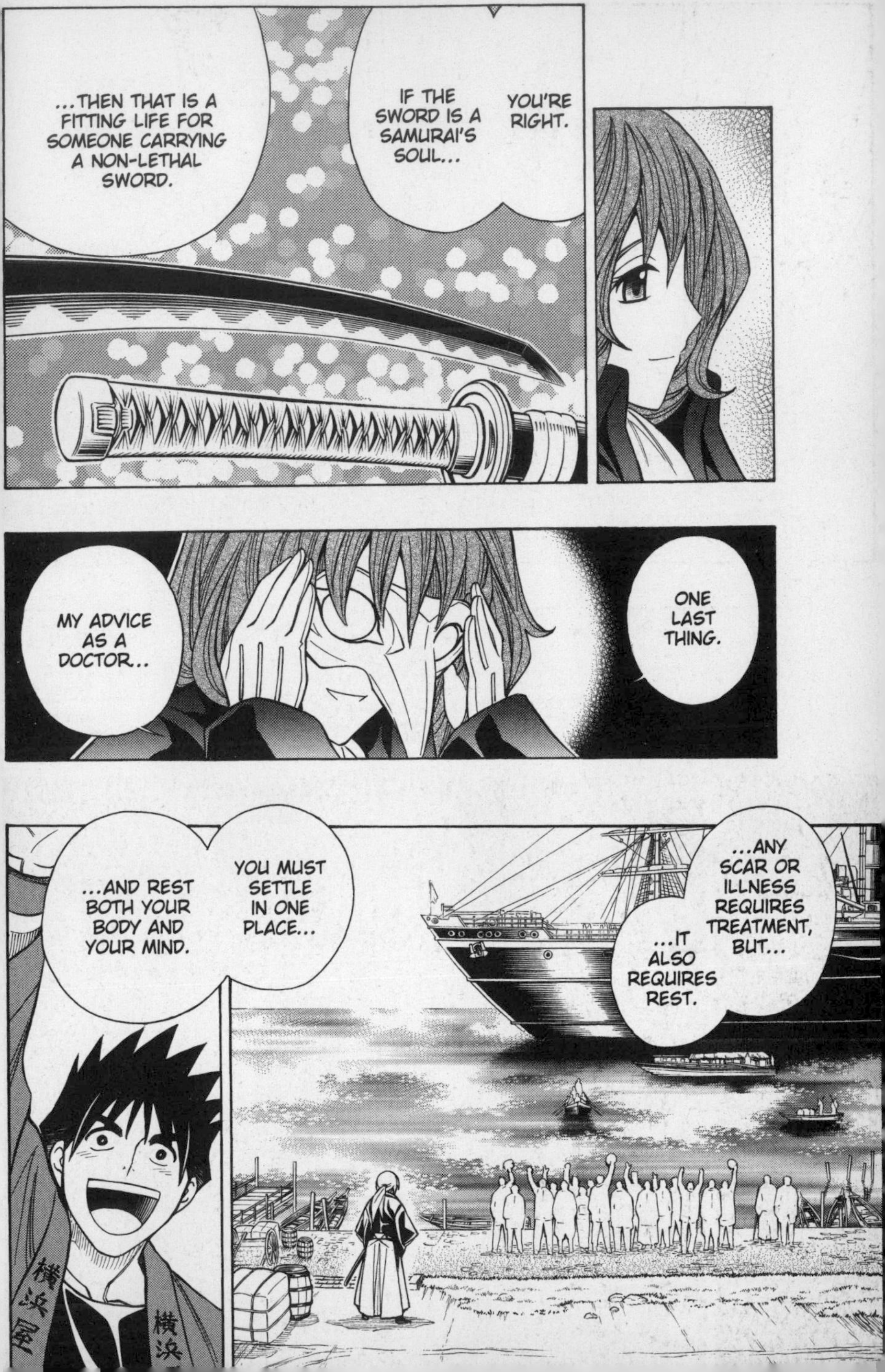
YOU'RE RIGHT.
IF THE SWORD IS A SAMURAI'S SOUL...
...THEN THAT IS A FITTING LIFE FOR SOMEONE CARRYING A NON-LETHAL SWORD.
ONE LAST THING.
MY ADVICE AS A DOCTOR...
...ANY SCAR OR ILLNESS REQUIRES TREATMENT, BUT...
...IT ALSO REQUIRES REST.
YOU MUST SETTLE IN ONE PLACE...
...AND REST BOTH YOUR BODY AND YOUR MIND.

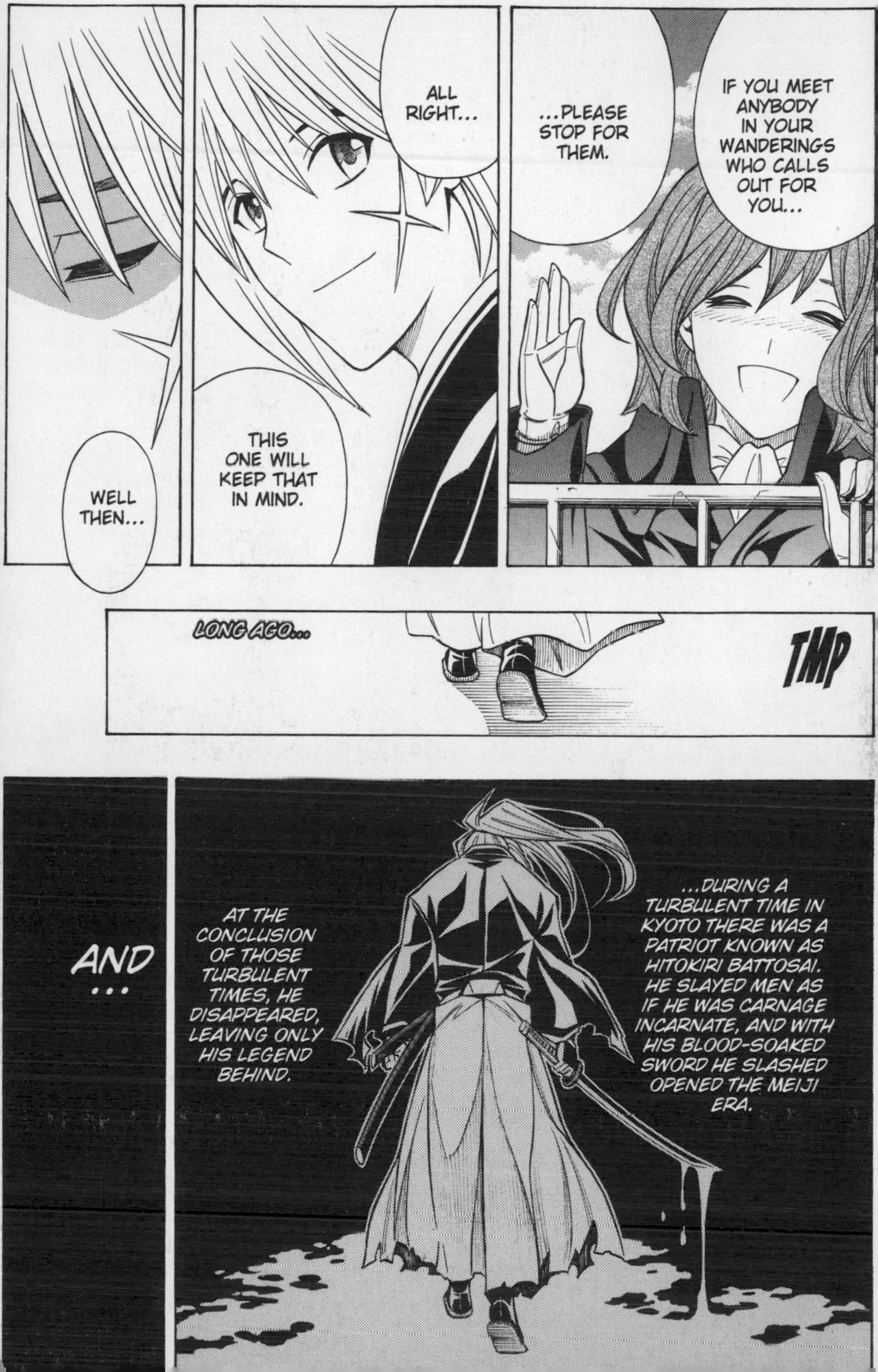
IF YOU MEET ANYBODY IN YOUR WANDERINGS WHO CALLS OUT FOR YOU...
...PLEASE STOP FOR THEM.
ALL RIGHT...
THIS ONE WILL KEEP THAT IN MIND.
WELL THEN...
TMP
LONG AGO...
...DURING A TURBULENT TIME IN KYOTO THERE WAS A PATRIOT KNOWN AS HITOKIRI BATTOSAI. HE SLAYED MEN AS IF HE WAS CARNAGE INCARNATE, AND WITH HIS BLOOD-SOAKED SWORD HE SLASHED OPENED THE MEIJI ERA.
AT THE CONCLUSION OF THOSE TURBULENT TIMES, HE DISAPPEARED, LEAVING ONLY HIS LEGEND BEHIND.
AND...

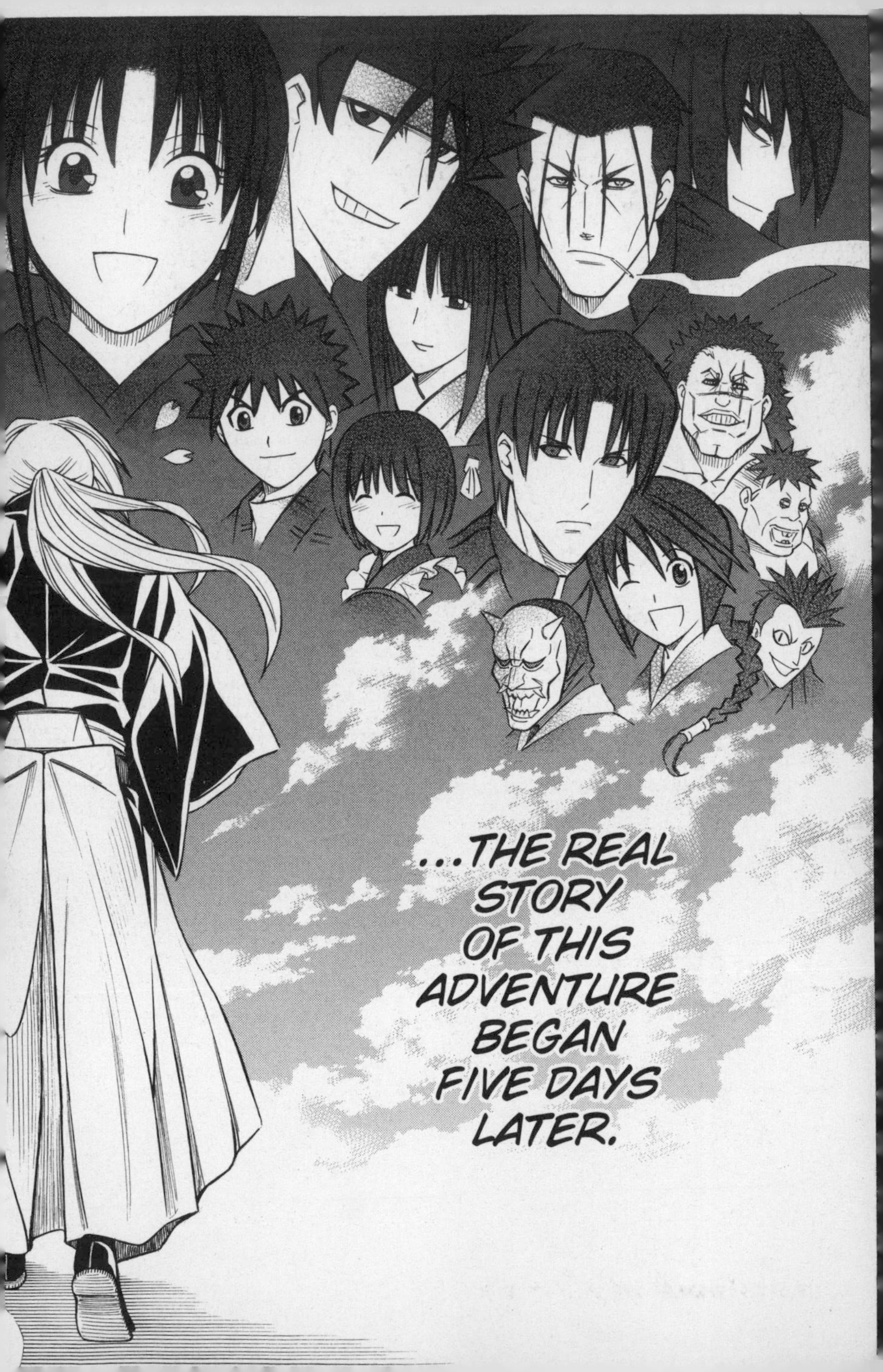
...THE REAL STORY OF THIS ADVENTURE BEGAN FIVE DAYS LATER.

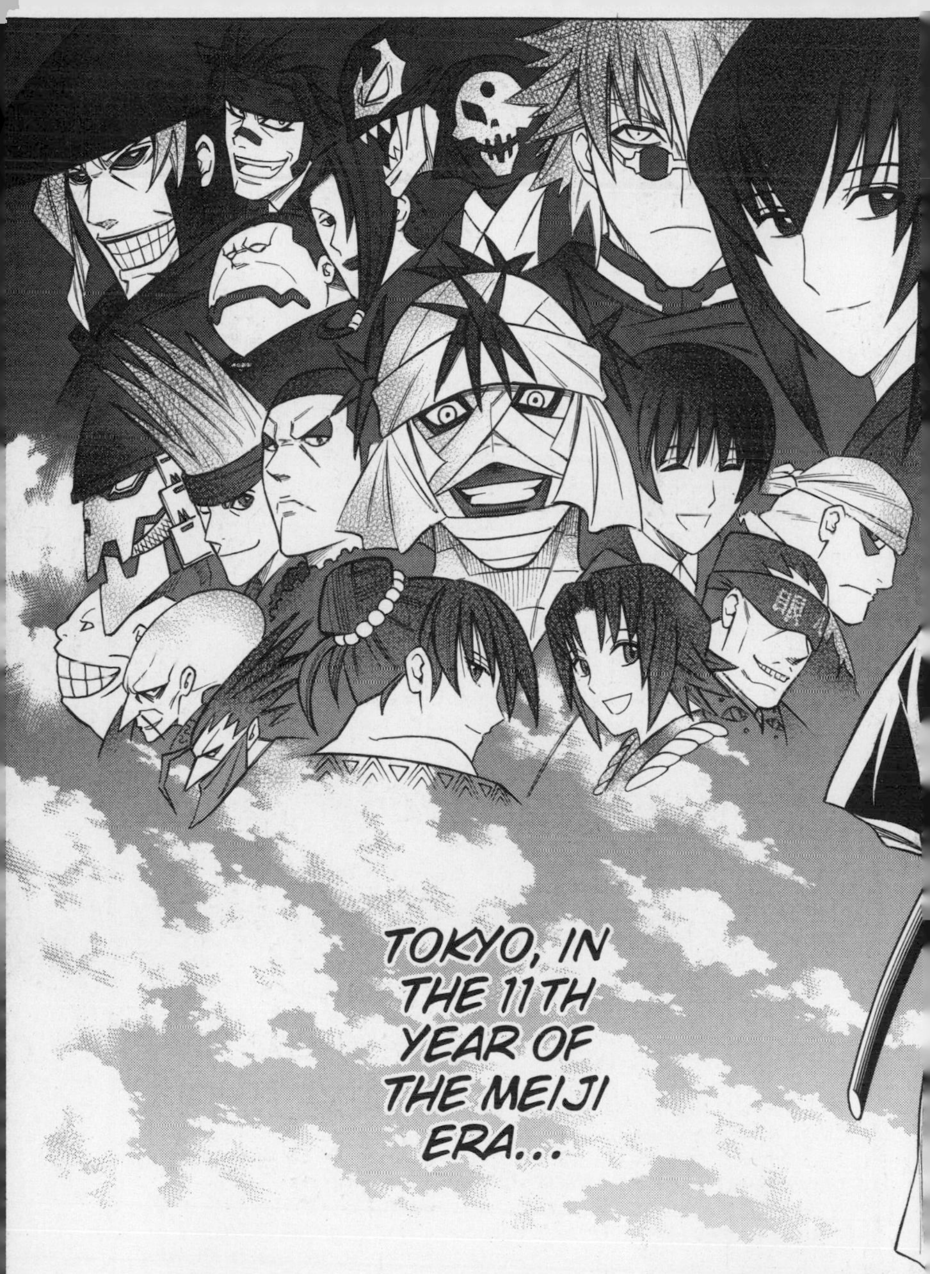
TOKYO, IN THE 11TH YEAR OF THE MEIJI ERA...

Continued in Act One...

FREE TALK 1

•It's been a while, Watsuki here.

It's been over one cycle of the Chinese zodiac since *Rurouni Kenshin: Meiji Swordsman Romantic Story* ended. I never dreamed I'd be writing another widely debated author's note again. Just to remind you, this note is simply a bonus. Not reading it won't affect your understanding of the actual manga, so to you readers who didn't like it or feel it's unnecessary, please feel free to skip it. Please.

•What led me to write *Rurouni Kenshin: Restoration* and *Act Zero*? In one word, because a live-action feature film was scheduled for release. Then why did you agree to a live-action feature film? Basically, Watsuki never turns down an offered project. Drama CDs, anime, games, novels, etc. I throw out suggestions and opinions, and then discuss them. Some offers don't pan out, but they are never turned away at the door. The one exception was an offer to turn it into a pachinko game. I turned it down simply because *Rurouni Kenshin* is a children's manga, so an over-18 medium was a bit... And because I'm just not a big fan of pachinko.

•The first offer for a live-action feature film came soon after the original serialization ended. It fizzled out even before we had any real discussions, so I honestly believed a live-action film was never going to happen. But three years ago, I received another offer. We discussed it at great length and it finally came to fruition.
Then Sasaki-san, my editor at the time and *Weekly Shonen Jump's* previous editor-in-chief, made a comment.
Sasaki-san: Now that the film's set to be made, you gotta start up *Kenshin* again, Wakky.
Watsuki: Huh?! (See author's comment)
Wife: Maybe you should?

So after some chaotic back and forth, I took up the pen again. But to be honest, Watsuki personally always harbored a desire to "write *Kenshin* again." A manga that to this day gets many requests for a sequel and remains loved ten-plus years after its conclusion. I always felt that if I was ever given the opportunity to meet those expectations, I would.
When the editorial staff and I came to a head at the end of serialization, Sasaki-san understood Watsuki's intentions and saw that I was at my limit physically and came to my defense. (Something similar is depicted in *Bakuman*, but this was for real.) I truly meant it when I said "I will never write *Kenshin* again." It was out of respect and appreciation for the readers to end a popular title while it was still popular. But when the live-action feature become a reality, it was time to lift the ban. An opportunity to write *Rurouni Kenshin* for longtime readers and potential new readers is what made me grab my pen again.

•What I was first told in making a live-action film was "unlike in anime and games, a live-action film belongs to the director and not the author." I see. Anime, games, and manga basically entail "creating" and "drawing." A live-action film entails "acting" and "filming." They are fundamentally different. I was a complete outsider, so I was only involved during the script-writing phase (writing the first half of the script, then checking the second half of the script they wrote), but I was told the script could be changed at the discretion of the director. A live-action film truly belongs to the director.

•Watsuki considers adaptations of his own work to be "family." The creator is the parent and the manga is the child. Anime, games, or novels born from the manga are grandchildren. Grandchildren have their own parents, namely their producers. From the grandchildren's perspective, the author is their grandfather. It's not right for a grandfather to constantly interfere with his grandchildren's upbringing so he basically leaves it up to their parents. But when the grandchildren are neglected or raised in an environment where they are not loved, the grandfather, as the head of the family, will step in verbally and at times physically.
So this live-action film is like a child adopted by another family. Not that I won't put in a word or two, but it is the director's job, as head of that family, to put his body on the line. You can do it, director!!

•What I recommend about the *Rurouni Kenshin* film is its "feel." Thanks to the hard work of the entire production crew, the fantastical world of manga has been brilliantly adapted to a live-action film. The actors' performances, the costume designs, the amazing locations that make you say "I didn't know Japan still had sights that remind us of the good old Meiji-era," and high-end sets that are just as amazing. I can go on and on. A real-life world of *Rurouni Kenshin* is truly there. And the other thing that I have to mention is the action scenes. Thanks to the work of the sword teachers, the actors' performances, and particularly Takeru Sato's (who plays Kenshin) Kenshin-like speed, it turned out to be very realistic. Watsuki was by and large pleased (of course, as the creator, I'm biased). If I was left wanting more, I believe it would've been due to the shortcomings of the creator and the original work itself. For example, if the original work had been more popular there would have been an overflow of love from both the creators and the viewers and in turn done better at the box-office. The budget for the production would've been increased that much more. To be quite frank, it's difficult to create any good work of art without love or a product without expenses. That's what was missing. That's what I mean by shortcomings.

•What led me to writing *Kenshin* once again after ten-plus years all started with this live-action film. If any of you have any doubts, please go watch it.

FREE TALK 2

RUROUNI KENSHIN RESTORATION

•So then I was set to write *Kenshin* again. But there was a major issue: where and what do I write? First, the "where." Currently, Watsuki works with *Jump SQ*. But when taking into consideration promotion for the film, *Weekly Shonen Jump*, the original magazine the manga was published in and the highest circulated magazine in the country, was more desirable. However, with the current series and new writers as *Shonen Jump's* priority, there was only room for a one-shot. It was such a great opportunity that I wanted to at least write enough for a graphic novel and reach as many readers as possible. After much discussion, it was decided to run the one-shot in *Weekly Shonen Jump*, and a short series in *SQ*.

•Next up was "What do I write?" In terms of the short series for *SQ*, I knew the readers most likely wanted the Hokkaido arc that ended as a rough draft. However, the conclusion of the theme was the main reason the serial ended in the first place. Without an idea for a new theme, I couldn't write the Hokkaido arc, much less as a sequel with Kenshin as the main character. There was just no way... The next idea I came up with was a sequel about the next generation. A story about Yahiko, who takes over the Sakabato or combining Kenshin's child Kenji with Yahiko's child Shinya as 'Ken – Shin.' But that wouldn't be a story about *Kenshin*. It would be acceptable as a continuation of *Rurouni Kenshin: Meiji Swordsman Romantic Story*, but it wasn't suitable for *Restoration*... If a sequel was difficult how about a prequel instead? A prequel would allow for more flexibility. But the story would take place before Kenshin meets his friends. In other words, it wouldn't be possible for most of the major characters to make an appearance. The look of the short series would've been a bit skimpy. In fact, a structure where Kenshin is the only pre-existing character was more suitable for the one-shot. The last idea I came up with was a parallel story. Many ideas and scenarios were rejected during the script-writing phase of the movie. One of mine that was rejected was a thirty-week story I envisioned before *Ruruoni* was published. A story based on a template so to speak. It would have been worthy of another *Kenshin* story and also in line with promoting the film. That is how *Restoration* was born. By the way, the novel version that will go on sale around the same time is based on Kurosaki Sensei's rejected idea.

•Watsuki's view of the parallel story.
Honestly, Watsuki does not disapprove of parallel stories. Maybe it's because I'm an avid reader of American comics where parallel worlds are common, but also because to me anime, games, novels, and live-action film adaptations are all parallels.
A parallel is "another" or "a separate" story and not a fake. I consider it as a pleasant gimmick that allows you to enjoy a piece of work in a different form. One thing you can't do is change the character's foundation. If you do, that would make it fake. And fake is not okay.

Parallels are okay as long as the characters remain fascinating. Kenshin and the other characters could be in school or fight dragons in a fantasy world and it would still be okay. (Although it would be very difficult.) Perhaps there is no parallel that would top the original, in this case *Rurouni Kenshin: Meiji Swordsman Romantic Story*. But it'd be a shame to reject all parallels outright. I think it's great to passionately love the original, but refusing to recognize anything else is a shame. Please enjoy a parallel world that is not possible in reality, a beautiful trick only made possible through creativity.

• Various topics about *Rurouni Kenshin: Resoration* will be featured in the next volume where the story will conclude. It'd be great if you could take another look at it...

RUROUNI KENSHIN: ACT ZERO

• As I was about to write the prequel, the following thoughts ran through my mind. 1) To make sure current *Weekly Shonen Jump* readers that have never read *Kenshin* would enjoy it. 2) To make sure existing readers would enjoy it. 3) To fill in the gaps of one element I missed. 4) Include an element I never included before. 5) Make sure to tie the ending into the First Act.

To address #1, I narrowed down the pre-existing characters to Kenshin, the main character, and made it easy to read by choosing a familiar story structure. I also made an effort to include elements of comedy.

For #2, I connected Kenshin's flashback scene in the middle with the spread at the end. I chose characters that were included in the cover of the complete collection.

With #3, I elaborated on the common question of "Why would Kenshin, who wandered for ten years, suddenly stop wandering in the First Act?" Elder notices Kenshin's deep, unhealed emotional scar. Her kind advice has a slight effect on Kenshin, thus becoming the motivation for his behavior in the First Act. Something like that.

#4 was, to put it bluntly, a Westerner. Surprisingly, there were no Western characters in *Rurouni Kenshin*. Even though it was an era of modernization and Westernization... That is why it was set in Yokohama's foreign settlement. I collected numerous materials on my research trip there in the spring. I regret not being able to introduce the Yokohama Foreign General Cemetery.

And as for #5, I used a recurring narration for this. Oh, the number of times I've written that narration...

• I struggled and struggled to decide on the above five points for this one-shot. Just when I had no clue what to do, when I was in the doldrums, I had an opportunity to eat with my very first editor, Sasaki-san. The subject of this one-shot came up while in a cab to the restaurant and we started talking. We came up with the framework in only fifteen minutes. I was reminded that Kenshin would not have been possible without him. Watsuki still has a lot to learn.

CHARACTER CREATION UNTOLD STORIES PART 55 PEOPLE OF ACT ZERO

•Elder = Peaberry
At first glance she seems like a gimmicky character, but she is the end result of a long period of planning.

First off, we needed a heroine for Kenshin to save. In addition, a doctor who gives Kenshin advice was necessary. We also needed to fulfill the criteria of including a Western character. A character pursued by the bad guys as well. Just when I was about to lose it, thinking "Can we really include all these characters?!" I had an opportunity to share a ride with novelist/supervisor Kurosaki Sensei, and it naturally led to a discussion. He made the bold suggestion of "combining" them. After much struggle, Elder was the character I came up with. By the way, the idea of a pretty girl in a mask concealing her sex was Kurosaki Sensei's. A lot of progress seems to be made while in a car...

A kind and earnest girl who everybody would like once her identity is revealed and since the mask is gimmicky she had to be somewhat plain. I didn't really have a specific motif for her design. I chose a trendy soft wavy hairstyle. Considering the look when lined up alongside Kenshin when in disguise and the setting, she is rather small. Somewhere in between Tsubame and Misao. I took the name Elder from a medicinal herb. She is a distant relative (not acquainted) of Hildegard Peaberry who appears in *Embalming*, which Watsuki is currently working on.

•Asahiyama Dankichi

My initial thought was for him to be a soldier and the lover or older brother of a heroine. Once Elder was decided on as a character, he was no longer a major character. He instead was reborn as a character familiar with the settlement, helpful during travels, one of Elder's few allies and guide.

Perhaps due to him being a macho rickshawman, he ended up almost overshadowing the main character even during the early stages, so I ended up having to reduce his role. It's a pity.

I took his last name from a mountain back in my hometown. And since he pulls a car, his first name had to be Dankichi. His design was impromptu. I regret that his face and hairstyle are slightly different from frame to frame.

•Espiral = Rotación

Plays the role of the (villain) Western character. How about Kenshin vs. a Western sword-style? That is how he came about.

He was initially more of a rival character than a villain, living in the West where the sword had become obsolete, and thus wanting deeply to fight a samurai. A man with a kind of resignation to dying and an obsession with the sword. In the end, he mends his ways after being saved by Elder and returns back home with Elder as her bodyguard. That how I imagined him at first, but... He would have taken eight pages in the epilogue, about 1/6th of the entire page count. I just didn't have enough pages!

As a result, he ended up being the kind of villain you see in the story. Although I believe a simple villain was better for a one-shot, it's a pity in a different sense from Dankichi. His name is Spanish for "spiral," and all his technical moves are related to that word. Basically, his design is the opposite of Kenshin. Short black hair, white top and black leggings, as well as a long glove on his right arm to emphasize his dominant hand.

Rurouni Kenshin
RESTORATION

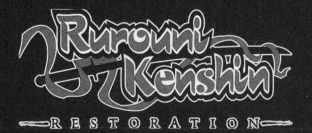